Railroad Development Programs in the Twentieth Century

Railroad Development Programs in the Twentieth Century

ROY V. SCOTT

THE HENRY A. WALLACE SERIES
ON AGRICULTURAL HISTORY AND RURAL STUDIES

IOWA STATE UNIVERSITY PRESS • AMES

First edition, 1985

Library of Congress Cataloging in Publication Data
Scott, Roy Vernon, 1927–
    Railroad development programs in the twentieth century.

    (The Henry A. Wallace series on agricultural history and rural studies)
    Bibliography: p.
    Includes index.
    1. Railroads—Economic aspects—United States—History—20th century. I. Title. II. Series.
HE2751.S345 1985   385′.068   84–22552
ISBN 0–8138–1506–1

CONTENTS

EDITOR'S INTRODUCTION

THE HENRY A. WALLACE SERIES on Agricultural History and Rural Studies is designed to enlarge publishing opportunities in agricultural history and thereby to expand public understanding of the development of agriculture and rural society. The Series will be composed of volumes that explore the many aspects of agriculture and rural life within historical perspectives. It will evolve as the field evolves. The press and the editor will solicit and welcome the submission of manuscripts that illustrate, in good and fresh ways, that evolution. Our interests are broad. They do not stop with Iowa and U.S. agriculture but extend to all other parts of the world. They encompass the social, intellectual, scientific, and technological aspects of the subject as well as the economic and political. The emphasis of the series is on the scholarly monograph, but historically significant memoirs of people involved in and with agriculture and rural life and major sources for research in the field will also be included.

Most appropriately, this Iowa-based Series is dedicated to a highly significant agriculturist who began in Iowa, developed a large, well-informed interest in its rural life, and expanded the scope of his interests beyond the state to the nation and the world. An Iowa native and son of an agricultural scientist, journalist, and secretary of agriculture, Henry A. Wallace was a 1910 graduate of Iowa State College, a frequent participant in its scientific activities, editor of *Wallaces' Farmer* from 1921 to 1933, founder in 1926 of the Hi-Bred Corn Company (now Pioneer Hi-Bred International, Inc.), secretary of agriculture from 1933 to 1940, and vice president of the United States from 1941 to 1945. In the agricultural phases of his wide-ranging career, he was both a person of large importance in the development of America's agriculture and the leading policymaker during the most creative period in the history of American farm policy.

At first glance, this book by Roy V. Scott may appear to be an inappropriate volume for the Wallace Series. The first two volumes dealt with the American farmer and the New Deal and with Roswell Garst, a man who had ties with Henry A. Wallace and a large impact on agriculture. This volume, on the other hand, the third in the Series, emphasizes railroads, not farming, and devotes a substantial amount of space to minerals, forests, and manufacturing.

Yet railroads have been very important in agricultural history and rural life, and much of this book illustrates that, as one would expect from a work by Scott. His valuable contributions to agricultural history include *The Reluctant Farmers: The Rise of Agricultural Extension to 1914* (1970) and (with J. G. Shoalmire) *The Public Career of Cully A. Cobb: A Study in Agricultural Leadership* (1973). Like Extension and Cobb (and also like the New Deal for agriculture, Henry A. Wallace, and Roswell Garst), the railroads contributed to the triumph of modernization over the agrarian tradition. Focusing his attention on railroad development activities, Scott shows the railroads, inspired by recognition that their profits depended upon the prosperity of the country they served, promoted economic development and much of their promotional effort centered on agriculture. I suspect if he were pressed to do so, Scott might argue that this is his most important contribution to agricultural history. Such an argument would necessarily include the very difficult tasks of measuring and comparing the impacts on farming of Extension, the New Deal cotton program, and railroad development work.

Agricultural history is the study of the development over time of farming and farm people and of the institutions and activities linked directly and significantly with them. This book gives us such a study—and more.

Richard S. Kirkendall

PREFACE

This study deals with an important but little known aspect of American economic history in the twentieth century. Scholars are fully aware of the tremendous role that railroads as a mode of transportation played in the economic growth of the United States. It is the contention of this book that rail carriers also made substantial contributions to the shaping of the economies of the territories they served through the activities of their development departments. Beginning with the efforts of the great land-grant roads to settle their lands and extending to the diverse programs of the recent past, railroads were a positive force in promoting economic development. These activities, of course, were inspired by good business judgment; railroads could not be profitable unless they had adequate volumes of traffic, and development programs were formulated with that fact in mind.

Historians have studied in some detail the first phase of railway development work in which the major transcontinentals sold and settled their land grants. The pioneer works of James B. Hedges, Paul W. Gates, Richard C. Overton, and Howard F. Bennett come readily to mind, and in recent years a number of dissertations and scholarly articles have sharpened our understanding of the procedures by which such roads as the Northern Pacific and the Burlington peopled the prairies.

On the other hand, historians have devoted little attention to the promotional activities of railroads in the twentieth century. In 1933 Chu Chang Liang published in Peking, China, his University of Pennsylvania dissertation entitled *A Study of the Industrial and Agricultural Development Departments of American Railroads*. Copies of that study are rare, and the book is encyclopedic in character, contains factual errors, and is outdated. Almost thirty years ago the late Mildred Throne called for an examination of the role of railroads in modern agricultural development and suggested some of the patterns such a study might take. C. Clyde Jones's superb dissertation stands as a model for those interested in twentieth-century agricultural programs and willing to dig into railroad company records for material. From his research Jones gave us several significant articles. In 1974 David D. Daniels completed at the University of North Carolina a dissertation that deals with the role of selected railroads in the location of certain kinds of manufacturing enterprises. More recently, Howard L. Dickman used the records of the Great Northern Railway Company to survey the development programs of that railroad.

I first became aware of railway development work more than two decades ago when I was given the task of examining the agricultural programs of a major carrier. Later, in writing the history of early agricultural extension in the United States, I discovered the role of the railroads to have been an important one. With a general concept of the character of development work in mind, I determined the outlines of the topic in a pamphlet published by Oklahoma State University (1963) and in an article in the New York Academy of Sciences's *Transportation: A Service* (1968). This book then is an attempt to produce a reasonably comprehensive survey of railway development programs in the twentieth century.

Some readers will note that in the preparation of this study I have not used railway company records. I make no apologies for the decision not to do so. Substantial experience in railway archives convinced me that, given their bulk, no one historian could hope to examine thoroughly the records of the several companies now available to scholars. On the other hand, I learned much from executives of several Class I carriers who were kind enough to answer my queries with lengthy discussions of their roads' development programs and in a number of instances to provide me with company memos dealing with the histories of their development offices.

I hope that this study will serve at least two purposes. First, by sketching in outline the character of railway development work since the disposal of the great land grants, this book should add to our knowledge of agricultural and railroad history in particular and American economic history in general. Second, it should serve as a guide to future historians who will undertake the detailed studies of development programs of individual railway companies that we need.

As is usual with authors, I must express my appreciation to those people who helped me to produce this study. The editors of *Business History Review, Agricultural History, Journal of Forest History, National Railway Bulletin,* and *Journal of Transport History* permitted me to use material and ideas that had previously appeared in their publications. Ralph W. Hidy of Harvard University first introduced me to railroad history; C. Clyde Jones of Kansas State University provided me with a copy of his dissertation so that I could study it at my leisure; and Fred A. Shannon of the University of Illinois remained a source of inspiration, although he probably would not have liked this book. The American Philosophical Society generously gave me two grants that permitted me to visit libraries in Washington and elsewhere. Personnel at the library of the Association of American Railroads, the Library of Congress, and the University of Illinois Library went out of their way to aid me in my research. I must also record my gratitude to George R. Lewis and Frances N. Coleman of my university library, who through many years have never failed to come to my aid. Mississippi State University, through its Development Foundation and its Office of Graduate Studies and Research, gave summer support on more than one occasion, and the Department of History provided me with as much secretarial help as I could use. Among my student workers, Gloria Cummings Cartwright, Linda Land Hilton, and Debra Marie Brown deserve special mention. Ann C. Chenney, who twenty years ago typed the manuscript of my first book, produced the final draft of this one with her usual efficiency and good humor. Finally, I must thank the personnel of Iowa State University Press, most notably Suzanne Lowitt, who did so much to turn a manuscript into a book.

Of course, I remain solely responsible for any errors in fact or interpretation that sharp-eyed reviewers or other readers may discover.

Railroad Development Programs in the Twentieth Century

CHAPTER ONE

Patterns in Railroad Development Work

IN THE TWENTIETH CENTURY freight traffic has been the lifeblood of American railroad companies. Perhaps few railway officers would agree with James J. Hill's earthy and unprintable observation concerning the value of passenger operations, but most rail carriers survive only as long as they can obtain enough freight business to produce operating revenues adequate to meet operating expenses, pay fixed costs and taxes, and leave a balance that will compensate invested capital. Railroad operations are characterized by high fixed costs, and unit costs decline rapidly as volume increases. There are, therefore, heavy pressures on railroad managers to maximize the flow of business, and the generation of freight traffic is a matter of considerable importance. Executives recognized quite early the need for formal programs to produce new business, and the traffic-generating activities of the railroads have been a significant factor in American agricultural and industrial development.

Traffic generation may be either creative or competitive in character. In the nineteenth century most new traffic came as the result of the physical expansion of the rail system. Pioneer lines built through developed country inevitably attracted business, and their construction represented the primary form of creative traffic generation. Commonly used forms of competitive traffic generation, which increased in significance as the century neared its end, included construction of lines in areas served by existing roads, solicitation, rate cutting and rebating, and the provision of better service.

Other methods of traffic generation became necessary when railroad managers discovered that the traditional approaches no longer sufficed. Programs instituted wholly or in part to build new traffic in creative ways first appeared in clear and distinct form when land-grant railroads were

3

built in advance of settlement. Only by contributing to the process of settlement could these railroads obtain satisfactory volumes of traffic within a reasonable period of time. Moreover, since settlers moving into new areas after the Civil War often had to make major changes in farming methods, railroad managers found that it was to the advantage of their companies to help in such adjustments. To their transportation functions western railroads thus added colonization and educational responsibilities.

By the first years of the twentieth century still other forms of creative traffic generation had made their appearance not only in the West but throughout the United States. The age of construction was nearing its end, public regulation had reduced substantially the possibilities of producing new traffic through rate cutting and rebating, and there were limits to the amount of new business that could be attracted by solicitation and the provision of better service. Programs of creative traffic generation proved to be one route to greater volumes of business. Increased and diversified agricultural production, for instance, would strengthen the economic position of rural shippers, result in heavier outbound and inbound traffic, and produce a better balanced flow of freight shipments that would ease the problems of seasonal traffic, excess capacity, and car supply. A new manufacturing plant or warehouse usually meant new business, while the industrialization of a region generally could be counted on to increase business, enhance economic conditions, and help stabilize traffic flow. The greater utilization of mineral and forest resources was certain to produce increased shipments. With such considerations in mind, railway executives throughout the United States instituted sophisticated programs in creative traffic generation and regional economic development that collectively constituted an important facet of railroad history.[1]

Nineteenth Century Origins of Railway Development Work

Between 1850 and 1871 railroad companies received federal land grants that ultimately aggregated some 131 million acres. State grants added approximately 49 million acres, including 32 million in Texas alone. A century later historians were yet to reach a consensus as to the wisdom of the land-grant programs, but probably a majority would agree that the grants represented a valid use of a cheap resource, they made a substantial contribution to the growth of the nation as a whole, and they speeded the settlement of the West by from ten to fifteen years.[2]

Regardless of the outcome of the debate among historians, the railroads that received the land grants had the problem of what to do with the real estate thus obtained. With some variations in timing, the answer was to sell it. Funds arising from sales were used to retire bonds and for other purposes, but more important to the companies in the long run was the traffic that was generated when raw land was converted into producing properties.

No doubt the roots may be found elsewhere, but the Illinois Central is given credit for launching the first extensive colonization program. Its methods were so successful that they were subsequently adopted by other roads. In due course the Union Pacific, Northern Pacific, Southern Pacific, and Santa Fe—indeed all land-grant roads—instituted colonization programs that were similar in broad outline, differing only in specifics.[3]

The Illinois Central's campaign to sell its 2.6 million acres began in 1854. The first true advertising pamphlet was issued that year, and soon promotional literature went out to easterners and squibs appeared in eastern newspapers. Agents visited agricultural fairs and other places where farmers might be encountered, met immigrants as they arrived at New York, and recruited in Europe. The railroad disposed of practically its entire grant by the end of the century. Management estimated that between 30,000 and 35,000 heads of families purchased land.

The Hannibal and St. Joseph received some 600,000 acres in Missouri; it adopted the land disposal procedures of the Illinois Central and transmitted them to the Burlington. That company appointed an agent in 1859 to survey its grant in Iowa and later in Nebraska and to lay the foundation for a sales campaign. By the early 1870s the work was in full swing; by 1905 when the land department closed its books the Burlington had sold 2.7 million acres for an average of $8.09 an acre.[4]

The Union Pacific, with its 12 million acres, lost little time in recognizing the need for "developing a population." A land office opened in 1869. Between 1873 and 1885 the company issued 9.1 million pieces of literature, not counting *The Pioneer,* a periodical that appeared in 1874 and for a time was edited by J. Sterling Morton, later a secretary of agriculture. Exploration tickets and tours of the West helped to attract settlers, while exhibits at agricultural fairs and the Centennial Exposition at Philadelphia pointed to the productivity of company lands. By 1880 the company had sold approximately 2 million acres.[5]

In the Northwest the most important colonizing road was the Northern Pacific. Its grant aggregated 40 million acres. The road's land department commenced operations in 1871; the next year the energetic James B. Power became head of the office. Under his leadership the company scattered agents throughout the United States and northwestern Europe, turned out millions of pamphlets, and established immigrant newspapers. When Henry Villard took control of the Northern Pacific in 1881, he strengthened the colonization program and extended it to the Pacific Northwest. These efforts produced a flock of settlers in the 1880s, with about 90 percent of the new arrivals coming from the states west of the Alleghenies.[6]

The Santa Fe first directed its colonization efforts to its almost 3 million acres in Kansas. Under the leadership of David L. Lakin and later A. E. Touzalin, who assumed direction of the land department in 1872, agents roamed throughout the East, broadcasting the usual promotional literature. Business was sufficiently brisk to justify the establishment in 1880 of an office in London to supervise activities in the British Isles and on the Continent. The company attracted members of certain religious sects, especially after C. B. Schmidt, a recent arrival from Germany who joined the Santa Fe in 1873, established friendly contacts with Mennonites. The great bulk of the original grant was gone by 1886, but by that time the company had done much to create "its own business by colonizing a wilderness."[7]

The Southern Pacific was active at both ends of its long line. The company poured out literature, including writings by Charles Nordhoff, advertised widely, cooperated with the California Immigration Union, and stationed agents at various points in the United States and abroad. One representative in London claimed to have visited every country in Europe except Russia and Turkey. Officials in charge of the company's three immigrant houses in Texas gave free board and often helped new arrivals obtain temporary jobs. Immigrant movable cars transported settlers' belongings at reduced rates.[8]

While the great transcontinentals were busily peddling lands, other western and midwestern roads were also at work, if on a smaller scale. The Texas and Pacific was active in settling West Texas. James J. Hill's St. Paul, Minneapolis and Manitoba received 21,000 inquiries from prospective settlers in 1883, and even such carriers as the Dakota Southern issued circulars and pamphlets. In the 1860s and 1870s railroads that later became the Frisco were selling lands in Missouri. Highlighting the efforts of the Fort Worth and Denver City was the Texas Spring Palace, an extravaganza staged in Fort Worth in 1889 and 1890. The Wisconsin Central worked closely with state immigration agencies, maintained exhibits of farm products in Milwaukee, and stationed an agent in Europe. Railroads in Michigan peddled land, using the standard methods.[9]

Southern railroads also used the colonization procedures of western carriers. In 1869 officials of ten southern roads met to consider how they might attract settlers, and during the next decade several southern railroads undertook advertising campaigns. They cooperated enthusiastically with state immigration agencies, which flowered in the New South. In the fall of 1888 the state of Alabama and the Louisville and Nashville sent a three-car exhibit train on a tour of the Middle West. Reportedly, a quarter of a million people visited the train and carried away 30 million pieces of literature. The Illinois Central promoted settlement in the Mississippi Delta in the 1890s, having taken title to more than a half million acres there in 1892. In the eastern part of Mississippi the Mobile and Ohio used the standard techniques a decade earlier, while the Fort Smith and Little Rock and the St. Louis, Iron Mountain and Southern distributed in Europe literature extolling the attractions of Arkansas, offered reduced rates to homeseekers, and worked with church leaders thought to be influential with members of their faiths. In the 1890s the Nashville, Chattanooga and St. Louis employed Joseph B. Killebrew, a pamphlet writer and lecturer whose abilities to paint in appealing colors the attractions of the South found few equals.[10]

These colonization programs in the West and South were soon supplemented by a variety of activities calculated to help farmers adjust to their new environments or to encourage them to improve and diversify their operations. There was, after all, nothing to be gained if settlers so laboriously placed failed in their new locations.

Again the Illinois Central was a leader. During the Civil War President William H. Osborn tried to promote the growing of cotton and sugar beets in Illinois to offset the loss of southern production, and in 1865 the road made a chemical analysis of Illinois soils. Later the railroad encouraged the fruit business in the southern portion of that state and in the 1880s it helped to develop tomato growing in Copiah County, Mississippi, by furnishing tomato plants to farmers and by settling experienced truck growers in the area. The company also claimed credit for the development of profitable agriculture in Tangipahoa Parish, Louisiana. In 1883 when the road began to operate its newly acquired line to New Orleans, Tangipahoa Parish was considered so poor that it would produce "not a . . . thing but crawfish." Undaunted, the company advertised the area, attracted people from Iowa and elsewhere, and promoted the development of strawberry growing and dairying. Other southern roads did some agricultural development work before 1900, but apparently they were less active than the Illinois Central.[11]

West of the Mississippi River the work of James J. Hill is best known. Convinced that hard times in Minnesota and North Dakota in the early 1880s were due in part to reliance on wheat growing, the Empire Builder distributed to farmers over 7,000 head of livestock, including 800 purebred bulls. To encourage scientific farming he transported farmers to state experiment stations at reduced rates and donated land at Crookston, Minnesota, for a branch station. Hill was also interested in the draining of Red River valley lands and offered to pay half the cost of required surveys, provided the counties would contribute an equal amount. Later in

1893 Minnesota made an appropriation for the work, and the Great
Northern gave $25,000 to aid in the development of a comprehensive
drainage system in the valley.[12]

Hill's reputation as a developer of the Northwest was well deserved,
but he was by no means alone in pre-1900 agricultural development work.
In the 1870s the Kansas Pacific distributed seed and broke prairie land to
encourage settlement and to test the productivity of the soil. The
Burlington gave seedlings to prairie farmers, donated alfalfa seed in Nebraska as early as 1875, sponsored educational exhibits at state and local
fairs, and beginning in 1895 published a promotional and educational
paper, *The Corn Belt.* The Northern Pacific established at Fargo a nursery that provided cuttings to farmers at cost, distributed a variety of rye
seed suited to the northern plains, and extended aid to the Montana Arid
Land Commission, an agency established to carry out the provisions of
the Carey Act of 1894. In the Southwest, as elsewhere, railroads were
enthusiastic supporters of agricultural fairs, providing funds, helping
with exhibits, and offering reduced fares to visitors. In 1899 the Oregon
Railway and Navigation Company cooperated with the Washington Agricultural College in arranging and holding a series of farmers' institutes
devoted to dairying.[13]

Prior to 1900 western railroads began to wrestle with the problems
of farming in the area beyond the 20-inch rainfall line. Railroadmen were
no more misinformed about the nature of the High Plains than a great
many other observers. Even as sober an authority as the *Army and Navy
Journal* announced that the coming of the railroad had altered the electrical condition of the atmosphere and increased the rainfall, and many
other spokesmen were thoroughly convinced that rain followed the plow.
In any event, western railroadmen embraced enthusiastically the theories
of Hardy W. Campbell, a noted exponent of dry farming. His work first
caught the attention of officials of the Northern Pacific, who asked him to
manage five experiment farms in North Dakota as a means of instructing
settlers in his methods of producing crops with little moisture. By 1896
Campbell was working in the same capacity for the Burlington and the
Soo, and the next year he managed forty-three farms in five states.[14]

Evolution of Railway Development Departments

To manage these programs and others that came later, new officers
and later distinct departments emerged within railway company organizational structures. Land agents and departments came first. The Illinois
Central created its land office only a year after the road was incorporated,
and other land-grant carriers were almost as prompt. When the roads
embarked upon extensive campaigns to attract settlers to their lands,

colonization agents made their appearance among railroad officers. Most of these men were connected first with the land offices of their companies, but in time distinct colonization departments emerged. When the effectiveness of colonization work became evident, railroads having no land for sale adopted similar procedures to increase the rural population along their lines. Before the end of the century most of the carriers in the West and South and a few elsewhere had colonization or immigration offices or departments.

Specialization also appeared in agricultural development work. In the nineteenth century such activity tended to be opportunistic and sporadic. Land, colonization, and freight and passenger department personnel were often engaged in it, and in some instances high company officials took a personal interest. But soon after the turn of the century distinct agricultural departments appeared. Effective 6 September 1905 Hal B. Fullerton became director of agriculture on the Long Island, charged with the task of generating agricultural traffic on that line. Other roads followed, in several instances urged on by land-grant college officials who recognized that railroads could be valuable allies in their efforts to educate farmers.[15]

The ten years that preceded American entry into World War I saw a flowering of agricultural development departments. The Santa Fe and the Rock Island, for example, hired agricultural experts in 1910, and the Missouri Pacific did so in 1911 after having one temporarily on its payroll earlier. The New York Central and the Lehigh Valley appointed agricultural agents in 1911, the Baltimore and Ohio created a bureau of agriculture in 1912, and the Burlington established its agricultural department in 1913, naming agronomist John B. Lamson of the University of Minnesota to fill the post. By that time the Southern Railway's department of farm improvement work had been in operation for several years, engaged in activities not greatly different from those of Seaman A. Knapp, a pioneer in agricultural extension work. By 1917 even the 32-mile Prescott and Northwestern in Arkansas had an agricultural agent.[16]

A decade or more before railroads added agricultural specialists to their staffs, some carriers appointed men who were charged with the specific task of attracting new business firms to their territories. Industrial location was not a new function of rail carriers; senior officers, at least, had always made known to enterprisers the potentialities of the country traversed by their railroads. Routine work of this nature gradually fell to superintendents and general freight agents, who in addition to their other duties sought out businesses likely to relocate, promoted the opening of mines, located new saw mills and packing houses, and otherwise did what they could to increase the number and diversity of firms served by their companies.

As early as the 1880s executives of a few roads had become convinced that the location of new businesses was too important to be left in the hands of officers whose primary responsibilities lay elsewhere. Industrial development work required skills not found in every railroad officer, and it appeared that the men involved should not also be responsible for the establishing of rates, providing of service, and other traditional aspects of railroad operation.[17]

The first industrial agent seems to have been appointed by the Milwaukee. In the 1880s E. P. Ripley, an official of the Burlington, became convinced that eastern manufacturers could be attracted to the West and directed a subordinate, Luis Jackson, to begin a preliminary study of the matter. Later when Ripley left the Burlington to join the Milwaukee, he took the idea and Jackson with him. Jackson's appointment as industrial commissioner was effective 1 January 1891.

Other roads were not far behind. In 1887 President Samuel Spencer of the Baltimore and Ohio employed M. V. Richards, a veteran western immigration agent, to take up work that would involve the location of industries. Before Richards could begin, Spencer resigned. Later when the Southern Railway was organized in 1894 and Spencer was chosen its first president, he appointed Richards land and industrial agent of that road. Within a decade several other roads established such offices or extended activities of their land and immigration departments to include the location of industries.[18]

As late as the outbreak of World War I, when at least fifty of the major carriers had development departments of some nature, there was no uniformity among railroads as to organizational structures for handling immigration, agricultural, and industrial work. The St. Louis Southwestern, which organized an agricultural and industrial department in 1908, divided the responsibilities in 1917. On the other hand, in 1913 the Frisco combined its immigration, agricultural, and industrial work in one office, known as the department of development, and in 1917 the Baltimore and Ohio concentrated all of its development work in its newly established commercial development department. Seemingly, differences were determined by the inclinations of senior executives and by the needs of the territories served.

Nor did the titles of departments indicate clearly the type of work being carried on. The Gulf and Ship Island's immigration and industrial department did a great deal of agricultural work; the Delaware and Hudson's industrial department promoted dairying.[19]

Illustrative of the evolution of development department organization before 1917 was that which came on the Illinois Central. That railroad traced its development work to its land department, established promptly after the road was incorporated. Soon the road had its colonization program in operation, and some of its senior officers were encouraging the improvement of agriculture. By the 1880s John F. Merry was general immigration agent, but his activities were not limited to the recruiting of settlers. "He was in fact agricultural agent, industrial agent, immigration agent, and publicity representative rolled into one," reported a historian of the company.

Specialization soon came. In 1892 the Illinois Central joined the ranks of those railroads having an industrial agent, appointing George C. Power to the post. He was succeeded by J. C. Clair, who in 1911 claimed that primarily "the work of the Department is to locate manufacturing plants." That year industrial and immigration activities were combined in a single department. Meanwhile, the Illinois Central's agricultural development work was increasing rapidly in scope and importance, and in 1907 the company established an agricultural department. Finally, in 1917 the Illinois Central placed all development work in Clair's office, and Clair was given the title of general development agent.[20]

World War I interrupted development work and led to the curtailment of programs and the disbandment of many development departments. With the return of the railroads to private control in 1920, the departments were reestablished and their programs resumed, but there were significant changes in functions. The 1920s was the great decade for railroad development work in agriculture. Colonization declined in importance, and industrial development men tended to be found in combined departments where the emphasis was on agricultural promotion. Some railroads began to employ industrial development specialists, geologists, and foresters, thereby suggesting the directions that development work would take in subsequent years.

Changes continued in the 1930s and later. The Great Depression forced a severe contraction in expenditures for development activities. The New Deal's farm program called into question some aspects of agricultural development work, and adverse business conditions limited the opportunities for successful industrial development work. Colonization work enjoyed a brief revival, but hopes in that area soon faded and disappeared. The post-World War II years saw a continuing decline in agricultural development work, in part because the proliferation of public agencies engaged in work with farmers eliminated the need for railway efforts. On the other hand, the spread of industry from its historic home in the East to the South and the West, combined with decentralization and other trends in business, afforded great opportunities for industrial location. In this area, in fact, came the major thrust of railway development efforts after 1945.

Changes in railway development departments after 1920 clearly reflected these trends. For example, in 1920 the Illinois Central had a combined department headed by H. J. Schwietert, who stated that the department was responsible for agricultural development and colonization, but it was also to "cooperate . . . in promoting new industries." In 1929 the industrial and agricultural functions were divided, and separate departments were created for each. The inauguration of systematic work in forestry promotion in the 1940s caused the agricultural department to become the agricultural and forestry department, and in the 1950s the Illinois Central claimed to have the largest and most comprehensive program in those areas of any railroad in the United States. But effective 30 June 1970 the company discontinued its agricultural and forestry department. Merger with the Gulf, Mobile and Ohio gave the resulting firm a forestry agent stationed at Louisville, Mississippi, but very clearly an age was at an end.[21]

The evolution of development departments on the Great Northern followed a similar pattern. Prior to World War I agricultural development and colonization were combined in an agricultural development department. This arrangement continued in the 1920s, while industrial development was in the hands of a subordinate officer in the freight traffic department. Not until the late 1930s did the company place major emphasis on industrial development and create a department for the work. In 1941 Great Northern hired its first geologist, and in 1945 agricultural and mineral promotion were combined in a new department. That organization proved to be unsatisfactory, and the functions were divided in 1951. Five years later industrial and agricultural work were merged, but by that time industrial work was by far the more important. This arrangement, with promotional work handled in the industrial and agricultural development and the mineral research and development departments, continued until 1967. Then in a wholesale reorganization, which had parallels on other lines, all development personnel as well as real estate men were grouped in a new office headed by a vice-president.

The roots of the Norfolk and Western's development department originated in the late nineteenth century when the road began to serve coal deposits in Virginia, West Virginia, and Kentucky. A necessary step toward the utilization of those resources was the recruiting of miners, so a bureau of immigration and mining was established. Later the bureau was reconstituted as the department of agriculture and immigration, which undertook typical colonization and agricultural promotion programs. About 1910 the office became the agricultural and industrial department; immigration work was largely abandoned. Interest in industrial development grew in the 1920s and 1930s; agricultural work gradually declined and ultimately disappeared. After World War II, engineers, economists, and other specialists were added to the department staff, and there was a concerted effort to upgrade the work and make it more sophisticated and effective. Finally, in 1971 industrial development and the handling of industrial property were assigned to a newly constituted industrial real estate department.[22]

Something of prevailing trends in development work was demonstrated by the changing size of promotional departments. In 1914, for example, the Frisco's seventeen-man department of development included twelve agricultural agents. Three years later the Southern claimed, apparently correctly, that it had the largest railway development department in the United States. Headed by the veteran M. V. Richards, it numbered fifty men and operated on an annual budget of approximately $225,000. The New York Central employed nine men in its agricultural development department in 1929, but by 1946 the number had declined to six. In 1940 the Louisville and Nashville's industrial and agricultural department had twelve members, six of whom were agricultural men. The agricultural and industrial functions were divided in 1949, but as late as 1952 the railroad employed four agricultural agents. Not until 1961 was the agricultural development department abolished. In 1960 the Rock Island's industrial development department consisted of six agents, located at Chicago and Dallas.[23]

Early colonization men tended to be publicists, propagandists, and promoters pure and simple, but in building their agricultural development departments after 1900 the railroads turned primarily to the land-grant colleges for manpower. The carriers sought a particular type of agricultural college man, one whose practicality and ability to establish rapport with farmers balanced his technical knowledge. In 1912 when the Rock Island was looking for a man to add to its staff, company officials stated that they did not want a scholar whose mind was "cluttered up with a lot of book knowledge, much of which often is not practical." Two years earlier, to head its agricultural development department, the road had selected Henry M. Cottrell, an authority on dry farming who had been director of the Colorado Agricultural Experiment Station and who had substantial experience in farmers' institute work.[24] Other roads followed similar recruiting practices, although there were exceptions, and reliance upon land-grant college men continued as long as agricultural development work remained an important railroad activity.

Industrial agents came from more diverse backgrounds. Probably a majority of the early agents were career railroadmen, although a few had had other experiences. J. C. Clair of the Illinois Central and M. V. Richards of the Southern had worked for several railroads in various capacities before they became industrial agents, but another of the pioneers had been a Dakota farmer and lawyer before he went to work for a railroad. Some of the same diversity of experiences characterized industrial men in the 1920s and later. Some men were recruited from chambers of commerce and other promotional groups. Certainly the work required a different type of man after World War II than it had a half century earlier. No longer was it sufficient for an agent to be little more than a salesman with charisma. For example, in 1972 the Norfolk and Western employed people in its development department who were trained in business administration, real estate, finance, economics, engineering, geology, and related areas. Like their less sophisticated predecessors, modern industrial development agents had to be able to maintain good public relations, but now they had to be markedly more knowledgeable in a variety of specific fields.[25]

In 1962 *Railway Age* estimated that close to 1,000 men were employed by railroads in the United States in their development programs. The number per railroad in 1966 ranged from 1 or 2 men up to 29 on the Southern Pacific, plus others who devoted part of their time to development work. On some small roads development work was supervised by the president or the vice-president of traffic, but on the great majority of roads the work was headed by individuals specifically assigned those duties. Titles varied as they had from the outset. Heads of development departments generally reported to the president or the vice-president of traffic, most commonly the latter.[26]

Organizations of Development Personnel

As more railroads undertook development activities, men involved in the work established their own organizations. After J. C. Clair of the Illinois Central proposed such a step, a charter meeting in Chicago in 1906 attracted representatives from seventeen railroads, including most of the pioneers in railroad development work. In addition to Clair, the group included Luis Jackson, then of the Erie; the Burlington's W. H. Manss; D. E. King of the Missouri Pacific; F. H. LaBaume of the Norfolk and Western; and G. A. Park of the Louisville and Nashville. The group drafted a constitution, elected a slate of officers headed by Manss, and chose a name for the new organization – the American Railway Industrial Association.

The group held its first annual meeting in Chicago in 1907. It subsequently met annually, except for 1918, 1919, and 1942, when national emergencies forced cancellation. Semiannual sessions were held until 1934. The annual meetings came to be scheduled in May and in different cities; the semiannual conclaves were generally held in Chicago in conjunction with the International Live Stock Show. In 1911 the name of the organization was shortened to Railway Industrial Association; two years later it became the Railway Development Association; and in 1920 the modern name, American Railway Development Association, was adopted. [27]

The association was never a large group nor was it able to enlist all of the men employed by railroads in development work. Membership rose from 46 in 1907 to 155 in 1917 and to 207 a decade later. The Great Depression cut membership to 92 by 1938, but the post-World War II industrial boom swelled it to 216 in 1962. That figure represented little more than 20 percent of the total number of railway officers with developmental duties. Meanwhile the wave of mergers that swept the railroad industry in the 1960s as well as the deepening economic difficulties of the decade cut membership to 195 in 1971.

In a general way, membership of the association reflected the prevailing emphasis in development work. At the outset the organization was primarily interested in the location of industries. Colonization and agricultural development men soon entered the organization in substantial numbers and they tended to dominate it until the 1930s, when they were again overshadowed by agents involved in industrial work. In the 1970s industrial men were holding their own in the organization, but real estate and marketing agents were increasing in numbers.

For a time in the 1920s and after World War II the American Railway Development Association had its own publication. Known as the *ARDA News*, it was a monthly in the 1920s and a quarterly in 1945 and 1946. Prepared by the secretary of the organization, the publication carried notices of appointments and promotions as well as articles describing the work done by different railroads. The need for economy forced the organization to downgrade the *News* in 1949 to a mimeographed newsletter issued three times a year.[28]

At various times railroad development men also organized themselves on a regional basis. In fact, the Southeastern Railway Land and Industrial Agents' Association predated the national group, having been established in Miami in 1903. Its announced purpose was "to develop and build up the States within our territory by increase of population and industrial enterprise," but the organization soon disappeared. The Southwestern Railway Development Association originated in 1915, apparently as an organization of railway development men in Texas. By the 1920s the group included agents stationed in several southwestern states. It survived until 1932. Finally the Railway Development Association of the Southeast was formed in 1920. It met regularly until 1931 and enjoyed a brief revival in the early 1950s.[29]

Whether national or regional in scope, organizations of railway development men had common objectives. In the 1920s the constitution of the American Railway Development Association stated the organization's goals plainly: "To foster the advancement of the industrial, agricultural, immigration, colonization, publicity, real estate, and other development activities of the railway companies." The emphasis shifted from time to time, reflecting changing needs, but the basic thrust of association goals remained constant. Meanwhile, the annual and semiannual meetings permitted the interchange of ideas that promoted the effectiveness and importance of railway development work and afforded members opportunities to hear talks by other men whose interests paralleled those of the railroaders.[30]

Expenditures for Development Work

The scope of development work over time is suggested by the expenditures for the purpose. Beginning in 1908 the Interstate Commerce Commission published figures indicating amounts spent for development work, and commencing with 1911 these data are available by districts. Account No. 356 includes the "cost to the carrier of industrial and immigration agents, and exhibit agents, their clerks and attendants and their office, stationery and printing, traveling and other expenses."[31] Quite obviously, these figures are only illustrative of general trends, since they do not include railway outlays for such development-related purposes as land purchases, sidetrack installations, and other items.

Between 1908 and 1971 inclusive, Class I railroads in the United States spent $223.3 million for the support and operation of their development offices. Outlays amounted to $699,000 in 1908, but reflecting the carriers' growing interest in agricultural promotion and land settlement, they rose to $1,753,000 in 1913, the peak figure for the pre-World War I years. Governmental operation led to sharp reductions in expenditures; in 1919 outlays aggregated only $891,000, the bulk of which went for colonization work. With the return to private management in 1920, the railroads resumed and expanded their development programs, pushing outlays from $1,354,000 in 1920 to $3,158,000 in 1929. Expenditures declined markedly during the Great Depression, and there was no great resurgence in the early World War II years. Outlays did not reach the 1929 level until 1946. The sharp upturn that began in 1944 continued, with only minor pauses, into the 1970s.

RAILWAY EXPENDITURES FOR DEVELOPMENT WORK BY DECADES

Decade	Expenditures, Current Dollars	Expenditures, 1967 Dollars
1911–1920	$13,972,000	$31,854,000
1921–1930	23,560,000	47,436,000
1931–1940	18,481,000	47,477,000
1941–1950	29,794,000	46,057,000
1951–1960	58,320,000	63,893,000
1961–1970	69,393,000	69,669,000

In general, southern roads seem to have been most deeply committed to the promotion of economic development of their territories. From 1911 through 1971 development department expenditures of carriers in the Southern District consistently represented a larger percentage of total operating expenses than of those railroads in the Eastern and Western districts. Western District roads were in second place, falling behind eastern carriers only in 1971.

The same patterns existed when development outlays were related to miles of road or volume of freight traffic. In terms of expenditures per mile of road, the Southern District was regularly the leader, although after the 1930s outlays in the Eastern District approached those in the area south of the Ohio River. Expenditures in the Western District trailed by a substantial margin, except during the decade before 1921 when they exceeded those in the East. The Southern District also spent more per million ton miles of revenue freight except for the 1930s when the West surged into the lead. The East lagged behind the other districts until the 1940s, when expenditures approximated those in the West.[32]

EXPENDITURES PER MILE OF ROAD, DECADE AVERAGES

Decade	Eastern District	Southern District	Western District
1911–1920	$ 4.06	$10.93	$ 5.47
1921–1930	9.65	15.12	8.22
1931–1940	8.91	10.72	6.31
1941–1950	18.10	18.42	9.06
1951–1960	34.67	38.37	18.23
1961–1970	41.31	44.11	24.63

EXPENDITURES PER MILLION TON MILES, REVENUE FREIGHT, DECADE AVERAGES

Decade	Eastern District	Southern District	Western District
1911–1920	$ 1.51	$ 8.35	$ 6.71
1921–1930	3.29	7.92	7.74
1931–1940	4.20	6.96	7.88
1941–1950	4.51	6.12	4.54
1951–1960	9.73	12.03	7.61
1961–1970	9.93	12.23	9.31

In authorizing the expenditures of company funds for development work, railway executives were certainly inspired by the profit motive. They recognized clearly that "prosperous communities meant prosperous railroads" and acted accordingly. A Burlington pamphlet stated the matter plainly in 1872: "It is not to be supposed that railroad corporations surpass other men in disinterested benevolence, but it is beyond question that they know their own interest, and so will take pains to help you earn a dollar whenever they can make two for themselves." Seventy-five years later the Illinois Central's Wayne A. Johnston wrote that "Our aim was, and is, to develop the prosperity and well-being of the territory we serve, for as the prosperity of the people along our line increases, the fortunes of the Illinois Central also climb."[33] For almost a century other railroad executives have shared and acted upon the same principles, and the industry as a whole has done much to shape the economic development and evolution of the United States.

Pere Marquette established in Lake County two experiment plots to attract settlers. In Wisconsin, the Omaha, Soo Line, and Wisconsin Central were still peddling land in the early twentieth century, including some from which the timber had been cut. Comparable work went on in eastern and northern Minnesota.[10]

Northeastern railroads mainly sought to attract farmers to abandoned farms. They emphasized the relative price of land. President William C. Brown of the New York Central reported that farms in New York could be bought for from $13 to $50 an acre, as compared to the going prices of from $100 to $150 in the Middle West. Some roads in the Northeast promoted the settlement of cutover land; the Maine Central, for example, had ambitious plans in 1911 for a colonization program in Washington County, Maine. [11]

Recruiting and Handling Settlers

Regardless of their locations, railroads having active colonization programs had to make every effort to establish contact with potential settlers and to attract as many as possible to their territories. The work was highly competitive. Some railroads quite obviously faced greater difficulties than others, but all of them used essentially the same recruiting methods.

Useful in colonization programs were company magazines, which circulated in sizable numbers. The Burlington's *Corn Belt* was a pioneer; soon such publications were common. The Rock Island had its *Western Trail*, later *Southwest Trail;* the Louisville and Nashville, *North and South;* the Southern Railway, *Southern Field;* the Seaboard Air Line, *Seaboard Magazine;* the St. Louis and San Francisco, *Frisco Magazine;* the Southern Pacific, *Sunset Magazine;* and there were many others. Circulation varied widely, but the average for the *Corn Belt* was 27,000 while that of the *Western Trail* was 55,000. Objectives similarly varied, but the Kansas City Southern's *Current Events* summarized the goals of most of the papers when it stated that its "aim in life will be to bring the resources of the country to the notice of those who are on the lookout for something good."[12]

Advertisements in newspapers and farm journals were used to arouse interest among prospective settlers. The Louisville and Nashville, for example, claimed in 1903 that it was using 2,500 advertising outlets. Generally, such squibs were brief notices that pointed to the attractions of an area, stated the terms available for land, and invited interested readers to write company officials for additional information. Typical of many others was a Northern Pacific advertisement of Minnesota in 1910. Farms were available throughout the state, the railroad stated, while in the northern portion there was "a vast region of the most fertile soil still unoccupied, where homeseekers can get government lands, or state lands, or cutover timber lands at low prices."[13]

Promotional literature ranging from one-page fliers to large and attractively printed and illustrated booklets poured out of railway company offices in tremendous volumes. In 1914 the Northern Pacific listed 25 separate booklets in addition to a number of pamphlets and leaflets dealing with specific areas or communities. A Great Northern booklet on Montana was published in an issue of 210,000 copies. The Denver and Rio Grande's *Fertile Lands of Colorado and New Mexico* went through numerous editions, and by 1912 copies numbered over a quarter of a million.[14]

The titles of many of these booklets were descriptive of their contents. The Missouri Pacific had its *Home Builder in Arkansas;* among its literature in 1903 the Cotton Belt listed *Homes in the Southwest;* and the Northern Pacific distributed *Montana, the Treasure State.* The Burlington's *Big Horn Basin* pointed to the attractions of that famous valley; the Great Northern covered a much larger territory in its *Opportunities in the Northwest;* and the Soo's *A Competence from Forty Acres* sought to show the agricultural potential of northern cutover lands.

All such literature had but one objective—to arouse the interest of homeseekers to the point at which they would visit the area being promoted. As the Illinois Central expressed it, the company's literature "seeks only to *guide* its readers to portions of the South where, by actual experience, it has been fully demonstrated that Northern farmers . . . have been successful; and, by a candid presentation of the facts, lead the new homeseekers to investigate. . . ."

Railroad literature certainly improved in quality over time, but its objectivity usually left something to be desired. The Illinois Central's *Southern Homeseekers' Guide* claimed to "describe as accurately as possible the exact conditions as they exist today on the line . . . south of the Ohio River," but it fell short of that goal. The same generalization applied equally well to the great bulk of the railroads' promotional literature.

In booming lands in north and northwest Texas in 1910, for example, the St. Louis and San Francisco informed readers that nowhere else in the world could a man have a better chance to succeed than in Lamar, Hardeman, or Cottle counties. "Here is a soil and climate where a farmer can sometimes get two crops . . . the same season. . . ." There had "never been a crop failure" in those areas, the railroad proclaimed, but it implied that farmers should use dry-farming methods.[15]

In their literature, all western roads devoted a great deal of attention to the question of aridity. The Milwaukee, for example, reported that the deep black loam soil along its new line through South Dakota was little different from that farther east and that the "soil and climate of eastern and central Montana generally . . . are adapted to the raising of almost all grains raised in the middle western states." Some roads continued to embrace the old doctrine that settlement increased rainfall. The precipitation at Ione, Oregon, ranged from 18 to 22 inches a year, according to the Union Pacific, but "this is constantly increasing as more of the country is brought under cultivation." In booming the Lewistown, Montana, area, the Milwaukee maintained that while "it has been demonstrated that the rainfall at present is sufficient to raise wheat, it is bound to increase as the country is broken up."

Western roads rarely failed to mention the allegedly healthy and desirable climate of their territories. According to the Chicago and North Western, South Dakota possessed "a climate unusually attractive, free from extremes of heat or cold, with a bracing and invigorating air that is fast becoming favorably known for its health giving qualities." The Northern Pacific informed readers that the climate of Montana was surprisingly agreeable, lacking both high humidity and extremes of temperature. Below zero readings were rare, while summers were pleasantly warm. Spring was delightful. "At Missoula, buttercups are usually gathered in March and butterflies have been taken as early as the middle of February." [16]

Southern roads attempted to counteract the prejudices and misinformation about the region that made their work more difficult. The climate was pictured as pleasant, healthy, and certainly not oppressive as northerners believed it to be. Admittedly, there were some bad days in the South, the Illinois Central's *Southern Homeseekers' Guide* said, but during the "months of February, March, and April, while Northern people hug the stove, and never venture out except with overshoes and coats, our Southern friends are picking strawberries, every morning a fresh bouquet of roses is placed upon the mantel, all the doors are wide open, and the perfume from native woods and flowers fills every house with fragrance." The Missouri Pacific was equally eloquent in describing the climate of Louisiana.

Railroad writers were willing to admit that the "lands of the South are not . . . of as uniformly good quality as those of the Western States," but they argued that it was "utter folly to extoll the advantages of one section of the country at the expense of another." The Illinois Central described land in Attala County, Mississippi, as "quite fertile" and claimed that it would not "wash or gully out." In the case of Ballard County, Kentucky, the company acknowledged that "during high water portions of the county are overflowed" but claimed that these "lands . . . are exceedingly fertile, and produce great crops. . . ."

Nor was the South a backwoods, lacking conveniences and the

amenities and inhabited by people without ambition. Pass Christian, Mississippi, was the "Newport of the South." The Missouri Pacific reported that the schools of northern Louisiana were in "fairly good condition," and its writers ventured the opinion that they would improve when the country filled up. Southerners were not lazy and transplanted northerners need not fear that they would lose their energy and drive. The Missouri Pacific assured readers that in Louisiana it was not true that "one grows indolent . . . beneath the benign influence of this land of sunshine. . . . Labor is a pleasure rather than a dreary round of endless monotony."

Southern railroads also sought to dispel the notions that southern white people resented outsiders and that Negroes were troublesome. The town of Sharon, Tennessee, said the Illinois Central, like the rest of the South, was inhabited by a "class of people that cannot be excelled." Race relations were portrayed in a favorable light. According to the Illinois Central, "in her constitutional convention [Mississippi] solved for all time, upon terms of enlightened justice, the race problems in politics." A transplanted northerner, who had moved from Nebraska to Coldwater, Mississippi, was quoted in an effort to put at ease the minds of those who believed that "the darkies . . . carry off all the pigs." That commentator on race relations reported that, in reference to the Negroes in his community, "we would not know what to do without them; they are very necessary and we haven't lost a pig."[17]

Testimonials by settlers were important features of much of the railroad literature. Apparently, they were obtained in various ways. An agent of the Sante Fe involved in the colonization of the San Joaquin Valley visited farmers, listened to their success stories, and then wrote the letters. The Rock Island offered prizes for the best testimonial letters from its western territory.

Regardless of how they were obtained, testimonial letters were thought to be effective tools in convincing readers that they should relocate. One of Northern Pacific's settlers near Carrington, North Dakota, claimed that, while winters were cold, the inhabitants were little affected because of the low humidity. Her seven sons walked two miles to school in forty degree below zero weather but felt no discomfort, she reported. A writer from Hammond, Louisiana, after discussing at length the mocking and humming birds, jasmines, and azaleas common to the area, concluded that he was "well satisfied with this country."[18]

Exhibits of different types also proved useful in recruiting settlers. Most colonizing railroads maintained permanent displays in important cities, often in major terminals where they might be seen by large numbers of travelers. In 1901 the Great Northern had fixed exhibits of Montana products in ten middlewestern and eastern cities, while the Southern maintained displays of grains and vegetables in St. Louis and elsewhere. More elaborate were exhibits placed at the great expositions and land shows so common during the years before 1917. The Southern Railway had a large exhibit at the Massachusetts Charitable Exposition in the fall of 1902, while at least five southern carriers had displays at the Jamestown Exposition of 1907 that advertised the agricultural resources of the states from Virginia to Texas. Railroad exhibits were prominent at the United States Land and Irrigation Exposition in Chicago in 1910 and at the American Land and Irrigation Exposition in New York's Madison Square Garden in 1911. Indeed, these great land shows were for all practical purposes railroad creations.[19]

Some roads used movable exhibits. In 1912 the Southern displayed the same exhibit at the Canadian International Exhibit in Toronto and at thirty-two agricultural fairs in eight middlewestern and eastern states. In all, 237,000 visitors carried away some 250,000 pieces of literature, and Southern agents reported that they discussed opportunities in the South with 71,000 "high-class farmers." The Norfolk Southern was another road that placed exhibits at northern fairs.[20]

Common also was the use of exhibit cars that were sent on tours of districts where prospective homeseekers were expected to be found. A two-car Illinois Central exhibit train toured Illinois in 1908, carrying displays of farm products grown in the South by northern farmers who had located there. According to the company's general immigration agent, the train "was a most potent method of advertising . . . and as a result my mail is now filled with inquiries from parties who say positively they are going to locate in the South." Between 1912 and 1917 Atlantic Coast Line exhibit cars made annual tours of the Middle West and East.[21] The Great Northern, Northern Pacific, Milwaukee, and Southern Pacific were among the other roads that used exhibit cars to attract prospective settlers.

Excursions were another widely used advertising method. With the Illinois Central, excursions for farmers were annual affairs during the early years of the twentieth century. Always scheduled for November, when company officials believed northern farmers could travel most conveniently, these excursions took groups from the Middle West on ten-day tours of the Illinois Central's southern states. The railroad also took groups of northern realtors on tours of the South, a practice inspired by the knowledge that the great bulk of farm sales was handled by real estate agents. The Frisco ran regular excursions into the Southwest from St. Louis, Memphis, and Kansas City, while in 1903 the St. Louis Southwestern took a group of farm journalists on a tour of Texas.[22]

While they were much less active, eastern roads used most of these standard techniques to attract new farmers to abandoned lands in their territories. In 1906 the Delaware and Hudson compiled and distributed a list of some 600 farms for sale, mostly in northern New York. The Pennsylvania issued typical promotional literature, including a booklet entitled *Farming Possibilities on the Delaware-Maryland-Virginia-Peninsula*. Like western roads, the New York Central and the Lehigh Valley sent exhibit cars into middlewestern states, and the New York Central was apparently the prime force in the organization in 1910 of the Agricultural Improvement Association of New York City, a group that published and distributed lists of farms for sale.[23]

Promotional literature, exhibits, and excursions might arouse the interest of prospective homeseekers, but railroad managers believed that personal contact was imperative if settlers were to be moved. The standard practice was to employ a number of colonization agents and enlist a much larger group of men who worked on commission, all of them under the supervision of a general colonization agent. The Frisco had 650 men at work in twenty-two states in 1904. Included were realtors, bankers, and clergymen. Organized as the Frisco System Land and Immigration Association, most of the men worked in their own communities, using their acquaintance with individuals to identify those who might be willing to move. Soon after the turn of the century the Southern Pacific's general immigration agent for Louisiana and Texas supervised the work of 600 men from his office in Chicago. In 1902 a central colonization bureau in the same city managed settlement work for all of the Harriman lines.[24]

Several roads continued to maintain agents abroad. In 1904 the Frisco had an agent in Zurich, Switzerland, to recruit gardeners, dairymen, and grape growers for the Ozark sections of Missouri and Arkansas. By 1907 that road and the Rock Island had men in London, Rome, and Bremen. For several years the Southern Pacific was represented in Hamburg, and the Santa Fe had men in various European countries. Southern roads also sent men to Europe, although M. V. Richards of the Southern Railway complained that it was difficult to compete with American and Canadian roads having land grants. Still, in 1905 the Illinois Central maintained agents in Norway, Sweden, Holland, and other north European countries. At least one road, the Southern Pacific, placed in Japan a recruiter who urged Japanese investors and rice farmers to purchase land and settle in Louisiana and Texas.[25]

The objective of all immigration agents was to contact as many prospective homeseekers as possible, convince them that opportunity awaited in the territories served by their roads, and arrange for their departure. Modes of operation varied greatly, but probably those of the Great Northern were typical. In 1902 that company had "34 men at work in the country east of Chicago." Confining their activities to rural districts, they gave lectures, illustrated by slides, in country school houses and town halls. At each lecture, "quantities of literature concerning the Northwest . . . are distributed and in addition each of . . . the agents carries with him products, fruits, vegetables, etc., all of which are placed on exhibition." Other agents spent a great deal of time attending meetings of agricultural societies, state and county fairs, and other rural gatherings. Probably most successful agents had their own tricks of the trade. One railroad had men who did "nothing but follow circuses. The circus collects a crowd and our men take advantage of the opportunity to distribute their information to a large number of people. A bundle of literature is slipped under the seat of each farmer's wagon. It is not thrown away, but is taken home, usually before it is discovered, and it is safe to say that it is then read."[26]

After 1900, as earlier, some railroads succeeded in moving groups of people of the same religious faith. The Great Northern enjoyed substantial success in placing Dunkards from Indiana and elsewhere in North Dakota, beginning that program in 1893 and settling over 10,000 of the sect by 1902. The Sante Fe established a Dunkard colony in the Texas Panhandle in 1904 and earlier worked with a national committee of Quakers to place members of that faith on irrigated sugar beet lands in Colorado.[27]

More significant after 1900, apparently, were nationality groups. Southern roads were especially interested in Italians. The carriers established warm relations with the Italian government and in 1904 arranged for the Italian ambassador to make a tour of Italian colonies in the South. The Illinois Central claimed to have put a substantial number of Italian families in Mississippi and in Louisiana's Tangipahoa Parish, while the Georgia Southern and Florida had an Italian colony at Valdosta, Georgia. Meanwhile the Illinois Central counted Danish, German, and Polish colonies in Mississippi and Hungarian and Swedish settlements in Louisiana. The Northern Pacific placed some "Hollanders" in Washington and Montana, and the Southern Pacific reported the movement of a colony of Norwegians from Iowa to Texas. The Frisco apparently succeeded in putting several hundred Swiss in the Ozarks.[28]

After settlers were recruited, railroads were faced with the task of facilitating their movement to their new homes. In the case of immigrants the problem involved also the handling of the new arrivals through East Coast ports to western gateways. In the main, procedures had been worked out before the turn of the century. In 1886 the Trunk Line Association, in conjunction with authorities at Ellis Island, organized the Immigrant Clearing House to insure the protection and proper handling of new arrivals. Later the trunk lines serving New York and Chicago and Mississippi River points established a pooling arrangement to handle the immigrant traffic and to serve as an evener for all passenger business.

West of Chicago and Mississippi River points pooling arrangements also existed; apparently, only southern roads failed to establish such systems.[29] The western pools survived numerous crises during the first years of the new century.

Meanwhile railroads improved facilities for the handling of immigrants. The Chicago and North Western station in Chicago that opened in 1912 was designed in part for the convenience of those passing though on their way to the West. It featured a laundry, baths, rest rooms, restaurants, and special attendants, all to make the station a temporary home for the "stranger within the gates."[30] The new Union Station in St. Paul, which was planned before World War I, also had special immigrant facilities.

Finally, most railroads offered a variety of special rates. All western roads sold homeseekers' tickets. These round-trip tickets carried generous stopover privileges to permit holders to visit different localities. Some roads sold the tickets the year around, but most offered them only during certain months and for use on specific days, such as the first and third Tuesdays of each month. Cost approached the regular one-way fare. In 1912 and 1913 homeseekers could go from Chicago to California and return for $65.00, from St. Louis for $62.50, and from Missouri River points for $55.00.[31]

Homeseekers' rates made cheaper the exploration of lands by potential settlers; colonist fares reduced the cost to settlers of taking their families to their new homes. Colonist fares provided for transportation in one direction only and were generally offered during those seasons, usually in the spring and the fall, when most settlers wanted to move. Again, cost was kept low. The Santa Fe fare from Chicago to California was $33.00 and from Kansas City $25.00, substantially below the regular second class fares of $52.50 and $40.00, respectively. These special fares were continued until the outbreak of World War I, although rates were adjusted from time to time.[32]

Some southern railroads also offered reduced rates to homeseekers. In 1904 the Nashville, Chattanooga and St. Louis, the Louisville and Nashville, and the Frisco, acting through the Memphis Passenger Bureau, announced homeseekers' rates to all points on their lines in the Southeast. Soon the Mobile and Ohio was another line that offered rates comparable to those in the West.[33]

Colonizing railroads also gave reduced rates for the movement of settlers' personal possessions, such as household goods, farm machinery, and livestock. The Kansas City Southern was more specific, stating that immigrant movable rates applied to tools and implements, livestock up to ten head, trees and shrubbery, one portable house, seeds, feed for livestock in transit, and "a sufficient quantity of furniture to make the intention of permanent residence at destination evident." Rates varied, but the Denver and Rio Grande claimed that it transported "carload lots of immigrant movables practically at cost."[34]

New Problems in Colonization

After 1900 railroadmen knew that energetic advertising campaigns and cheap transportation would not, by themselves, produce the results the carriers wanted. Conditions were different from those of an earlier era, and executives in charge of colonization programs recognized that the work now required more attention to details. Agents could no longer be mere propagandists, and those who hustled settlers into an area without determining that they had a reasonable chance of success were doing more harm than good. Moreover, the nature of much of the country being settled generated a variety of problems unknown to earlier colonization agents.

According to the Northern Pacific's C. W. Mott in 1903, the "wide-awake . . . agent must know the country he wants to settle, not only what it is, but what it can be made to be, and what class of people are most likely to be successful in developing it." Some individuals should be avoided "as we would a pestilence." These included the "ne'erdo-well, who can always be found at the crossroads general store, sitting on a cracker box and dividing his time between expectorating tobacco juice . . . and blaming the political conditions for his poverty. . . ." Such men "would have starved to death in the Garden of Eden" and were a "detriment to 'any community."[35]

Colonization in the new century involved cooperation with a diversity of groups and agencies, some of which had objectives not always in accordance with those of the railroads. Railroad officials were often critical of the activities of land locators, claiming that such men had no real interest in seeing that homeseekers were placed on desirable land. Other difficulties arose with the herd of realtors with whom all railroads worked. Some of them, according to railroaders, had a tendency to oversell land, locate people who were unsuited to the land they bought, and take prices that were unrealistically high. Some carriers tried to establish procedures to control the most obvious excesses of such men, but apparently with little success.[36]

Nor were relations always satisfactory with the multitude of private land companies that flourished in the years before World War I. In the South a large number of these firms were busily peddling cutover land to settlers. In 1907 the Hawley-Moore Land Company offered near Waverly, Virginia, 25-acre plots equipped with three-room cottages for from $300 to $500, while the Chicago Mill and Lumber Company had on the market large tracts of land in the Blytheville, Arkansas, area. In west Louisiana, along the line of the Kansas City Southern, several major companies were selling land. The Pineland Manufacturing Company had extensive holdings in Vernon Parish, in 1916 the Long-Bell Lumber Company placed on sale 300,0000 acres in Beauregard and adjoining parishes, and other firms had over 100,000 acres in Sabine and Calcasieu parishes. Understandably enough, the desire of such firms to sell land conflicted at times with the railroads' goal of establishing successful farms.[37]

In other instances some railroads and railroad officials worked closely with private land companies. In 1902 the Union Pacific sold over 50,000 acres to one such company, and some carriers in the Southwest were making every effort to induce investors to "buy up the land and afterwards drag the homeseeker down there." Meanwhile in 1903 the Southern Pacific was closely allied with three land companies created to sell lands in Louisiana and Texas, while the Santa Fe worked with a firm engaged in the handling of rice lands that numbered among its officers General Nelson A. Miles of Indian and Spanish-American war fame.[38]

Railroads seemingly had more friendly relations with public agencies that were engaged in colonization work. State immigration bureaus still existed in many western and some southern states, doing work that was much like that of the carriers, and railroads often cooperated with them. James J. Hill's son Louis was only one of many railroadmen who urged state legislatures to be generous in supporting such agencies. Chambers of commerce and comparable groups were also useful allies in colonization work.[39]

Where state and regional promotional agencies did not exist, railroads moved to create them. The Immigration and Industrial Association of Alabama and the Georgia Bureau of Industries and Immigration apparently were railway creations. Railroaders were also prominent in such southern groups as the Four-State Immigration League, the Southern Immigration and Industrial Association, and the Southern Cutover Land Association. In the West railroads contributed generously to the support of the American Immigration Association of the Northwest, the Wisconsin Advancement Association, formed in 1910 to "promote Wisconsin agricultural interests . . . and to attract immigrants to the unsettled lands of northern Wisconsin," and the Northwest Development Congress, established to aid in the more rapid development of the country between Minnesota and Puget Sound.[40]

The most difficult problems that colonization men faced after 1900 were those that were associated with the territories being boomed. Southern railroads wrestled with those conditions that historically had handicapped efforts to induce people to move into that section, while in the

West colonizing railroads found that it was no small task to convince farmers from Ohio and Illinois that they could prosper on irrigated land or in areas of light rainfall.

While southern roads recognized that they labored under huge handicaps, their spokesmen professed to believe that they were on the threshold of overcoming those hindrances. In 1902 J. T. Harahan, vice-president of the Illinois Central, proclaimed that the "tide of immigration . . . has shown a steady growth. A few years ago we were sending all of our immigrants to South Dakota, but homeseekers have turned southward, and we are bringing them to Louisiana and Mississippi." In reality, the bulk of potential homeseekers continued to think of the South as exclusively cotton country, inhabited by Negroes and unfriendly whites, and no amount of railroad effort could completely dispel those notions.[41]

Western roads that sought to attract men to irrigation districts also encountered serious problems. Irrigated farming was new to midwesterners, it was heavy work, and irrigated land was expensive. In answering the latter of these objections, railroadmen stressed the greater value and productivity of irrigated land. According to the Denver and Rio Grande, "If a poor man buys poor land . . . he is still poor, but if a poor man can buy good land, no matter what the price, on terms he can meet with sure-fire crops, then, when he gets it paid for, he is no longer poor."[42]

But for western roads it was the High Plains country that offered the greatest challenges as well as opportunities for colonization work during the years before 1917. Never before, said one observer in 1907, had there been "a movement comparable to that now in progress either in vast extent of the territory involved, the number of investors and homeseekers attracted, or the variety of causes contributing to its rise and progress." Certainly a variety of factors contributed to the rush to the High Plains, but overshadowing others was "the discovery that a very large proportion of the semi-arid lands are . . . well adapted to wheat growing . . . provided rational methods of preparing the soil" were used.

Those "rational methods of preparing the soil," most railroadmen believed, had been discovered by Hardy W. Campbell, whose achievements, enthusiasts maintained, exceeded those of Luther Burbank. Dry farming was a "phrase of hope," and by using its methods farmers could grow wheat in "the natural habitat of the cactus." Nor was wheat the only crop that flourished with dry farming: "Every crop that grows in the rain countries grows in eastern Colorado," reported one advocate.[43]

The problem, of course, was to convince prospective settlers that the High Plains would produce. The area had long tempted settlers, but many early arrivals could be found who could testify to the difficulties encountered in developing a farm west of the 20-inch rainfall line. Nevertheless, shortly after the turn of the century railroadmen concluded that the only thing the country needed was people, and they set out to supply that need.

The question of the value of the land for farming gave western railroaders pause until they convinced themselves that the country could be settled. In 1904 the Northern Pacific took its Montana lands off the market, and the next year it joined with the federal government and the state in conducting experiments to determine whether the plains could be made to produce. In 1906 the Montana Agricultural Experiment Station managed six test farms, and by 1908 the scientists were willing to state that Montana lands would grow satisfactory crops without irrigation. Meanwhile a similar program was underway in North Dakota, the railroads first contributing funds for that purpose in 1906. By 1910 the Great Northern had forty-five tests in progress in North Dakota and Montana under the direction of Thomas Shaw, James J. Hill's agricultural adviser. Shaw was a former professor at the University of Minnesota and farm paper editor who went to work for Hill in 1905. By 1910 he was considered an authority on dry farming and while he did not accept Hardy W. Campbell's ideas without reservation, he was fully convinced that dry land farming on the bench lands of northern and eastern Montana and in western North Dakota was totally feasible.

An important propagandizing tool in the settlement of the High Plains was the Dry Farming Congress. Created in 1907, the organization consisted of scientists as well as laymen, but railroads apparently provided much of its financial support, at least until 1911. Prominent participants at its annual sessions included Shaw and Thomas Cooper, land commissioner of the Northern Pacific, as well as James J. and Louis Hill.

The nature of the organization and the purposes to which railroadmen wanted to put it were demonstrated clearly in 1911 when a controversy arose concerning the name of the group. Railroadmen objected to the use of the word "dry" in its title, contending that "scientific" would be more descriptive. "We know that Montana is neither dry or arid," said the Northern Pacific's Howard Elliott, "and we do not want the idea to go to Indiana and Ohio and all through the East where they are looking for new places to go." Louis Hill was equally specific. "Those of us who are acquainted with the country . . . know that there is just as good an opportunity and as good a chance to harvest a crop with as great a certainty as in any of the states east of the Mississippi. . . . [44]

The scientists in the Dry Farming Congress managed to preserve its name, but the carriers soon abandoned the organization and turned their attention to the immediate task of attracting people to the plains. Montana, according to Howard Elliott, contained 20 million acres suitable for cultivation by "better methods of farming." Production figures in the hands of railroadmen showed that the Treasure State was truly the farmers' last frontier. The average wheat yield in 1907, Elliott pointed out, was 29 bushels per acre, more than double the national average, and the yield of barley and oats was on a par.

In a sense the crusade culminated in 1912. That year James J. Hill, then at the peak of his influence as the voice of the Northwest, stood before a crowd at Havre, Montana, and informed his audience categorically that northern Montana was suitable for family-sized farms. By that time his men had done their work well. Homesteaders took 4.8 million acres in 1910, and between that year and 1922 they claimed 42 percent of the state.[45]

Elsewhere on the High Plains and in intermountain areas, comparable, if less well-known, propagandizing work went on. Thomas Shaw was certain that dry farming would transform central Oregon. In 1912, he said, there were more than "10,000,000 acres of land as yet unplowed, on which can be raised 62,000,000 bushels of wheat annually," provided dry farming was practiced. In northwest Texas settlers were told they could produce cotton if they used dry farming methods; there "has never been a cotton failure," the Frisco informed readers. The Sante Fe's H. M. Bainer maintained that it "is not the mean average rainfall that will make a crop, but it is rather the amount of moisture that can actually be saved and made available to our crops." Numerous farmers in the Santa Fe's eastern Colorado and west Texas territories produced from 20 to 25 bushels of wheat with no more than 4 inches of rainfall because they followed "an intelligent system of farming."

The problems of colonizing the High Plains was one of the factors that encouraged railroads to move energetically into the promotion of better farming. H. M. Bainer noted that on the High Plains "the only successful way to handle corn is to forget it," thus indicating his recognition that midwestern farmers moving to the Texas Panhandle or to Montana would have to make significant adjustments in farming methods if they were to succeed in their new environment.[46] Western railroaders thus concluded after 1900 that it was to the advantage of their companies to do all that they could to help settlers make those adjustments, while railroads in other areas of the country decided that they could do much to stimulate greater output of farm commodities by encouraging the adoption of better farming methods. The result was the establishment, soon after 1900, of remarkably comprehensive agricultural development programs by most major carriers.

CHAPTER THREE

Railroads and Better Farming, 1900–1920

A VARIETY OF MOTIVES induced railroads throughout the United States to institute in the first decades of the twentieth century broad programs in agricultural development. Almost without exception railway executives believed that outbound traffic could be increased through agricultural diversification and the use of newer and more progressive farming methods. Greater agricultural output would increase both rural income and inbound shipments, thus generating additional revenues and helping to solve the perennial problems of imbalanced traffic flow, car shortages, and excess capacity. An increased volume of business would help railroads meet a new challenge, the cost-price squeeze created by Progressive legislation and regulation. As the Northern Pacific's H. W. Byerly expressed it, "the ever-increasing cost of operation and taxes, and the downward tendency of rates . . . have made it imperative to increase traffic."[1]

Railway development work with farmers was also inspired by political considerations. After Populism lost its power, some industry leaders decided that it would be wise to enlist the rural population on the side of business. In 1905 officials of the Missouri, Kansas and Texas suggested to stockholders that a favorable rural sentiment might help to restrain the tendency of state legislatures in Kansas and Missouri to enact "drastic legislation." B. F. Yoakum of the Frisco stated plainly that considering the drift of political affairs, "the safest way for a railroad to proceed was to work with the farmer. . . ."[2]

In their efforts to improve farming, railroads enjoyed a great deal of assistance. During the early decades of the twentieth century the nation was swept by a crusade aimed at the improvement of farming methods and rural life, the establishment of the Country Life Commission by

Theodore Roosevelt being only one manifestation of the movement. Under the leadership of Iowa's James Wilson, the U. S. Department of Agriculture increased its activities. Modern agricultural extension originated with Seaman A. Knapp's work in Texas in 1903 and became a national system of rural education with the enactment of the Smith-Lever Act in 1914. Other men began to think of teaching agriculture to school children. Agricultural high schools were established in a few states, but more common was the introduction of agricultural courses in traditional high schools. The Smith-Hughes Act of 1917 provided federal money for a nationwide program.

Businessmen soon joined the crusade for rural improvement. Bankers, farm machinery manufacturers, grain buyers, and fertilizer companies cooperated with public agencies engaged in the work, contributed funds, and occasionally implemented their own programs. No industry was more deeply involved than were the nation's railroads.[3]

Railroaders generally believed that their companies could make their greatest contributions to the better farming crusade by acting as vehicles for the transmission of information to farmers. As the Frisco's Frank Anderson explained to the University of Missouri's F. B. Mumford, "My idea has always been that the railroads . . . should confine their efforts towards demonstrating and carrying to the farmer the methods already developed and pronounced as successful by various agricultural agencies . . . it is not part of our business to expound theories or to experiment. . . ."

Certainly railroads did not attempt to conceal their motives under the guise of philanthropy; their spokesmen emphasized that development work was strictly a business proposition. Some railroad officials on occasion talked like agrarian fundamentalists, but most were more practical. Speaking before a group of farm leaders in 1902, the Southern's M. V. Richards noted simply that "the prosperity of the railroads is inseparable from the prosperity of the farmer" and that "the success of the railroads depends . . . largely upon the success of the farmer." J. C. Clair put the matter even more bluntly. "We don't claim a special credit for what the Illinois Central has done; we are not in this for philanthropy; we have a selfish motive," he wrote.[4]

Influencing Farmers

To achieve the goal of increased agricultural production, railroad executives knew that their companies had to develop effective teaching methods if farmers were to be induced to make the desired changes in their operations. Enterprising development men responded with a remarkable diversity of programs, but like all agricultural educators they found some techniques to be of more value than others in influencing farmers.

The use of exhibits at state and local fairs was an educational technique that was borrowed from colonization work. By 1912 the Southern Railway had at fairs in seven southeastern states horticultural and agricultural exhibits that were educational in character, showing what progressive farmers could produce on their own land. The Illinois Central and Yazoo and Mississippi Valley roads used displays at fairs in Mississippi to demonstrate the corn-growing potential of that state, and the Central of Georgia adopted the technique as one means of encouraging cotton farmers to shift to legumes and livestock.[5] Regional, national, and international expositions also attracted numerous railway educational exhibits.

The awarding of prizes to farmers who excelled was another method widely used to stimulate better agriculture. In 1906 James J. Hill gave awards of from $75 to $300 for good farming in each congressional district in Minnesota and the Dakotas. Awards were based on rotation of crops, quality of cultivation, control of weeds, and crop yields as well as the raising of at least two kinds of livestock. Roughly comparable were awards offered in Louisiana and Texas in 1915 by the Southern Pacific. The Bangor and Aroostook used prizes to encourage potato growers in Maine. At the American Land and Irrigation Exposition in 1911 the Northern Pacific awarded 160 acres of Montana farm land and $500 for the best display of apples, while Hill's Great Northern gave a silver cup valued at $1,000 for the best 100 pounds of wheat.[6]

Reduced rates for farmers attending a variety of types of agricultural meetings were also common. The Mobile and Ohio gave special rates to persons attending programs at the Mississippi Agricultural and Mechanical College, and in 1908 the Western Passenger Association set a rate of 1.5 cents a mile to persons going to state fairs, a reduction from the standard 2 cents a mile then prevailing. Farmers attending such gatherings as the International Live Stock Show in Chicago and other meetings having a distinctly agricultural flavor also benefited from less than standard rates.[7]

In their efforts to increase production along their lines, most railroads relied heavily on the printed word. Railway literature ranged from regularly issued periodicals to bulletins, folders, short articles prepared for newspapers and farm journals, and other items. Many of the same kinds of literature were used in the carriers' colonization programs; in fact, the distinction between colonization and agricultural improvement objectives was not always clear, and a given piece of railroad literature was often used for both purposes.

Among the roads using dual purpose periodicals, the Burlington and

Santa Fe were pioneers. The former company's *Corn Belt* and the Santa Fe's *The Earth* were aimed primarily at homeseekers, but both carried some educational matter and circulated among farmers in the companies' territories. More educational in purpose were the Baltimore and Ohio's *Messenger of Agricultural Development* and the Long Island's *Long Island Agronomist.* The Boston and Maine's *New England Farms* carried typical educational articles and in addition sought to plant the idea among New England farmers that the West had no attractions that could not be matched by those of their native region.[8]

Much more numerous were booklets and pamphlets that dealt with single crops or groups of crops or with some aspect of livestock production. By 1912 the Frisco had available a half dozen different booklets on as many crops. One of the most active publication programs was that of the Pennsylvania. Beginning in 1907 and continuing until World War I, the road flooded its territory with brochures and bulletins. In 1911 it issued a 112-page booklet entitled *Increase the Crop per Acre* that the road claimed was the most elaborate piece of farm literature produced by a railroad. The same year it turned out its *The Essentials of Soil Fertility* and other items that dealt with alfalfa growing, orchard development, potato culture, seed grain selection, and the use of dynamite on the farm. By 1912 the company claimed that it had placed more than 200,000 copies of various publications in the hands of farmers.[9]

The Pennsylvania and other railroads also produced short informative articles for publication in newspapers and farm periodicals. One of the Pennsylvania's agricultural agents claimed that he wrote 400 such items in 1910 alone. An agent of the Rock Island performed the same task for that line, and almost a decade earlier the Illinois Central's J. F. Merry was producing one-page articles for newspapers in the company's southern territory.[10]

Railroad literature was compiled from a variety of sources and was written by both railroadmen and outside experts. Some railroads distributed bulletins issued by the U. S. Department of Agriculture or the state agricultural experiment stations. Others distilled such items into more readable language. The Chicago and North Western used publications turned out by the Middle West Soil Improvement Committee, while the Soo simply gave subscriptions to *Hoard's Dairyman* to selected farmers along its line. The Pennsylvania, Southern, and Wabash arranged to have pamphlets written for them by professors at the agricultural colleges in their territories. On the other hand, the Missouri College of Agriculture found some of the material produced by railroadmen to be of sufficiently high quality to distribute it to students.[11]

Of all the teaching methods used by railroads, however, none was more popular or widely used than the educational or demonstration train.

Like most teaching methods educational trains had diverse origins. In 1891 the Ontario, Canada, Agricultural College sent two lecturers intó the countryside in a wagon loaded with equipment to instruct farmers in dairying, and later in the decade the Great Northern placed better farming exhibits on a train that visited stations in Minnesota. In 1902 John T. Stinson of the Missouri Fruit Experiment Station used a boxcar to haul spraying equipment to points in southern Missouri where he held demonstrations. The Missouri State Board of Agriculture subsequently employed Missouri Pacific and Frisco cars to transport display materials for farmers' institutes.

More significant in the later development of educational train work was an experiment conducted by the Minneapolis and St. Louis. In the winter of 1896–1897 prices for Iowa grain fell, and railway revenues declined. At the suggestion of a railroad official, the carrier and Henry Wallace's farm paper held jointly a series of creamery-promotion meetings in northern Iowa in February 1897. A few weeks later officials of the Des Moines and Fort Dodge branch of the Rock Island sponsored similar meetings.

These programs were not continued but in 1904 the precedent was put to use. Bad weather in 1903 reduced the Iowa corn crop, causing the seed for next year's planting to be of poor quality. Speaking before a group of grain dealers, Perry G. Holden of Iowa's agricultural college warned of the impending problem and pointed out that careful seed selection and other simple procedures could increase production substantially.

In Holden's audience was a Rock Island official who recalled the lecture program of 1897. A conference between railroadmen and farm leaders followed, and the first true educational train took shape. It consisted of three coaches and two business cars, the latter to accommodate the speakers. Each coach served as an auditorium and was equipped with a speaker's platform as well as lecture charts and other demonstration materials. The lecture crew included personnel from the agricultural college, the railroad, the rural press, and the grain dealers' association. The carrier assumed primary responsibility for advertising meetings and making local arrangements. The three-day tour of the Seed Corn Special, as it was labeled, began 18 April 1904, covered more than 400 miles, visited 50 communities in 15 counties, and attracted an estimated 3,000 farmers. Such favorable response induced the Burlington to arrange a similar tour over its lines in southern Iowa during the last week of April.

Following the appearance of the trains in Iowa, their use spread rapidly and the educational train became the most successful means of presenting basic agricultural knowledge to large numbers of farmers. The Burlington was an early leader in the work, sending trains into four states during a three-month period beginning in December 1904, but other lines were not far behind, and soon educational trains were a common sight throughout the United States.

The first educational trains were devoted to seed corn improvement, but later trains took up other topics so that all aspects of farming were discussed from their lecture platforms. Nor were the farm wife and her concerns ignored. Programs gradually became more elaborate, with sufficient lecturers to cover a wide array of subjects in more than superficial detail. Displays of prize-winning livestock and modern farm machinery carried on some trains enabled lecturers to improve their presentations.

Educational trains were most often operated in conjunction with the agricultural colleges or other agricultural agencies. They provided a majority of the lecturers. The railroad furnished motive power, cars of different types, and operating crews. The companies also handled most of the advertising necessary to attract farmers. At the outset, train schedules were arranged so that several stops—perhaps eight or ten—were made each day, but later it became common to spend a day or more at each community visited. As the trains became more elaborate, several lectures might be given simultaneously in as many cars. There also came to be a greater effort to shape programs to the needs of specific communities.

Educational trains attracted farmers in droves. In one month in 1910 University of Missouri speakers reached 40,000 people, far more than could have been contacted by any other means. During the 1911 fiscal year a total of 62 trains carried 740 speakers more than 35,000 miles and brought them into contact with almost a million people.[12]

The great majority of educational trains, like the original specials, sought to show farmers how to grow new or better crops or how to raise more or better livestock. Land clearing and good roads trains had other objectives.

Land clearing trains were as closely related to colonization as they were to agricultural improvement. They sought to show how cutover land might be made ready for the plow. The first operated in Wisconsin in the spring of 1916. Six cars transported stump-pulling machines and dynamite to eighteen points on the Chicago and North Western and Omaha lines. University of Wisconsin personnel staged demonstrations, and in the evenings the experts met with neighborhood farmers to discuss general problems related to land clearing. Other land clearing trains appeared elsewhere in the state later. Speakers on one train that operated on the Soo Line urged farmers to organize land clearing associations so they might obtain machinery and dynamite at lower cost. Land clearing trains also made tours in 1917, 1918, and 1919.[13]

Understandably enough, railroads were active participants in the good roads movement that swept the United States during the early years of the twentieth century. Country roads were viewed as feeders for the railroads; according to Samuel Spencer of the Southern, railroads were the arteries and the roads the veins of the body. Other officials pointed out that better roads would encourage agricultural diversification, and it was almost an article of faith that there was a favorable relationship between the condition of the country roads and the volume of railroad traffic. Finally, all-weather roads would allow farmers to move products to markets throughout the year, thereby helping railroads to avoid seasonal fluctuations in traffic volume.

During most of the nineteenth century, Americans were little interested in improved roads, but attitudes began to change in the 1890s. The League of American Wheelmen and other groups demanded road improvement, and in 1893 the Office of Road Inquiry was created in the Department of Agriculture, an event that marked the reappearance of the federal government as a positive force in highway improvement. Railroads joined the crusade when they began to operate good roads trains to dramatize the need for better roads and to demonstrate road-building techniques. Such trains were generally arranged by the National Good Roads Association and the federal highway agency. Manufacturers supplied road building machinery, and railroads provided rolling stock to transport the machines and personnel to operate them.

The first of the good roads trains was operated by the Illinois Central. The twelve-car train, which included eight cars of road equipment, was assembled in Chicago and moved to New Orleans where in April 1901 the first demonstration was staged. Using machines carried on the train, a crew of men rebuilt a street in the city's suburbs. Later the train made a tour of company lines, stopping at communities in five states to conduct demonstrations. The train completed its tour at Buffalo, New York, where it was a feature of an International Good Roads Congress held in conjunction with the Pan-American Exposition. Among other railroads that operated good roads trains between 1901 and 1905 were the Lake Shore and Michigan Southern, the Southern, the Burlington, and the Northern Pacific. There were reports that such demonstration trains visited thirty-six states in 1905.[14]

Despite enthusiastic responses in some areas, farmers still dependent on horses and wagons were not sufficiently aroused to accept the increased taxation necessary to pay for better thoroughfares. What was needed, apparently, was some cheap method of making existing rural roads passable during most of the year. D. Ward King, a farmer from Holt County, Missouri, developed what he believed was the answer to that problem – the split log drag. That simple tool was built by splitting a 7–9 foot log, placing the two halves parallel to each other with the flat sides facing the front and spaced about 30 inches apart, and connecting them with bars to make the implement rigid. According to King, any farmer could build a split log drag and with two or more horses keep a country road smooth and greatly improve its drainage.

Henry Wallace, a strong proponent of King's invention, concluded that it could best be popularized by means of a special train. The management of the Chicago and North Western shared his views, and the first split log drag train operated over that line in Iowa in 1905, stopping at sixteen towns. Later in the year the Burlington arranged for a series of programs along its lines in southern Iowa, and in 1906 the Chicago and Alton ran a split log drag train in Illinois. A few years later the Norfolk and Western built six of the drags in its shops and donated them to as many communities.[15]

A second surge of good roads train operation came between 1909 and 1912. The Nashville, Chattanooga and St. Louis, the Atlantic Coast Line, the Pennsylvania, and the Southern operated trains during those years, but it was the Frisco that was most active, keeping a good roads train in service almost constantly from the summer of 1910 to the fall of 1912. A Missouri state highway commissioner praised the "missionary" aspect of the work, saying that the Frisco was providing a service to Missouri that the state could not afford to provide for itself.[16.]

In addition to the operation of good roads trains, railroads sought in a variety of other ways to help farmers get out of the mud. In 1909 B. F. Yoakum of the Frisco took a group of Farmers' Union members on a tour of New England so they might see the improved roads there. The Pennsylvania distributed a pamphlet setting forth D. Ward King's road-building ideas, while some railroads transported road materials and machinery at reduced rates. The Illinois Central constructed in 1911 and 1912 in each of the states of Illinois, Iowa, and Louisiana a mile of "standard improved wagon road" to show how adequate roads could be built from materials easily available. Finally, in 1911 the Great Northern provided a twelve-car train for the convenience of drivers involved in an automobile race between St. Paul, Minnesota, and Helena, Montana, an affair that was expected to popularize a demand for better roads by showing the reliability of automobiles.[17]

The different types of educational trains were highly successful propagandizing and popularizing techniques, useful in dissolving some rural prejudices and in awakening some farmers to new ideas. Dean F. B. Mumford of the Missouri College of Agriculture noted that they constituted an excellent means of "taking the University out to the people." But as early as 1910 some railroad officials and academic men were coming to the conclusion that as a teaching device educational trains were not the final answer. Farmers proved to be reluctant to accept oral teaching, and it appeared that only practical demonstrations in their own fields and barnyards, or at least in their own neighborhoods, could induce the great majority to adopt new methods.

Railroadmen recognized the value of the object-lesson farm before the turn of the century. Some industry leaders maintained private estates that served as examples for less affluent neighbors, but true demonstration farms proved to be more useful. They were generally established by companies whose tracks extended through undeveloped territory or through districts with sparse rainfall or other problems. The purpose of such farms was often dual in nature: to improve the practices of farmers already in an area and to attract new settlers by demonstrating the potential of a region.

The latter was clearly the objective of the Cycloneta-Model Stock and Agricultural Farm that the Georgia Southern and Florida established near Tifton in south Georgia in 1889. The company hired a college professor to manage the property and invested a substantial sum to "demonstrate to . . . settlers what it is possible to do in this piney woods."[18]

In the twentieth century the Long Island Railroad was a pioneer in demonstrating farm work. When Ralph Peters became president, large areas of Long Island were undeveloped and considered useless for agriculture. Determined to change these perceptions, Peters arranged for the purchase in 1905 of an 18-acre tract of "scrub oak waste" land near Wading River on the north coast of the island. A year later, the company acquired a second farm.

Work on the first farm began in the fall of 1905 under the direction of Hal B. Fullerton, the company's agricultural agent, and his wife Edith. The first step was to clear the property and remove the stumps by dynamiting. Amused natives claimed that "they're plantin' dynamite an' raisin' hell, an' that's all they will ever raise." Nevertheless, the Fullertons succeeded in demonstrating that the land would produce a variety of truck and garden crops as well as the hay necessary to maintain a livestock industry. They publicized their accomplishments by displaying farm products at agricultural fairs, launching the *Long Island Agronomist,* and writing a "human interest" account of their work. Within four years over 4,000 families had been added to the island's rural population, and company officials noted a new balance in traffic flow and a decline in the company's dependence upon its passenger business.[19]

Several other roads soon established similar demonstration farms along their lines. In 1909 the Pennsylvania purchased a 50-acre tract near Bacon, Delaware, installed a Cornell University graduate as manager, and gave him the task of renovating the badly rundown property. The next year, after President W. C. Brown announced that "I am going to recommend . . . the purchase of farms, to be operated . . . at the expense of the railroad, but under the auspices of the agricultural college . . . ," the New York Central acquired two properties, one at West Bergen and the other at Chittenango, New York.[20] Other carriers using experimental farms included the Buffalo, Rochester and Pittsburgh; the Norfolk Southern; the Toledo, Peoria and Western; and the St. Louis Southwestern.[21]

The single demonstration or model farm, however, suffered from distinct weaknesses as a teaching device. Too often farmers could not or would not visit a model farm, and if they did they were likely to discount methods used there, saying that they were economically unsound or that they were unsuited to other localities. A series of small plots answered some of these criticisms.

Precedents for the use of scattered demonstration plots had been set before the turn of the century. Some of the dry farming work of Hardy W. Campbell fell into that category, and in 1899 an official of the Seaboard Air Line reported that the carrier had twenty-two "experimental farms" that had played some role in the settling of more than 400 families along the line the previous year. There were also some early experimental plots in Oregon established by the Oregon Railway and Navigation Company.[22]

During the years before World War I the Illinois Central and its subsidiaries were among the leaders in the use of demonstration plots. The parent company established twelve 40-acre plots in Mississippi and Louisiana in 1912. In each case, the carrier entered into a contract with the landowner that required the latter to farm the plot in accordance with instructions and to use properly the seed and fertilizer provided. In return, the railroad guaranteed the farmer against financial loss. For guidance in working out plans, the Illinois Central turned to the land-grant colleges in the two states, and the carrier detailed three men to supervise the work in the fields. The primary goal was to show the value of diversification and crop rotation, and according to J. C. Clair, the "operations are confined strictly to practical farming, the idea being to afford a practical demonstration of what any average farmer can accomplish." By 1916 the company had thirty-two plots in five states, and the Central of Georgia maintained almost as many.[23]

Only slightly different were projects undertaken by several other southern and southwestern lines. When H. M. Bainer joined the Santa Fe in 1910, he rejected a proposal to establish a central demonstration farm, insisting that plots on properties of farmers would be far more effective. Under his plan the Santa Fe supplied farmers with enough improved seed to plant 10 acres of a crop and required that recipients follow such instructions as might be offered. Most of the farmers who participated were residents of the Panhandle and South Plains of Texas. The Missouri Pacific had several demonstration plots in Missouri, Arkansas, and Louisiana; the Nashville, Chattanooga and St. Louis maintained some in Tennessee; and the Frisco had almost a hundred small plots in Missouri and Arkansas.[24]

The Northern Pacific and the Great Northern, which earlier had used small plots to study the agricultural potential of the northern Great Plains, resumed their use for educational purposes in 1911. The Northern Pacific concentrated its efforts in western North Dakota where problems stemmed from the prevailing reliance upon wheat growing and a tendency among farmers to seed the crop in stubble. The inevitable result was crop failure in drought years as well as an increasingly serious weed infestation. The company established seven plots of 6 acres each to demonstrate those tillage methods best calculated to conserve moisture and to show the value of crop rotation, with alfalfa, corn, and livestock production supplementing wheat raising. Each cooperating farmer received free seed, an analysis of his soil, necessary fertilizer, the crop produced on the land, and a cash payment. In later years, the number of plots varied, reaching fifty in 1913, and by 1916 the company claimed to have shown its better farmers that diversified farming was practical in North Dakota.

The Northern Pacific program, however, was overshadowed by that of the Great Northern. James J. Hill was an early advocate of small plots scattered among farmers, so beginning in 1912 the Great Northern leased for $8 an acre a number of 5-acre plots in western Minnesota and in North Dakota. The company supplied high quality seed and fertilizer; cooperating farmers received the crop as well as the rent. The next year the program grew, and Great Northern experts used Hill's private greenhouse to test varieties of seed and to analyze soil samples. Between 1912 and 1914 some 780 farmers in the two states cooperated with the railroad, and in 1915 there were 987 plots in the program, giving the carrier what some observers claimed was the largest private agricultural extension system in the world.[25]

Promoting Diversification

To a great many railroadmen agricultural improvement meant diversification. Officials of southern and western roads especially believed that one-crop farming with emphasis on cotton or wheat should give way to a more balanced agriculture featuring a variety of crops and livestock. All farmers should maintain gardens, keep dairy cows and poultry, and raise as much other livestock as their operations permitted. Blooded or at least improved animals and silos were recommended enthusiastically. Both old and new crops should be produced with approved methods, including crop rotation, deep plowing, use of high quality seed and adequate amounts of fertilizer, conservation of moisture, and better control of erosion and weeds.

In their efforts to promote livestock raising and dairying, railroad development men paid homage to the pioneer work of James J. Hill, and they profited from his unhappy experiences. Few carriers after 1900 were prepared to give farmers purebred stock without protective provisions, but they were perfectly willing to try any number of other approaches.[26] The Central of Georiga, for example, loaned purebred shorthorn bulls to selected farmers who agreed to install dipping vats and to acquire one or more purebred heifers. According to company spokesmen, the program produced "more actual results . . . than all the bulletins and lectures on stock-raising for the last fifty years." In 1916 the Illinois Central set out to improve dairy herds in its territory by loaning purebred bulls to farmers in Illinois, Tennessee, and Mississippi, distributing twenty-four Holsteins at Carbondale, Illinois, as the first step. Farmers receiving the animals were allowed to keep them for two years, but recipients were required to care for the animals properly and to keep records showing the service to which the bulls had been put. The Nashville, Chattanooga and St. Louis and the Big Four were other railroads that had comparable programs.[27]

Railroadmen held innumerable meetings with farmers, urging them to obtain cattle. At times, they arranged livestock sales and acted as purchasing agents. As early as 1902 the Oregon Railway and Navigation Company, in cooperation with the American Shorthorn Breeders' Association, took several carloads of stock into Whitman County, Washington, where the animals were sold to farmers. More than a decade later, the Nashville, Chattanooga and St. Louis reported that it had placed about 3,000 head of purebred cattle on farms through sales that it organized.

Credit was a necessity for many farmers if they were to purchase stock. The Illinois Central's J. C. Clair urged country bankers to loan money on cattle, and although southern bankers preferred cotton as collateral, an official of the Iron Mountain claimed that some 700 head of purebred stock had been purchased by farmers in his territory, mostly with bank loans. Earlier, the Burlington asked bankers to obtain cattle and sell the stock to farmers, offering each purchaser credit up to $1,500 to be secured by the cattle and land.[28]

The Illinois Central was especially active in promoting the development of a dairy industry in its territory south of the Ohio River. At Martin, Tennessee, and Mayfield, Kentucky, the company organized boys' and girls' purebred Holstein dairy clubs, induced local bankers to extend credit to members, located cattle in Wisconsin, and later contributed purebred bulls to the communities. In Mississippi the company encouraged the establishment of creameries by offering to furnish skilled butter makers and business managers to communities meeting certain requirements. The town of West, in Holmes County, was the first to accept the offer, doing so in 1914. Later the Illinois Central fought the cattle tick, printing and distributing primarily in Mississippi a booklet describing methods by which the pest could be eradicated and sending out agents to conduct dipping demonstrations. The railroad also took southern livestock men and agricultural educators to the International Live Stock Show and arranged side trips into the Wisconsin dairy country.[29] This kind of promotional work was quite common, many roads using tours to inspire and instruct farmers.

Several roads made major efforts to popularize silos as the best means of providing winter feed for dairy and other cattle. The Burlington and the Santa Fe were perhaps the leaders in this work, but the Southern claimed credit for many of the silos built in its territory.[30]

A few roads encouraged the formation of livestock associations, and most carriers produced and distributed widely literature dealing with all aspects of livestock production. The Frisco was one of several roads that encouraged farmers to test for butterfat and keep accurate records on each cow; a dairy car equipped with lecturers and Babcock testers carried the message into the Ozarks and elsewhere. In the Middle West some railroads waged war on hog cholera, and the Great Northern was one railroad that used the standard techniques to promote the raising of sheep.[31]

The promotion of diversification also involved the introduction of new crops. No single crop attracted more interest than alfalfa. The growing of alfalfa contributed to soil improvement and made livestock raising and dairying more profitable, so railroads set out to popularize the crop. After making a careful study in 1913 the Rock Island produced a map of Iowa showing the treatment that land in different sections of that state needed to grow alfalfa. The Chicago and North Western distributed a booklet that presented "the practical view . . . and testimonials" concerning the growing of alfalfa in South Dakota, while in Nebraska it leased much of its right-of-way to neighborhood farmers who agreed to plant alfalfa. The Chesapeake and Ohio organized alfalfa clubs, provided instructions for the growing of alfalfa, and donated seed and a carload of lime to each club. More elaborate was an alfalfa campaign conducted in the summer of 1913 in Iowa and Missouri by the Burlington in conjunction with the International Harvester Company and the agricultural colleges of those states. The Burlington provided a special train to transport speakers and equipment to fifty-five towns where meetings attracted almost 13,000 persons.[32]

Railroads in the Southeast and elsewhere promoted the growing of fruit and truck crops. The St. Louis, Brownsville and Mexico did much to transform the lower Rio Grande Valley from ranching to truck farming, while the St. Louis Southwestern claimed credit for developing an east Texas tomato industry. On its farm near Alto, Texas, the railroad grew tomato plants that it provided to farmers at cost. The Missouri, Kansas and Texas told its stockholders that it was generating a large amount of high-class tonnage through work with fruit and vegetable growers, and the Southern reported that its agents were promoting the growing of all kinds of common fruits and vegetables as well as figs, quinces, Japanese persimmons, and pomegranates.[33]

Several other crops received attention in specific areas. The Missouri Pacific and the Rock Island promoted rice growing in Arkansas through the establishment of demonstration plots and the introduction of varieties of seed suited to the area. The Santa Fe helped to strengthen the sugar beet industry in Colorado by testing soils, encouraging a sugar company to put up a refinery in the area, and recruiting labor. The Frisco, in cooperation with Kentucky growers, tried to introduce hemp into the Ozark region of Missouri and Arkansas but was more successful in promoting the growing of fruit and truck crops there.[34]

Railroads in different parts of the country improved the output of standard crops by introducing better seed or new varieties. The carriers in North Dakota, for instance, converted some farmers there to durum wheat, despite the opposition of millers who favored softer varieties. The Burlington for a time operated a seed exchange for its patrons, while the Southern Pacific distributed samples of new varieties of wheat, barley, and oats to growers in Oregon and elsewhere.[35]

Railroadmen soon found that it was not enough to encourage the growing of a crop; if a promotional project were to be successful, marketing had to be strengthened. The Southern Railway, recognizing that cotton farmers were not going to shift to truck and fruit crops unless there were reasonable assurances that their output could be sold profitably, established a marketing office in 1913. Four agents stationed in Washington, Cincinnati, St. Louis, and Atlanta sought outlets for southern-grown fruits and vegetables and helped producers and buyers establish contact with each other. The Frisco organized marketing associations for growers of fruit and truck crops, surveyed urban markets to determine the most desirable type and size of shipping containers, and instructed farmers in proper grading and packing procedures.[36]

Railroads also encouraged production of fruits and vegetables by providing better rail service. The Pennsylvania emphasized the value to growers of its preference freight trains that operated on fast schedules so arranged as to deliver produce to urban markets at the optimum time. As early as 1906 the Kansas City Southern ran a daily special strawberry train from Siloam Springs, Arkansas, to Kansas City during picking season, an arrangement which placed each day's picking on the city market the next day and cut almost twenty-four hours from the regular schedules. Faster service was also important in the development of fruit and truck crops in the lower Rio Grande Valley.[37]

Railroads and Agricultural Education

Quite obviously, much of the work undertaken by railroads paralleled or supplemented the efforts of the U.S. Department of Agriculture, the land-grant colleges, and other agencies involved in the general improvement of farming. Nowhere, however, was this similarity of interest stronger than in the area of agricultural education. Railroadmen almost without exception equated formal training in agriculture and the growth of agricultural science with increased production and heavier traffic, so they were eager to aid those institutions engaged in agricultural teaching and research. They were even more enthusiastic about the efforts of educators and others to find a teaching device effective with adult farmers, so the industry became an important force in the development of an agricultural extension system.

The offering of free transportation or reduced rates was a common method used by many railroads to aid formal agricultural education. Some roads gave less than standard rates to teachers and scientists attending professional meetings, and agricultural educators often carried free passes for transportation within their states. The extending of such aid was not without its problems. Requests in some instances were extreme, while evolving state and federal legislation placed restrictions on the offering of such services. By 1914 some roads were refusing to give passes to agricultural educators, while others evaded the letter of the law by placing agricultural college personnel on their payrolls at nominal salaries.[38]

The offering of college scholarships was another kind of aid given to formal education in agriculture. In Missouri beginning in 1910 at least four lines gave scholarships of $50 or $100 to students in agriculture at the university who resided in counties served by those roads' tracks. More ambitious was the scholarship program announced in 1912 by the Southern Railway. Details were left to the agricultural college officials concerned, but each recipient was required to agree to spend the first three years after graduation in practical farming, in the teaching of agriculture, or in other agriculture-related work in the territory served by the Southern or its subsidiaries. A few years later the Southern established a loan fund of $1,000 at each of the agricultural colleges in nine states.

In various ways the railroads displayed their interest in the teaching of agriculture at other levels. The Gulf and Ship Island supported the agricultural high school movement in Mississippi, and the Missouri Pacific encouraged the teaching of agriculture in the public schools. At least one railroad was directly involved in instruction. Early in 1910 in cooperation with the Missouri College of Agriculture, the Frisco conducted for several months in St. Louis its "Night School of Agriculture."[39]

Since railroads recognized the value of the state agricultural experiment stations, they often extended aid to them. Following the precedent established earlier by James J. Hill, the Florida East Coast gave a 20-acre tract near Boca Raton to the Florida station for citrus research, and in 1906 the Southern Railway donated 300 acres to Clemson College for experimental purposes. In the first years of the twentieth century the Illinois Central urged the Mississippi legislature to establish a branch station at Stoneville, and the Rock Island used its influence for a similar purpose elsewhere. Some railroads provided grants of money to supplement experiment station financial resources. The Burlington gave substantial sums to the stations in Colorado and Wyoming, while the Nashville, Chattanooga and St. Louis underwrote specific experimental work at the University of Tennessee.[40]

It was in the new area of agricultural extension, however, that railroads made their greatest contribution. The emerging extension programs formulated by the U.S. Department of Agriculture and the agricultural colleges sought the same ends and used many of the same methods as did the railway agricultural development departments, so it was logical that the carriers would prove to be the most useful allies as the public agencies moved toward the establishment of a nationwide system of county agents under the Smith-Lever Act of 1914.

Railroadmen were enthusiastic supporters of the farmers' institute movement, believing correctly that the first widely used extension technique was a promising method for exposing farmers to new ideas. In some cases the railroads were pioneers in the work, the Illinois Central arranging at least two institutelike conclaves in Mississippi several years before the institute system was firmly established in that state. Railroads throughout the country provided free transportation for institute workers until it was prohibited by law. In many instances railroadmen helped to make local arrangements and to advertise the meetings. Some railroad development men were popular speakers at institute programs.

Still, many railroadmen recognized the inherent limitations of farmers' institutes and the need for a more effective teaching device. Even before Seaman A. Knapp launched his boll weevil work in Texas in 1903, officials of such lines as the Texas Midland had appealed to the U.S. Department of Agriculture for help for farmers, so the carriers responded eagerly when Knapp opened an office in Houston in January 1904 and asked for assistance. Knowing that railway development agents were familiar with conditions and people along their lines, Knapp put them in charge of the territories served by their companies and sent them into the countryside to enlist demonstrators. In this manner the Farmers' Cooperative Demonstration Work was launched in a large area of east and south Texas in time to have an impact on the 1904 crop. In later years, as the work extended throughout the South, railway agents were relieved of their primary role, but the carriers continued to make important contributions, especially in the form of free transportation for Knapp and his subordinates and in advertising the work.[41]

Impressed with the impact of the Farmers' Cooperative Demonstration Work, some lines in the South set out to supplement Knapp's efforts by placing men in the fields to work directly with farmers. In 1910 Knapp made a tour through the territory of the Southern Railway, giving his message on boll weevils and how the pests might be controlled. Later that year the Southern created its cotton culture department and assigned six field men the task of visiting farmers and offering advice concerning the growing of cotton under boll weevil conditions. When farmers reacted favorably, the Southern in 1912 expanded the service to cover its entire territory and broadened it to include all aspects of agriculture found in the Southeast. A new department of farm improvement ultimately employed as many as sixty men. According to President Fairfax Harrison, the agents "visit the farmer on his farm, find out what he wants to know, help him solve the problem on his individual farm, and demonstrate how he can obtain the best results on his own land and with his own resources."[42]

Railroads also participated in the emerging county agent movement in the North. There the effort was led by William J. Spillman of the U.S. Office of Farm Management in cooperation with the land-grant colleges and groups of local businessmen and farmers who raised funds to support a county agent and otherwise aided him in his work. Railroads often joined this combination of forces. The Lackawanna played an important part in placing John H. Barron, often considered the first county agent in the North, in Broome County, New York, in 1911.

Hoping to halt the decay in agriculture in southern New York State, the Lackawanna early in 1910 approached the state department of agriculture and the agricultural college at Cornell, offering to purchase two farms and turn them over to the state for demonstration purposes. By September the Binghamton, New York, Chamber of Commerce had agreed to join the railroad in the project, but before proceeding, representatives of the chamber and the railroad visited the U.S. Department of Agriculture in search of advice and possible assistance. There they met Spillman who suggested that the idea of demonstration farms be abandoned and that the two agencies employ a single agent who would devote his full time to the problems of farmers in the Binghamton area. Spillman pledged the support of the Office of Farm Management. A memorandum of understanding was signed 20 March 1911, and Barron soon went to work in Broome County.

When the success of the Broome County experiment became apparent, the Lackawanna offered to extend similar aid to other counties, and other railroads took up the work. The Lackawanna helped to place agents in Chemung and Cortland counties, New York, and Sussex County, New Jersey, while the New York Central contributed in Oneida, Montgomery, Oswego, and Jefferson counties, New York. Elsewhere in the North the Santa Fe agreed to pay 80 percent of the salary of a man stationed at Dodge City, Kansas; the Rock Island made the same contribution to the maintenance of an agent at Norton, Kansas; and the Burlington offered to contribute $150 annually for two years to any county in its territory employing a county agent. Later, as public funds became available, the size of railroad contributions tended to decline. In Broome County the Lackawanna carried one-half the cost the first year, but in other counties its contribution was generally less, and in some instances railroads contributed only to the extent that they placed the agent on their payroll at a nominal salary so they could provide him with free transportation.

The most comprehensive effort by business interests to place agricultural agents in individual counties, however, came in North Dakota. By 1910 business leaders had become concerned with deteriorating agricultural conditions there, and they determined to undertake a program to produce changes in farming methods. The Better Farming Association of North Dakota, which began operations in November 1911, was supported financially by a wide variety of business interests, but the organization in its goals and early planning reflected the ideas of James J. Hill, a leading advocate of the county agent system. Hill's Great Northern contributed at least $15,000 to the association, an amount that was matched by the Northern Pacific and the Soo. The purpose of the organization was to take "personally to the individual operating his own farm the results of investigations as obtained by the Department of Agriculture, the Experiment Stations, and similar agencies." Men of broad training and experience were to be placed permanently in counties or districts where they were to teach by general farm advising and by arranging demonstrations with cooperating farmers.

The first agent went to work in Bottineau County in January 1912; soon 13 men were located in the eastern part of North Dakota. The next year, the number of agents increased to 25 and of cooperating farmers to more than 5,000. The Better Farming Association also worked with farm wives. Spokesmen claimed that it contacted directly or indirectly 40 percent of the state's rural population. Meanwhile the Office of Farm

Management began providing technical and financial assistance, and in 1914 the entire program was taken over by public authority. During its existence the association inspired the establishment of similar groups in South Dakota and western Minnesota.[43]

While aiding in a variety of ways the development of an agricultural extension system for adult farmers, the railroads also worked with the early rural youth clubs that were the forerunners of modern 4-H. Railroadmen recognized that one of the most effective means of insuring the existence of better agriculture in the future lay with the proper training of country boys and girls; they also knew that by aiding the development of rural youth clubs they could gain substantial benefits in terms of long-term goodwill.

Some roads assumed an active role in organizing the clubs. The Illinois Central was on the scene when in 1907 William H. Smith founded the pioneer corn club in Holmes County, Mississippi. Elsewhere, agents of the Norfolk and Western, the Oregon Railway and Navigation Company, and the Rock Island actively promoted the launching of rural youth clubs. The Santa Fe's Henry M. Bainer was apparently an innovator when he organized a boy's kaffir corn club at Sweetwater, Texas, in 1912. After the club movement was well established, railroads encouraged the work by contributing prizes for club winners, the Great Northern giving $10,000 in a single year in Montana.[44]

Railroads made a final contribution to the development of an agricultural extension system by lending their influence in the struggle to obtain passage of the Smith-Lever Act. Railroadmen participated in at least two organizations – the Crop Improvement Committee of the Council of North American Grain Exchanges and the National Soil Fertility League – which sought to crystalize opinion in support of a measure that in time would install a county agent and the demonstration technique in every agricultural county.

The Crop Improvement Committee was established at a meeting in October 1910 of the Council of North America Grain Exchanges. The group, which included J. C. Clair of the Illinois Central and H. M. Cottrell of the Rock Island, was given the responsibility for promoting agricultural betterment by the most feasible methods, including the establishment of a county agent system. It campaigned actively for legislation on the subject and administered a $100,000 grant by Julius Rosenwald of Sears, Roebuck to promote the work.

More important as a propaganda and lobbying agency, however, was the National Soil Fertility League. Formed in 1911, the league listed among its sponsors many of the national political figures of the time, but business leaders, including James J. Hill, provided its support and direction, and railroad officials were especially interested. The Wabash, for example, donated $1,000 for its first year's work. The league enjoyed the advantages of singleness of purpose; the only way to promote agricultural betterment, it steadfastly maintained, was to place in each agricultural county a trained agent who would carry scientific information to farmers in their fields, modify it to suit local conditions, and help the individual farmer to put it to use. This lesson the league constantly drove home, and Howard H. Gross, president of the group, became a well-known figure in Washington where he lobbied successfully for the Smith-Lever bill.[45]

By 1917 agricultural development departments had been in existence for a decade or more. Railroads had expended a great deal of energy and substantial sums of money in implementing a variety of programs expected to generate new traffic through agricultural diversification and the wider application of more modern farming methods. The roads also had participated in a movement to establish under public auspices a teaching method in the countryside that in time would do much to revolutionize American farming. Unexpected opportunities for agricultural development departments to play a new role came when the United States found itself involved in a great war in Europe.

Development Programs in World War I

Agricultural development departments made their greatest contributions in World War I through programs to increase food production. Soon after the declaration of war, President Woodrow Wilson declared that "upon the farmers of this country . . . rests the fate of the war," thus calling upon American farmers to do their part in the great crusade and giving railway development departments an opportunity to be of service to the nation.

The different railroads undertook their wartime task of increasing food production in various ways. Most company officers believed that the emergency called mainly for an intensification of existing programs. Some considered colonization work to be of special importance because it would increase the amount of land in production. Others thought that the effort to promote diversification and better farming need only be pushed with renewed energy. In any event, during the first year of the war educational literature continued to pour from railway development offices, railway agents continued to busy themselves in the countryside, and educational trains continued to tour company lines, their purposes in most cases altered to bring them into line with the war effort. Some emphasized the preservation and conservation of food. Several railroads discontinued their demonstration farm work, believing the properties could be put to more productive use.[46]

Some new programs were inspired by wartime conditions. As one means of stimulating food production, many roads encouraged the planting of crops or war gardens on their right-of-ways and other unoccupied lands, in some instances providing the wartime gardeners with seed and instructions. Several roads undertook to help farmers obtain adequate quantities of seed for field crops. Others tried a variety of ways to assist farmers in meeting their labor needs, in some cases allowing section crews and other employees to work on farms during planting and harvesting seasons. The Buffalo, Rochester and Pittsburgh acquired several large tractors that it leased to farmers.[47]

The government's takeover of the railroads late in 1917 brought some of these activities to a halt. Officials of the Railroad Administration, the agency established to manage the railroads, believed that under governmental control the work of railway traffic departments was at least partly superfluous. The agency suspended their operations and thus called into question the existence of development departments. A few railroads abolished temporarily their development agencies. Government authorities ultimately decided that since increased agricultural production was needed, agricultural development departments could continue those activities that were directly related to the war effort. To provide general supervision, in July 1918 the Railroad Administration created within its Division of Traffic an Agricultural Section, headed by J. L. Edwards, a former railroader.[48]

Many of the programs carried on under Edwards' supervision differed from prewar work only in quantity. There were fewer educational trains, but livestock and crop promotion continued with only minor changes. There was some emphasis upon those commodities that were most in demand. Colonization work was restricted, although there were notable exceptions.[49]

The end of the war brought a reversal of policy regarding colonization. Some government officials, concerned with the availability of suitable employment for returning servicemen, proposed that veterans be settled on the land. Secretary of the Interior Franklin K. Lane claimed that there were millions of acres in government and private hands that could be converted to profitable farms through irrigation, draining, and clearing. The South as a whole presented great opportunities, he thought.

Partly in response to such ideas, in January 1919 a Homeseekers' Bureau was established in the Agricultural Section of the Railroad Administration. J. F. Jarrell, the head of the new office, instituted a colonization program modeled after those of the prewar period. The Homeseekers' Bureau placed advertisements in farm and other papers across the country and in the Paris edition of *Stars and Stripes*. In addition to typical brochures and pamphlets, the bureau published booklets on twenty-nine states, mostly in the West and South. Since these booklets were compiled with the aid of railway development men, they resembled those that railroads had been turning out for a half century. Like their predecessors, the government-issued booklets resorted to extravagant language, occasionally overstated the case, and perpetuated some ideas that were questionable. The booklet on Montana, for example, gave little indication that the railroads' efforts to settle that state's dry lands had been based on false premises.[50]

The federal government's role in such activities ended in 1920. Despite the hopes of some, the Transportation Act of 1920 returned the carriers to private management, effective March 1. The legislation proved to be a watershed in the history of the nation's railroads, but railway development men assumed the end of government control meant that they could resume the programs of the past. That assumption proved to be only partly valid.

CHAPTER FOUR

Origins of Industrial Development Work, 1900–1945

INDUSTRIAL DEVELOPMENT WORK was inspired by the same motives that led railroads to promote the settlement of farmers and the improvement of agriculture in their territories. The basic goal, the generation of new traffic, was certainly the same. Few railroad executives doubted that the location of firms along a rail line would increase the business handled on that line or that the industrialization of an agricultural region would both increase and stabilize the flow of traffic.

Railroads were always factors in industrial development. As soon as rail transportation, with its lower costs and greater reliability, became available in a region or community, some development inevitably occurred. Where the population was relatively heavy, as in the northeastern United States, pioneer railroads found that organized promotional efforts on their part were unnecessary, although in informal ways senior officers often called the attention of businessmen to the attractions of their railroads' service areas.

But as intramodal competition in the older regions increased and as the economies of other sections matured, a more active role became imperative. As one of the early industrial agents explained, railroads discovered that in some ways they were like manufacturers; they produced a commodity—a service—and good business judgment suggested that they should "create a market" or "manufacture a demand" for that commodity.

As a rough generalization, organized industrial development work appeared first in the Middle West and the South, later in other sections of the country. This pattern was due largely to the character of the economies of the different sections. The Middle West was industrializing rapidly at the end of the nineteenth century, affording great opportunities for industrial work, and railroads there were highly competitive. In the South railroadmen embraced with vast enthusiasm the ideals and goals of the New South, and they were determined to do what they could to speed change in the region and to get for their companies a fair share of any new business that might become available. Eastern roads took up industrial development work only a few years later, inspired in part by the competition offered by middle western carriers. In the West, on the other hand, opportunities in the first years of the twentieth century were limited. As C. W. Mott of the Northern Pacific acknowledged in 1908, "Our industrial work is largely in the future."[1]

Mechanics of Industrial Development Work

After the Milwaukee established the first clearly defined industrial department in 1891, other roads soon followed so that many of the major carriers had such offices by the time the United States entered World War I. Among the pioneers in the work, in addition to the Milwaukee's Luis Jackson, were M. V. Richards of the Southern, George C. Power of the Illinois Central, and Thomas L. Peeler of the Missouri, Kansas and Texas.

These men formulated the general principles, objectives, and procedures that governed railway industrial development work a half century or more. According to Luis Jackson, when he went to work for the Milwaukee, his superiors told him that they had "no instructions to give" but they wanted him to "develop our territory." President Stuyvesant Fish of the Illinois Central appointed George C. Power to the post of industrial commissioner in 1892 "expressly to 'sell' Illinois Central territory to manufacturers" as the road's colonization agents were "already 'selling' it to immigrants. . . ."[2]

Although there were few guidelines for the new officers to follow, they soon discovered that their first task was to gather information. According to M. V. Richards, he made his office into "a great bureau of information" by accumulating and cataloging data concerning the resources of the territory, opportunities existing in the different communities, the amount and cost of labor, kinds of power available, and miscellaneous other factors important to business enterprise. Such information was available from many sources, including technical and trade papers and governmental publications, but most useful to the early agents was personal inspection.

After information had been gathered and assembled, it had to be placed in the hands of those who might be expected to use it, primarily eastern manufacturers and investors. To contact them, the early industrial men found brochures and advertising in trade papers to be of some value, but most of the pioneers in the business apparently relied most heavily upon direct contact.

Some examples illustrate well the character of early industrial development work. During his first six months on the job, Luis Jackson toured the Milwaukee's territory, acquainting himself with the people and resources. Along the Wisconsin River he found that pine and hardwood timber was being rapidly depleted, promising problems in the future, while hemlock lands were almost unsalable at any price. Jackson contacted eastern tanneries, pointed to resources available in Wisconsin, and in time was able to report the location of three tanneries on company lines in the state. He scored another success with brick manufacturing. In the 1890s brickyards were rare and bricks were expensive west of Chicago. Jackson circularized station agents within 100 miles of the city, asking for information concerning the availability of clay suitable for brick manufacture. When three agents reported deposits of blue clay near their stations, Jackson took several Chicago brick manufacturers on a tour of the localities. One of the manufacturers soon decided to put up a brickyard and in time competitors followed.

An early accomplishment of the Santa Fe is also illustrative. At Iola, Kansas, local businessmen, hoping to change the town from simply a farmers' market, discovered that the area contained substantial deposits of rock of unknown value. A letter to the president of the Santa Fe brought the industrial commissioner to Iola, where he ascertained that the rock in question was high-grade limestone, useful in the manufacture of cement. That information was circularized in the East, and ultimately a cement manufacturer from Michigan built the first cement plant in Kansas along the tracks of the Santa Fe.

Other early industrial men functioned in roughly the same manner. After the Illinois Central's George C. Power spent a year studying the country served by his company, he announced that his office "invites correspondence with all manufacturers who may be considering a change of location; will treat confidentially all applications for sites or information; and will lend its best assistance in aiding industries to locate to their best advantage."[3]

That statement described equally well the basic goals and mode of operation of industrial development departments for decades. Soon after the Erie established its development department in 1903, company officers wrote that the new office had

for its purpose the further development of the territory traversed by its line. The company seeks to increase the number of manufacturing plants on its system, the bringing of raw materials and resources to greater utility, and the general development of the commerce of its territory, so that the prosperity and growth of towns on its lines be augmented and the traffice returns of the company be increased.

Toward those ends the office had available information concerning the territory's "resources, adaptability, markets, and advantages for manufacturing" and it stood ready to "advise with manufacturers in relation to the most suitable locations." A quarter of a century later the Kansas City Southern stated that its industrial department had "for its object the location of new industries to develop the natural resources along the Railway, also the location of industries to manufacture commodities from the agricultural products grown in the territory served by the Railway. [The department] endeavors to assist existing industries to expand and grow, and to find wider markets for their output."[4]

In the 1920s, especially, industrial men found that they could also play a public relations role. With the memory of governmental operation still fresh in their minds and with the Plumb Plan—a proposal by the railroad brotherhoods that the government take ownership of the railroads—still considered a threat, high executives insisted that industrial development men help form "a better understanding of the railroad situation by the Public." According to President L. A. Downs of the Central of Georgia, since development men had "the confidence of the patrons of transportation, they could do much to make clear to the people the true position and aims and ideals of transportation management."[5]

If objectives of development work remained constant, so did methods of operation. The accumulation of useful data continued to be a first prerequisite to a successful program, even if methods of gathering information changed. Some railroads, for example, found rather early that sophisticated industrial surveys were needed. The Baltimore and Ohio was one of the pioneers in this area, beginning a comprehensive study of its territory in 1916. Groups of men spent from a week to three months in towns and cities, gathering the data needed by businessmen considering new locations. The data thus accumulated was assembled and made available to industrial agents for their use as they dealt with prospects. World War I interrupted the survey, but it was resumed in the 1920s.[6]

Other roads were not far behind in systematic survey work, although some approached the task differently. In the early 1920s when the Seaboard Air Line arranged with a private engineering firm to make studies of cities along its line, the carrier required the cities involved to meet some of the costs. Later the Cotton Belt undertook a comprehensive survey of its line that included information on social, labor, and economic conditions in each community, as well as the general character of its government and its prevailing tax rates. From "the general survey, individual surveys covering every community served by the Cotton Belt were prepared and issued in pamphlet form" to prospective customers and to local chambers of commerce. In 1930 the Illinois Central employed Pace, a private consulting firm in Chicago, to make an industrial survey of that carrier's territory. When the survey was completed, the company expected to have "exhaustive files of information covering all factors governing industrial location."[7] Meanwhile railroads encouraged chambers of commerce and similar organizations to undertake on their own studies to determine the needs of their communities for new businesses and to discover those resources and other attractions that might be of interest to enterprisers.

After an industrial department had studied its territory and gathered data of different types, the next step was to put the information to use. Early industrial agents had relied heavily on personal contact, and that approach continued to be widely used. But in time, other methods became necessary, and industrial men turned to advertising and a variety of other techniques to attract the interest of potential customers.

Advertising in the early days of development work usually took the form of brief notes in trade and business magazines. In 1911 the Southern Railway was advertising the industrial attractions of the Southeast in 150 American magazines and newspapers as well as in a number of publications circulating in Europe. In a typical advertisement, the Lackawanna informed readers that its industrial department was prepared to provide "information concerning either a site for an industry or an industry for a site." The Chicago Great Western and the Burlington pointed out that there were opportunities in their territories for men interested in creameries, mills, general merchandising, hotels, banks, lumber yards, and factories.[8]

Some advertisements were more specific. In 1905 the Seaboard Air Line advertised for sale a woolen mill located on its line, available for $25,000. The Kansas City Southern was one of several roads that published lists of opportunities along their lines for small businessmen; the town of Lewis, in Caddo Parish, Louisiana, for example, needed a doctor and a general merchandise store to serve its population of 275.[9]

Some advertising continued to be used in the 1920s and later. A typical Burlington advertisement in 1929 pointed out that the road served an area "rich in agriculture, coal deposits, minerals and raw materials; a territory with a record of steady substantial development furnishing a steadily growing market, increasing each year as the center of population moves westward." Among the territory's other advantages were "a favorable climate, low taxes, raw materials, steady labor supply, low power rates, excellent transportation, and nearby markets. . . ." In the 1930s the Seaboard reported that its industrial department was prepared to "recommend specific locations and to furnish information on raw materials, plant sites, water supply, fuel, power, labor, shipping facilities and other factors of pertinent interest."[10]

By the 1920s several railroads used a variety of other means to call attention to their industrial development work. The Santa Fe advertised in folders issued by its passenger department, and the Frisco used the *Blue Book* published by *Manufacturers Record.* The Reading distributed widely an industrial map of Philadelphia, while the Kentucky and Indiana Terminal Railroad Company advertised in the Louisville newspapers and issued a pictorial industrial map of the city, giving aerial views of areas served by company tracks. Even before 1917 some development men had considered the use of a new medium – films – in their advertising work. The Santa Fe had rejected the idea, but the Southern Pacific was reported to have shown films to large groups of businessmen, with apparent success.[11]

When such advertising aroused the interest of businessmen and they contacted a railroad, its industrial development men stood ready to supply the additional data needed to enable interested parties to make an informed decision. As a tool for use in that stage of negotiations, most railroads produced a large number of industrial brochures and other items, all of which contained varying amounts of detailed data concerning resources, labor, and other locational factors.

Industrial brochures appeared almost simultaneously with the establishment of industrial departments. The Illinois Central's John F. Merry compiled his *Where to Locate New Factories* in 1892. A few years later George C. Power produced a pamphlet entitled *One Hundred Cities and Towns Wanting Industries,* and in 1905 came *Locations for Industries,* a 230-page booklet that described the principal towns and cities along the Illinois Central and Yazoo and Mississippi Valley railroads. In an introductory statement J. C. Clair explained that the later booklet was compiled for presentation to manufacturers and others considering location and he noted that he would be happy to provide further information upon request.

These early booklets described the towns they were booming in only general terms. In the 1905 volume Mount Olive, Illinois, was pictured as a thriving town of 3,000 people in the heart of good farming country, some forty miles from St. Louis. It boasted of two banks, six hotels, five churches, the largest volunteer fire department in the state, and an automatic telephone system. The town had four coal mines and a cigar factory, and according to the Illinois Central it was seeking firms of all kinds.

Although the county had a debt of $600,000, the town had no bonded indebtedness. Coal cost $1.50 a ton, and labor was $1.90 a day.[12]

Such accounts were typical of those in industrial brochures issued by other lines. In 1902 the Buffalo and Susquehanna produced a booklet describing the "magnitude and activity of the industrial enterprises" along its line. A decade later the Great Northern issued *Business Openings*. According to that booklet, "In the Great Northwest there are hundreds of opportunities to engage in various lines of industry. . . . It is doubtful if any place in the world offers as wide a range of opportunities. . . . It is to meet the demands for specific information relative to these opportunities that this book is published. . . ." Apparently much of the material that went into such volumes was gathered in various ways. The Delaware and Hudson's *Industrial Openings*, in use by 1912, listed opportunities that were reported by "reliable businessmen interested in the welfare of their communities."[13]

Seemingly, industrial brochures changed little in the 1920s. The Frisco's *Industrial Opportunities* and *Industrial Development* were similar to those that had been issued earlier, while booklets that agents of the Seaboard Air Line distributed discussed the advantages of the South in the usual manner.

The late 1930s and early 1940s brought a flood of new industrial brochures that were more sophisticated and contained more of the type of specific data needed by businessmen considering location. A number of items issued by the Union Pacific were typical of many others. Glossy pamphlets that described tracts of industrial lands owned by the company or adjacent to its lines near Portland, at various points in Washington, and in Los Angeles contained statistical information on power and transportation facilities, labor, natural resources, and markets, and included detailed maps based in part on aerial photographs. A brochure issued in 1941 showing the industrial properties that the company had for sale in such Nebraska cities as Lincoln, Beatrice, and Fairbury pointed to raw materials available in Nebraska, mentioned freedom from bonded indebtedness and from sales, income, and other "nuisance" taxes, and pictured the special attractions offered by each of the towns.

Other roads turned out comparable literature. *Chessie's Corridor* discussed the natural resources along the Chesapeake and Ohio. A pamphlet produced by the Lackawanna in 1941 reflected that company's awareness of the movement of industries from the core cities. In 1944 appeared the first of several brochures issued by the Nickel Plate to "present a complete picture of the territory . . . for the convenience, utilization, and interest . . . of those needing pertinent information and statistics." The booklet contained accounts of the history, development, recreational facilities, and industries of different towns and colorful maps that showed the location of natural resources, natural gas lines, water regions, generating stations, and transmission lines.[14]

A special type of brochure or booklet that appeared before World War I and became more popular later was the industrial and shippers' directory. The Norfolk and Western issued such a volume in 1905, revising it periodically later. At the outset the booklet apparently was little different from the other industrial publications of that time, but by 1917 it had evolved into a classified list of business concerns, industrial enterprises, coal mines, blast furnaces, fruit growers, stock raisers and farmers, and other businesses along the line. Among other roads using such publications in the early 1920s were the Delaware and Hudson, which turned the job of compiling a book over to an outside firm, the New York Central, the Pennsylvania, and the Missouri Pacific.[15]

In their efforts to attract the attention of businessmen to their territories, industrial development men at times adopted some of the methods of colonization and agricultural agents. Exhibits were as useful in industrial development work as they were in other areas of development activity. At the Jamestown Exposition in 1907 and the Appalachian Exposition in 1911, the Southern Railway maintained displays of mineral and forest resources. In the 1920s several roads had exhibits at the annual Southern Exposition, and the Illinois Central placed a permanent exhibit at the New Orleans International Trade Exposition.

Traveling exhibits served similar purposes. In 1923 the Missouri Pacific dispatched three baggage cars loaded with displays of Arkansas' industries and resources on a two weeks' tour of eastern cities. One of the prime movers in the project was Walker Power, president of the Arkansas Central Power Company, who was an early leader in the electrical power industry's interest in the location of new businesses.[16]

Industrial tours were also used by railroads to advertise their territories. As early as 1907 the Southern took more than a hundred representatives of the textile manufacturing interests of seven European countries on a tour of the South. In the 1920s the Kentucky and Indiana Terminal Railroad used industrial tours to educate businessmen of Louisville to the opportunities enjoyed by that city, while the Missouri Pacific, in cooperation with chambers of commerce and power companies, took a group of eastern businessmen on a tour of Arkansas as part of a campaign to attract textile manufacturers to that state.[17]

At the same time that railway development men were trying to attract the attention of businessmen, they needed to keep themselves informed of the plans of enterprisers to relocate. This was a difficult task, since enterprisers were hesitant to discuss projects until details were finalized. Some roads used clipping bureaus to gather tips, but industrial men generally found that technique to be of little value, since by the time an item appeared in the papers it was outdated. Real estate brokers specializing in industrial properties, trade associations, chambers of commerce, and boards of trade were other sources of tips.

More important was information provided by the rank and file of a railroad's employees, from the chairman of the board down to station agents. All employees were expected to be "constantly on the alert and report immediately . . . any information coming to their attention of any prospect." According to the Missouri Pacific, the objective was to insure that "no worthwhile industry or warehouse locates in Missouri Pacific territory . . . until the Industrial Development Department . . . has an opportunity to present the advantages of a Missouri Pacific location."[18]

After receiving a direct inquiry or determining by some means that a firm was contemplating a move, industrial men were then ready to contact the prospect, ascertain his specific needs, and offer him a location along the line that met his particular requirements. Most railroadmen were convinced that at this stage personal contact was an absolute necessity. On roads with small development departments, division freight agents often contacted prospective customers, escorted them to sites, and provided them with additional data. Other roads used development men for this purpose, since top management thought that traffic department personnel tended to lack the long-range view and the knowledge and personality to make the best presentations.

In the case of prospective customers of substantial importance, railway development departments worked up complete engineering reports on one or more sites covering all the topics outlined in the more general pamphlets, plus detailed data on the competitive situation, unit costs of production, freight rates to all significant points, and any other matters that appeared relevant. Suitable maps and charts illustrated these reports.

Inevitably these presentations became increasingly complex, a fact that served as a prime justification for the existence and expansion of railway development departments. As one of the pioneers in the work explained it, by the turn of the century locational decisions were based on such a multitude of factors that "it is almost impossible for the average businessmen . . . to collect sufficient data of a reliable and helpful nature. This is where the industrial development department of a railroad steps in." Moreover by the 1920s, at least, the growing complexities of locational decisions caused the nature of railway development men to change. The work was becoming less a "matter of glib salesmanship," and industrial departments began to employ metallurgists, geologists, chemists, and engineers. Industrial development men now needed to know more about industrial water than its costs, more about coal than its freight rates or BTU values. In fact if they were to perform satisfactorily, they needed to know as much about the customer's business as the customer himself.[19]

Land, Sidetrack, and Other Problems

Industrial development work by its very nature was complex, involving problems rarely encountered by most railroadmen. Among the most perplexing of the industrial development man's concerns were those involving land management, the installation of sidetracks to serve industries, and relations with other departments and offices within a railroad's organization.

A successful industrial development program quite obviously required land for the location of industries. Until the 1920s, however, railroads devoted little attention to this issue, since most roads had right-of-way and terminal properties that could be put to industrial uses, and land-grant roads often were able to utilize remnants of those grants in or adjacent to cities and towns. Far more important in the aggregate, moreover, were privately owned industrial lands that could be reached by rails. Industrial development men pushed the utilization of these properties with enthusiasm, since the foremost objective in any case was the generation of traffic.

By the 1920s railway development men began to perceive an approaching shortage of industrial land, and the conservation of real estate suitable to industrial purposes became a matter of serious concern. Some railroad leaders tried to impress upon city officials, chambers of commerce, and realtors the desirability of preserving industrial property and of restricting the use of such land for other purposes. As late as 1930 zoning was in no more than its infancy in many cities, but railroadmen were already alert to its dangers. They noted that once land was zoned for residential uses, for example, it was very difficult to obtain a reversal. Thus they became avid students of zoning ordinances in their towns and cities, with an eye toward protecting potentially valuable industrial property, and they missed few opportunities to impress upon city officials the wisdom of using restraint in enacting zoning ordinances. For the same reasons railroadmen in the 1920s and later established contact with state highway departments, seeking to prevent the building of highways in locations that would diminish the supply of industrial land.

Increasingly, too, railroadmen devoted attention to the best utilization of carrier-owned real estate. They examined their companies' physical facilities to insure they did not occupy land that could be better used for industrial purposes. Changes in operations occasionally made some land available. Finally some industrial development men began to argue that railroads should be more selective in placing industries on available land and should give priority to those that promised to maximize tonnage and revenues.[20]

Nevertheless, in time many roads were handicapped by a shortage of industrial real estate. One answer was the purchase of tracts suitably situated for the location of industries. A few roads apparently bought odd pieces of land early in the century, but the purchase of industrial real estate did not become a systematic policy until the 1920s and 1930s. In the earlier decade, for example, the Wabash announced the purchase of 216 acres of prime industrial land at different points, and the Akron, Canton and Youngstown bought 800 acres near Akron, Ohio, to be in a position to take advantage of the expected expansion of the rubber industry in the city. In the 1930s the Chicago Great Western acquired 50 acres at Rochester, Minnesota, and succeeded in locating two concerns on the property before the year was out.[21]

In the 1930s and the early 1940s the Union Pacific was especially active in buying land; almost every annual report mentioned acquisitions. In 1930, for example, the company bought 30 acres adjoining its Argo Yard in Portland, Oregon. Later it acquired additional land there, as well as 45 acres at Denver, 35 acres at Gering, Nebraska, and 540 acres at Omaha.[22]

The need to insure a supply of prime industrial land, combined with changes in the types of businesses likely to be attracted and pressures generated by the rise of highway competition, caused railroads to turn to the establishment of industrial parks. These planned industrial communities were "subdivided and developed according to a comprehensive plan . . . with adequate control of the area and buildings to protect the investment of the developers . . . as well as of industries" occupying them. In Great Britain, where industrial parks or districts were called trading estates or industrial estates, two of the better known ones were the Trafford Parks near Manchester, established in 1896, and the Slough Trading Estate near London, established soon after World War I. In the United States the pioneer was the Clearing Industrial District, launched in Chicago in 1885. Experience showed that such areas were ideal for the location of small manufacturing plants and warehouses and especially those types of concerns that could most easily move commodities by truck.[23]

In the usual procedure in the establishment of industrial districts, a tract of well located but raw land was acquired; it was then provided with utilities, streets, spur tracks, and other facilities. In some instances railroads encouraged the formation of industrial districts by others, but carriers also joined with developers or created industrial districts themselves.

The Union Pacific was one of the leaders in developing its own industrial districts. In the 1920s the company created its Fairfax Industrial District, consisting of some 1,300 acres located roughly a mile from the center of Kansas City, Kansas. Original plans called for the installation of 40 miles of spur and storage tracks, adequate streets, and utilities. Lots were 100 by 600 feet; firms could obtain as many as necessary. The railroad proposed to sell sites on time contracts, but in some instances it was prepared to make other arrangements.[24] In the same decade the Union Pacific created its Metropolitan Warehouse and Industrial District at Los Angeles, a 750-acre development, and in 1929 the Union Pacific and the Milwaukee jointly purchased 16 city blocks in Spokane for the purpose of establishing an industrial district.

A number of other railroads were interested in various ways in industrial districts. As early as 1922 the Western Pacific was developing a tract at Stockton, California, and the Lehigh Valley was trying to interest private developers in a 230-acre tract it owned at Buffalo, New York. The Chicago Produce Terminal, perhaps not a true industrial district, was created jointly by the Illinois Central and the Santa Fe. First occupied in 1925, the terminal was the largest of its type in the world. The Santa Fe also had extensive interests in Dallas and Los Angeles, including the Central Manufacturing District in Los Angeles that became a major enterprise with buildings alone worth $15 million. Meanwhile the Wabash reported in 1930 that it had worked with chambers of commerce in several cities to establish industrial districts, and the Katy played a role in the creation of industrial districts in San Antonio, Houston, Fort Worth, Oklahoma City, Tulsa, and Dallas. The Katy Wholesale and Industrial District in Dallas, one of the most successful, was the result of cooperation between the carrier, the city, and local businessmen.[25]

By the 1920s some railroads had begun to provide buildings for the specific use of shippers. Carriers had traditionally leased excess space in stations and terminals to others, but the construction or purchase of buildings for the use of customers was a new departure taken to generate traffic in the face of growing competition. As an early example, the Katy in the 1920s spent half a million dollars in constructing a freight storage warehouse in Dallas for use by a freight forwarding company. Almost two decades later the Mobile and Ohio put up a freight house at Mobile for the United Fruit Company.

By the late 1930s the Union Pacific was quite active in this kind of work, generally operating through subsidiaries. In 1937 its Portland Terminal Investment Company built a warehouse at Portland for lease to a packing company; the Las Vegas Land and Water Company built one warehouse and purchased another at Los Angeles; and the Oregon and Washington Railroad Company constructed two warehouses at Seattle. The Union Pacific put up a building in Council Bluffs in 1938 for lease to the U.S. Post Office Department. The next year the Oregon and Washington erected another building at Seattle and one at Portland, while the Las Vegas Land and Water Company added one in Los Angeles. During the first years of the 1940s the Union Pacific constructed five warehouses at Denver and enlarged five others, while the Kansas City Industrial Land Company constructed additions to two structures in the Fairfax Industrial District.

Some railroads, unable or unwilling to tie up their own capital in rental properties, worked through third parties. In the late 1920s, for example, the Cotton Belt found that some firms interested in locating in the carrier's territory were reluctant to make the necessary capital outlays. In this situation the Cotton Belt located banks and insurance companies that were willing to finance new structures.[26]

The sale or lease of industrial land and buildings took carriers into areas in which legal questions were complex and not easily resolved. In the early days of industrial development work, most carriers apparently were little concerned with amounts of rental income earned from industrial properties or with selling prices. The objective was to generate traffic; industrial properties were viewed as means to that end; and railroads charged only nominal rents and sold industrial properties at substantially less than prevailing market prices. These policies had to be altered following enactment and clarification of the meaning of the Elkins Act.

Prior to World War I the Interstate Commerce Commission undertook a study of leasing policies. Hearings were conducted at different points, and results of the investigation were reported in 1922. In the printed record the commission limited itself to the practices and procedures of the Northern Pacific, Great Northern, and Spokane International at Spokane, Washington.

Northern Pacific's industrial lands there consisted in the main of right-of-way land and remnants of its federal grant. Leases were for long or indefinite terms, the latter subject to from one to three months' termination notices. Long-term leases, some of which were for fifty years, were used in cases where permanent and expensive structures had been erected by the occupant and where it was reasonably certain that the land would not be used in railway operations. In granting leases, company officials considered primarily the traffic that would accrue to the railroad, and most contracts provided that when rates were favorable, lessees would route their shipments over the Northern Pacific. Leases negotiated at Spokane by the Great Northern and Spokane International were similar in most of these particulars to those of the Northern Pacific.

Rents varied, but it appeared that the roads were not greatly interested in rental income. The Northern Pacific claimed that it charged a rent equal to 6 percent of the value of a property, with the lessee paying all taxes and special assessments, but the Interstate Commerce Commission found that the railroad established values for its industrial properties that were unrealistically low. Of eight lessees, only one paid 6 percent of the value established by tax assessors; the others paid approximately 2 percent of those values. Apparently standard procedure was to agree with the tenant on the amount of rent to be paid and then establish a value on the property that would make the rent equal to 6 percent of that value. The Northern Pacific's rents, however, were high when compared with those of the Spokane International. That road charged a flat annual rent of $10, regardless of the size, value, or location of a property. The Great Northern's rents equalled from 2½ to 5 percent of the value of its properties.

Officials of the three roads were frank in stating that traffic considerations were foremost in the minds of those executives responsible for arranging leases. Nevertheless, spokesmen for the carriers maintained that their companies were getting as much in rents as the land could be expected to earn, although there was no clear explanation for the variations in rentals. In no case did tenants complain about the rents charged them; the only complaints that the commission found came from owners of other warehouses, who claimed that they were unable to lease their properties on advantageous terms because of the competition from firms located on railway-owned land.

Although the Interstate Commerce Act and subsequent legislation did not authorize the commission "to prescribe . . . the terms or conditions under which carriers may lease their lands to shippers," the agency concluded that indirectly it could exercise some control. "When a carrier permits a shipper to use valuable land . . . without charge or without reasonably adequate charge, the practical effect is to reduce that shipper's transportation charges, so that there results what amounts to a refunding or remission of some portion of the published rates." Under these circumstances the commission found that "there may be a violation" of several sections of the Interstate Commerce Act and of the Elkins Act.

Given the complexities of the issue, the commission decided that an order was unnecessary, but it established a number of guidelines which "should govern carriers in the leasing of lands to shippers. . . ." The commission stated flatly that no "justification exists for the leasing of railway lands to industries at a nominal rental charge." Such an arrangement almost inevitably meant that an illegal concession had been made to the shipper. When leasing lands to customers, carriers should make every effort to obtain "terms no less favorable than could be obtained, under similar conditions, and restrictions of use, were the land owned independently of the railroad." The commission also rejected traffic clauses and claimed that the common practice of determining land values by mutual agreement between the carrier and the shipper was "open to serious abuse" and should be abandoned.

The commission recognized that effective supervision of these matters would be difficult, but it believed that its investigation and resulting publicity would encourage the carriers to modify their policies. Meanwhile the commission invited those who felt themselves aggrieved to bring their complaints to its attention.[27]

Some railroadmen complained bitterly about the new guidelines, pointing out, for example, that chambers of commerce and nonrailroad owners of industrial properties could charge any rent or even give lands to industries while the carriers could not go below certain levels. Nevertheless, most railroads accepted the guidelines in principle, even if they at times deviated from them when it appeared to do so would best serve their purposes. The end result was that there were no uniform policies, but in general rents were established at roughly 6 percent of the "fair valuation" of a property, that evaluation to be determined in the main by the selling price of comparable land. There were a number of general exceptions to this rule. Where the 6 percent rent would amount to only a few dollars, some roads had a fixed minimum. In large cities where a 6 percent rent would make prohibitive the use of land for industrial purposes, some carriers used a flat charge per square foot that presumably equalled prevailing rates in the area.

In time, some railroads drew up regulations to be followed in the leasing of property, the Chicago and Eastern Illinois doing so in 1930. According to that guide, all land was to be leased at 8 percent of its value as determined by the market prices of adjacent land used for the same purpose. The railroad paid all normal taxes on the property, but taxes levied because of the use of the property were the responsibility of the lessee. Special taxes resulting from public improvements were added to the value of the property, and leases provided for an automatic increase in the rent to cover such adjustments. Leases could not be transferred without the consent of the carrier, and the railroad would make no lease that would have the effect of decreasing the value of the remainder of a tract of land. The company also had a system of minimum charges for miscellaneous intrusions of company property.[28]

Similar in many ways to the problems arising from the handling of railway industrial properties were the complexities of installing industry sidetracks. Again, the policy of the Interstate Commerce Commission seemed in the early years to be poorly defined. The Interstate Commerce Act provided that railroads would construct, maintain, and operate on reasonable terms switch connections with private sidetracks in those instances where such connections were feasible from an engineering point of view and could be operated safely and profitably. On the other hand, under common law, railroads were not required to receive or deliver freight off their right-of-ways nor were they compelled to build or extend a track beyond the right-of-way line for the benefit of a private shipper. In short, railroads were required in normal circumstances to put in switches, but they were under no legal compulsion to construct, maintain, and operate private sidetracks.[29]

At the outset railroads built spurs for shippers in response to requests for service, the decisions to do so usually being dictated by the volume of expected business. The enactment of the Elkins Act and subsequent findings by the courts forced modification of these policies. If a railroad constructed a sidetrack on terms that it did not offer others, questions of discrimination were inevitable, but at the same time railroads could not afford to build private sidetracks for all shippers who might apply for them. Nevertheless, as competition among railroads became more intense, railway companies found themselves installing and maintaining industry sidetracks on terms that were unfavorable to them and perhaps of doubtful legality.

Prior to World War I railroadmen decided that a uniform sidetrack agreement would free their companies from undue pressures and at the same time permit the carriers to provide those services needed to attract new businesses. Committees representing roads in official and western classification territories took up the problem, and by 1917 a committee of the Railway Development Association was able to announce that a final solution was near. According to the committee, "great savings of unnecessary expenditure" had already been achieved and hopefully in the not far distant future all roads would be induced to subscribe to a uniform sidetrack agreement.

No final agreement had been reached when the federal government took control of the railroads. On 26 March 1918 Railroad Administration Director General McAdoo issued General Order 15, a directive that was apparently based on the recommendations of the sidetrack committee of the Railway Development Association. The order provided that in the case of new tracks the railroad concerned would pay for, own, and maintain that portion of the track from switch point to clearance point, while the industry involved would be solely responsible for track beyond the right-of-way line. Track from the clearance point to the right-of-way line would generally be the responsibility of the industry, although "in special cases" the railroad might assume that burden. Existing arrangements were to be adhered to until otherwise ordered, but all new tracks were to be covered by written contracts.[30]

Minor changes came during the period of governmental operation, and after the roads were returned to their owners many of them continued to use General Order 15. Some roads urged all of their customers using sidetracks to sign uniform contracts based on the Railroad Administration directive. By 1925 the Delaware and Hudson claimed that it had 90 percent of its sidetracks under such agreements; the Missouri Pacific indicated that it was ready to cease operations on sidetracks not covered by the standard contract; but some roads reported that in the event of a refusal by an important shipper, they did nothing. For the railroad industry as a whole, arrangements still varied widely, with each road presumably adopting uniform policies and following them carefully to avoid charges of discrimination. The suspicion remained strong, however, that many roads made special arrangements when the competitive situation seemed to require them. In any case it was common practice for railroads to build to their standards all needed spur tracks and to maintain them, charging the customer for work performed on his portion of the track.[31]

While policies concerning sidetracks varied among railroads, procedures for handling applications were reasonably uniform. When an industry promising a satisfactory volume of business requested a sidetrack from the Kansas City Southern, for example, the railroad's industrial men asked the chief engineer to make a study of the proposed construction and to prepare an estimate of its cost. The operating department was consulted to insure that the new switch and spur would not interfere with the movement of trains. After these studies were completed, terms under which the railroad would construct the track were offered to the customer. If they were acceptable, both parties signed a standard sidetrack agreement. Time was of considerable importance in these negotiations. A common complaint among industrial men was that the handling of sidetrack applications took so long that some customers were lost.[32]

Many of the problems and frustrations of industrial development work stemmed from the fact that a successful program required the cooperation of many officials and several departments of a railroad. J. C. Carlisle of the Missouri Pacific was correct when he noted that industrial development work was not "a one man, one department task. It is one that calls for the hearty co-operation of our entire personnel – officers and employees alike."

Nevertheless, industrial development men often complained about the cooperation, or lack of it, that they received from personnel in other departments. In some instances they contended that top management failed to give the work the support it deserved; in other cases industrial men felt that they were not given the rank and prestige needed to permit them to meet top businessmen on common ground and that management too often appointed to industrial positions men lacking the necessary skill and personality.

Differing objectives also generated conflicts between industrial development departments and other railway officers. Operating and engineering departments often came in for criticism, either because they acted slowly or because they were too often inclined to object to the location of a spur on engineering or operating grounds. Traffic department men, according to development agents, tended to take an excessively short-sighted view of the traffic potential of a prospective customer and too often were slow in working up tariffs for new industries.

Real estate departments were special sources of complaints. These offices, the first of which was reportedly created by the Reading in 1866, were charged with the responsibility for handling tax matters and managing company lands, including industrial properties. In the latter capacity, they were inclined to strive for a satisfactory return on the value of property, while industrial men looked more to the traffic a firm using the property might generate. Recognizing this difference in goals, the Reading foreshadowed later developments in the industry when in 1935 it combined the two offices. Other charges leveled against real estate departments included their failure to maintain accurate and up-to-date blueprints of properties and a tendency to delay determination of an acceptable rent or sale price until the prospect was lost.[33]

Relations with groups and individuals outside of the railroad industry also produced problems. Industrial development men often worked with private real estate firms, but relations were difficult. Realtors, logically enough, were interested in the size of their commissions, a goal which did not always square with the railroadman's desire to locate an industry that would generate substantial amounts of traffic. Even more disconcerting to railway development men was the hostile attitude toward industrialization that prevailed in some communities. As late as 1940, for instance, the Illinois Central reported that businessmen seeking new locations avoided Mississippi, believing apparently correctly that many people in the state did not want industrial growth.[34]

Finally the appearance of vigorous intermodal competition in the form of the motor truck introduced an element of uncertainty in railroad development work. By the early 1930s trucks were beginning to make significant inroads in certain kinds of railway traffic, although few people in the industry envisioned the tremendous impact that highway competition would ultimately have on railroading. Indeed, some industrial development men believed that the use of trucks for short hauls would lead to the establishment of numerous branch plants and warehouses to serve smaller markets, thereby giving them new opportunities. Others were less optimistic, and some suggested quite correctly that expansion of trucking and improvement in the vehicles in use would change sharply the environment in which they worked.

In many ways industrial development work was difficult and frustrating to those engaged in it. Unlike other railroadmen who could expect to see concrete results of planning and effort, industrial men often worked for months only to see a prospect evaporate. As Edward J. Israel, industrial agent of the Pennsylvania in the 1920s, expressed it, "you work on a proposition for months . . . and years and put a great deal of time and effort on it and you work it up to a point where you think it is going to materialize into something, and then a beautiful gloom begins to settle over the whole thing and something touches a match to it and away she goes. Sometimes you have a number of prospects on your desk and they all fade away."[35] Other industrial development men could have reported the same discouraging results, but few of them, or their superiors, questioned the value of their work.

between a good father and his immediate family, the settler having the entire confidence of the agent, and the agent in turn being the adviser of the settler in all of his business and other affairs." According to a spokesman for the Northern Pacific, the road's "real interest in the settler begins at the time that he settles in its territory." The agent stood ready to help the settler if disaster struck, keep him out of the hands of those who would exploit him, and otherwise aid him whenever possible. Perhaps atypical was the experience of one colonization agent who reported that after he placed a group of farmers, he spent "nearly . . . three months telling them what to do and how to do it."[1]

No doubt practice fell short of the ideal, but a program undertaken by the Duluth and Iron Range Railroad to settle cutover lands in northern Minnesota constituted an example of the new approaches to colonization work. The company owned some 200,000 acres, the remnants of a state land grant. In the prewar period the population in the area was sparce, consisting in the main of former lumberjacks who accepted a primitive, subsistence existence and who opposed those changes that would permit development of a more settled society. In truth, the country was far from attractive. There were few roads, and the area needed draining. Reportedly, it was so wet that hardy residents "cut their hay in hip boots and spread it on the stumps to dry."

Nevertheless, the Duluth and Iron Range resolved to improve the property and settle it. Major efforts centered at a point some forty miles northwest of Duluth, which the railroad had named Meadowlands. The road began to clear the land, contributed financially to the building of drainage ditches and roads, and launched a colonization drive, with the usual exhibits and literature. Recognizing the problems facing new arrivals in such a raw country, the railroad detailed an agent to meet settlers and their families and to arrange temporary housing for them. It provided plans for houses, the most popular being a three-room structure of shiplap construction costing about $450, and helped settlers locate materials and carpenters.

After a settler's house was up, the new arrival and the railroad turned to other tasks. The land had to be completely cleared, a chore in which the state agricultural college and the federal government helped by providing technical advice and low cost or free explosives. The carrier joined in the work, clearing and breaking some of the land with its own crawler-type tractors and giant breaker plows. Meanwhile it encouraged settlers to establish a cooperative creamery and to explore markets in Hibbing for garden truck and it induced a sugar beet firm to set up a buying center in the area. The railroad also concerned itself with the development of educational and social facilities and with the installation of such modern conveniences as telephones.

In the course of its colonization drive, company spokesmen claimed that they made no effort to conceal the fact that carving a farm out of northern Minnesota's cutover country was difficult. They tried to make prospective settlers fully aware of the hardships while stressing that the land was so cheap and terms were so easy that men could buy farms who could not obtain land elsewhere. Everyone in the area was poor, the railroad noted, and a general shortage of money was fully understood, so families that accepted the conditions and had the proper pioneering spirit need feel no hesitancy in moving to the area.[2]

The first requirement for a successful colonization effort, of course, was suitable land, and railwaymen assured all who would listen that an abundance of it remained in the 1920s. Agents pointed out that homestead land remained in the West. The Burlington, for example, made known the availability of 640-acre homesteads in Wyoming. Irrigated land on both old and new projects attracted the efforts of such roads as the Burlington, Great Northern, Santa Fe, and others. Railroad spokesmen noted that almost 70 percent of the land area of twenty-seven counties in the eastern Colorado had never been cultivated and they professed to believe that the region was suitable for irrigated, dry-land, and grazing operations. The Northern Pacific and Great Northern stressed the attractiveness of established farms in the Dakotas and Montana. Middle western farmers should be interested in these properties, company officers believed, because of their relative low cost. In the fall of 1923 more than 200 tracts of Indian lands from the Pine Ridge and Rosebud reservations were sold at public auction.

The Great Northern spent considerable energy in booming Minnesota. That state, according to company writers, offered "unusual opportunities for every person seeking a farm home no matter what his tastes or abilities are. The man with plenty of capital can find highly improved farms and the man with very little means can find cheap land. There are opportunities for the man who wants to go into diversified farming as well as for the man who wants to specialize. . . ."[3]

Railroads serving the South Plains were still promoting that area. Ranches in the Lubbock-Canyon City region of Texas were being broken into 160-acre farms where, according to the Santa Fe, cotton could be grown without the problem of the boll weevil. The Burlington's southwestern subsidiaries were interested in a similar type of development. The Missouri Pacific and Southern Pacific were booming the lower Rio Grande Valley. The San Antonio and Aransas Pass claimed that there was room for 75,000 more farmers along its lines alone.[4]

In the South railroad colonization men stressed the wide diversity of crops, the long growing season, the cheapness of forage for livestock, and the low price of land as compared with that in the North. The Missouri

Pacific and the Kansas City Southern pointed to the attractiveness of the Ozark regions of Missouri and Arkansas. Mississippi still offered "almost unlimited opportunities to farmers willing to work," said the Illinois Central. According to the Southern Railway, highly productive lands along its lines should attract settlers from throughout the United States. The Gulf, Mobile and Northern and the Georgia and Florida were only two of the roads that were convinced that cutover lands of the Lower South had great potential, and a tiny short line was still enthusiastically promoting cutover lands in eastern Arkansas.

Eastern roads believed that there remained opportunity in their territories for effective colonization work. Luther D. Fuller, agricultural agent of the Erie, reported that the New England states and New York contained much vacant land, generally with good improvements and located near the nation's largest markets, that could be purchased at low prices. He attributed the availability of land to the lure of the industrial cities that drained the countryside of young people and left farms abandoned.[5]

There was little new railroad construction in the 1920s, but where new rails were put down railroadmen were quick to point out the attractions of areas opened to settlement. When the Northern Pacific announced plans to build a branch from Glendive to Circle and Brockway, Montana, it suddenly discovered the attractions of Redwater valley lands and commenced to advertise them. The Great Northern reacted in a similar fashion following completion of branch lines in northern Montana. A new line extending into the "Big Flat" country of Phillips and Blaine counties opened "one of the best farming and stockraising sections of Montana." Because of the region's good soil, water, and climate, settlers might expect to produce high yields of wheat at low cost. Meanwhile the Frisco promoted settlement along its new line south of Aberdeen, Mississippi.[6]

Although a few roads, including the Northern Pacific, still had land for sale, the great majority of the carriers sought to achieve full utilization of publicly or privately owned lands along their lines. Typical was the position of the Kansas City Southern, which announced in 1924 that it "does not own any farm lands, and has no farm property to sell. All of the land holdings along the line are the property of individual owners." Such owners were usually represented by realtors, who the railroad pointed out were not on its payroll but who had been recommended as "reputable men."

Not all realtors, of course, were "reputable men." Too often, according to an official of the Santa Fe, the single goal of realtors and landowners they represented was "to get the other fellow's money." Moreover he thought that generally "we take too much . . . money from the settler from the start." It would be wiser, many railroadmen contended, to minimize initial payments and allow the settler to conserve his funds for operating expenses.

In various ways a number of railroads tried to exercise some control over realtors. The Northern Pacific, for example, worked through boards of trade and chambers of commerce in an effort to force agents and sellers to restrain themselves. In 1924 the Central of Georgia agreed to advertise lands only if owners, realtors, and local commercial organizations accepted certain conditions. All farms had to be of a proper size, given the type of agriculture for which they were best suited. Lands had to be placed under option until the spring of the following year in order to guarantee price stability, and the price had to be reasonable as determined by an examination of the property by Central of Georgia agents. Terms of sale had to ask for no more than 15 percent down with the balance due in 15 or more annual payments. The San Antonio and Aransas Pass Railroad also worked closely with landowners, bankers, and others to reduce payments and to arrange low cost loans to cover improvements.[7]

Methods of recruiting settlers tended to be those of the past. Homeseekers' rates reappeared; the Great Northern claimed that it was the first railroad after World War I to reestablish such rates, doing so early in 1921. Shortly, the Western and Southwestern Passenger associations placed in effect a round trip homeseekers' rate that equalled approximately a one-way fare plus two dollars. These arrangements were retained with little change throughout the decade. Southern roads were more reluctant to offer reduced rates, despite considerable pressure to do so from realtors and others. According to railroad spokesmen, travelers took advantage of homeseekers' rates, and the Southern Railway quoted its former industrial agent, M. V. Richards, to the effect that homeseekers' rates had never been effective in producing migration into the South. Nevertheless, late in 1923 the Southeastern Passenger Association agreed to institute homeseekers' rates.

Advertising for colonists, much like that of an earlier period, reappeared in the 1920s. Western roads were most aggressive in this work, or so reported the *Manufacturers Record,* which claimed that all the roads of the South were spending less in 1923 to promote the area from Maryland to Texas than were the roads serving the single state of California. That year the Hill roads announced their decision to expend between $300,000 and $400,000 to advertise the Northwest. The campaign called for advertisements in national magazines, to be followed by a comprehensive set of brochures that were to be provided upon request.[8]

Much railroad advertising in the 1920s took the form of brief notices in the classified sections of farm papers and small town newspapers. In

1921, for instance, the Seaboard Air Line reported that such advertisements in 120 papers generated some 10,000 inquiries. A typical advertisement of the Louisville and Nashville urged midwestern farmers to "Go South to Prosper," and a similar blurb of the Northern Pacific labeled southeastern Montana the "New Corn Belt" where productive land could be purchased for from $10 to $25 an acre.

Some railroads went beyond brief notices in the classified sections. As late as 1929 the Missouri Pacific was placing half-page advertisements in such papers as the *Southern Ruralist* as part of its efforts to attract people to the White River valley of Missouri and Arkansas. That area was ideal for farm homes because "of its happy blend of rich soil, pleasing weather, beautiful scenery and unusual opportunities for successful farming, recreation and life in the open."[9]

Railroad-produced brochures continued to play their role in colonization efforts. Val Kuska, a Burlington agent, spent a good bit of his time in preparing them. Some publications were joint ventures. In 1923, for example, the Burlington and the Thurston County, Nebraska, Real Estate Board issued jointly a brochure, the railroad providing some of the material and arranging for publication in Chicago.

Railroad literature issued in the 1920s was certainly more objective than that in use earlier, but it still contained a great deal of pure boosterism. A folder circulated by the Missouri Pacific proclaimed that somewhere "in Missouri Pacific territory there is a farm that will meet your every requirement, where you can grow the crops you want to grow, where you can find the best educational advantages to your children, and where you can find happiness and success." Mississippi, according to a Mobile and Ohio brochure, was "a land of 'frontier opportunities,' where millions of acres of good lands are yet to be had at low prices, enabling the man of moderate means to gratify the home building impulse of the true American."[10]

As a means of attracting attention to their territories, a number of railroads operated or cooperated in the operation of regional promotional trains that were similar in many ways to the traveling exhibits of pre-World War I years. An Illinois Central Know Mississippi Better Train toured the Middle West each year from 1925 through 1929. The Milwaukee, Missouri Pacific, and Frisco also used exhibit cars or trains, while the Atlantic Coast Line placed movable exhibits at fairs in New York and the New England states in the late 1920s.[11]

Standard procedures for handling colonists seem to have changed slightly to meet the times. Fairly typical was that of the Seaboard Air Line. In answer to each inquiry, the railroad sent a collection of literature and a letter stating that the company wished to encourage only those farmers who were properly fitted and equipped for Seaboard territory.

Along with the literature went a questionnaire to determine a man's circumstances. On the basis of the replies, the company recommended that a prospective homeseeker either visit Seaboard territory or remain where he was. The railroad provided desirable prospects with lists of realtors, all of whom it had investigated, and it insisted that persons considering its territory examine personally any land before purchasing it. Finally the carrier promised to do all that it could to help the new arrival to settle in his new community. Programs of other roads differed only in details.[12]

Generally railroads concentrated their colonizing efforts on those specific parts of their territories where there was enthusiastic and energetic local participation. Local booster groups were useful, and where they did not exist railroads often created them. The Burlington was largely responsible for the establishment in 1925 of the Big Horn Colonization Association, and it was closely allied with the Nebraska Association of Real Estate Boards. The Great Northern and the Northern Pacific were supporters of the Greater North Dakota Association and the Northwestern North Dakota Development Association. The Pere Marquette helped to establish the Western Michigan Development Bureau, headquartered at Traverse City. The bureau "concerned itself with such problems as the development of suitable crops, the encouragement of new settlers, the opening up of the cutover timberlands and various other activities, each having a direct bearing upon agricultural expansion."[13]

Southern railroads cooperated with comparable organizations, as well as lumber companies, in promoting the settlement of their cutover lands. The Gulf, Mobile and Northern organized the Alabama-Mississippi Improvement Association for that purpose in 1923, while the Seaboard Air Line and the Central of Georgia continued to contribute financially to the Southern Settlement and Development Organization. Finally such roads as the Kansas City Southern and the Missouri Pacific were still working with the Long-Bell Lumber Company and other firms to dispose of Louisiana cutover lands to farmers.[14]

As part of their colonization and land utilization programs, at least ten railroads contributed financially to the support of the Institute for Research in Land Economics and Public Utilities, headed by Richard T. Ely, the famed economist from the University of Wisconsin. The institute was interested in formulating a "scientific settlement policy," and, according to M. T. Sanders, tax commissioner of the Northern Pacific, the carriers believed that the institute would "result in real benefit to all of us who are affected by progress in the general welfare."[15]

Railroads also gave their hearty approval to state efforts to aid colonization. California was deeply involved in community building, using state money, while Wisconsin provided for the careful supervision of private colonization companies. In Maryland the agricultural extension service was charged with the task of attracting new farmers. County agents compiled lists of farms for sale while headquarters personnel advertised the state. In 1922 part of the work was assigned to the Southern Maryland Immigration Commission.[16]

Railroadmen continued to believe that it paid to locate new settlers along their lines in the 1920s, although there was no consensus concerning the value of each new settler. Obviously the ability and determination of the man, the type of farming pursued, and a multitude of variables over which the railroad had no control entered into the equation. The Milwaukee figured that a settler in North Dakota was worth $250 in new traffic each year; in Montana the figure was $350. The Santa Fe set the value at $500, the Denver and Rio Grande Western established it at from $700 to $900, and some lines estimated it as high as $2,500. Nevertheless, there could be little doubt that colonization efforts in the 1920s were dramatically less rewarding than they had been earlier. According to the Burlington's Val Kuska, "the work was very much of an uphill proposition," and all the evidence suggests that his colleagues on other lines would have echoed his views.[17]

Colonization Work in the 1930s and Later

The decade of the 1930s, with its Great Depression, droughts, and new departures in federal farm policy, produced both opportunities and problems for railroadmen interested in colonization. The soaring unemployment in the nation's cities suggested that many urban dwellers might well return to the land, while dust bowl conditions caused some farmers to consider relocating in districts where inadequate rainfall was not a constant, nagging threat. The exodus of drought victims from the Great Plains presented railroads serving those areas with the need to find replacements, a task that presumably would be made easier by the deteriorating economic conditions in the older sections of the Middle West and elsewhere that drove men to seek cheaper lands. Meanwhile the crop reduction programs of the New Deal and the federal government's interest in the retirement of marginal lands produced obvious contradictions with railway colonization efforts.

The back-to-the-farm movement especially excited railroadmen. It was apparently substantial; the U.S. Department of Agriculture reported that net increase in rural population in 1931 was 656,000 and 263,000 during the first three months of 1932. The Northern Pacific's John W. Haw identified at least three classes of people in the movement. First was a migratory group, lacking funds and looking for cheap housing and space for a garden. Of more interest were sons of farmers who had lost jobs in the cities. Finally, Haw noted a class of economically substantial people, currently unemployed, who needed land for investment purposes until times improved.[18]

If numbers of inquiries received by railway colonization offices were any indication of the scope of the movement, it had great potential. According to Ralph W. Reynolds of the Milwaukee, the volume of mail proved that "there is a desire for farm homes by many men with the background of farm experiences . . . who have been employed in industry . . . and wish to get back to the land before their savings are dissipated." The Burlington claimed that the average number of inquiries received in 1931–1933 was almost a third more than in the 1920s, and in June 1931 a company official estimated that between 800 and 1,000 new settlers would locate in Burlington territory that year.

Other roads had comparable volumes of business. Not "since 1917 and 1918 have we had such a demand for rental farms," reported P. H. Wheeler of the Missouri Pacific in 1933. The high unemployment and the availability of cheap land and a large number of rental farms in the hands of federal land banks, insurance companies, and other farm loan agencies inspired most of the inquiries. In the South the Norfolk and Western found in 1931 that the purchase of farms in its territory was substantially heavier than in the previous year. Among the inquiries that came to the Northern Pacific were many from urban dwellers interested in cutover lands in Washington and Oregon.[19]

Recruiting procedures were in the main those that had proven themselves in the past. A new burst of advertising in classified sections of farm magazines appeared. The Louisville and Nashville informed northerners in 1932 that if they were interested in improving their condition they should "investigate the Central South, where hundreds of former northern farmers are enjoying longer growing seasons, wider diversity of crops, splendid climate, good water, and opportunity for recreation." The Santa Fe encouraged readers of farm journals to consider buying a farm in the South Plains of Texas and offered copies of the *Earth* to any prospective homeseeker. "Why pay rent when you can buy a farm in the Panhandle and South Plains of Texas at a low price and on very reasonable terms," asked the railroad in a typical advertisement. The Milwaukee advertised western South Dakota, the Moses Lake area of Washington, and the Judith Basin and the Greenfields Division of the Sun River Irrigation Project in Montana in publications having a total circulation of over 9.5 million. Included were foreign language papers through which the company hoped to reach the unemployed in the nation's industrial cities.[20]

Colonization brochures and other promotional methods of the past also enjoyed a revival in the 1930s. The Milwaukee especially seemed to produce literature in abundance, issuing in 1934 alone three new items describing available lands in Washington and Idaho, central Montana, and upper Wisconsin. As late as 1938 the Gulf, Mobile and Northern was still using its time tables to call attention to the agricultural attractions of the South. Several roads offered the usual spring homeseekers' rates.[21]

Probably the Missouri Pacific's mode of operation was typical of those of other lines. Through contact with the various agencies having land for sale or rent, the company kept an up-to-date listing of offerings for daily reference. Company personnel inspected some of the offerings of "reliable dealers." On the basis of information gathered by these means, the Missouri Pacific prepared mimeographed lists of available farms. These lists and illustrated literature dealing with the general agricultural characteristics of a region then went to homeseekers who contacted the railroad. The company also enclosed a questionnaire to obtain data from the prospect to determine his needs and capabilities. This information was then turned over to dealers, who contacted the homeseeker and tried to make a sale or arrange a lease. If terms were worked out, the dealer reported the details to the railroad so that its colonization men might be informed as to the amount of land involved, the terms, and the type of farming to be taken up by the settler. Soon after the family's arrival, a Missouri Pacific agent called upon the family to determine whether the railroad could render any assistance. When a family was located, the railroad developed publicity concerning the event, both to help the new arrival fit more quickly into his new neighborhood and to serve as a means of attracting other settlers.[22]

Heavy reliance upon realtors and others not connected with individual railroad companies led to many problems, as it had earlier. The Missouri Pacific, for example, considered misrepresentation to be the greatest deterrent to successful colonization. The Milwaukee noted that under the conditions of the 1930s, the road should make every effort to "protect new settlers against misrepresentation . . . regarding agricultural, climatic, and market conditions."[23]

The results of these efforts were difficult to assess, partly because most homeseekers in the 1930s traveled by automobile, but some railroads contended that they were getting reasonable returns on their work. Throughout the decade the Northern Pacific regularly informed its stockholders that people were moving into its territory. Colonization drives in the Ellensburg and Pasco districts of Washington and near Missoula and Sidney, Montana, reportedly produced "substantial results," and "large numbers" of new settlers found homes in northern Minnesota, on cutover lands in Idaho and Washington, and on several irrigation projects.

Other roads, too, reported successes. The Great Northern contended that considerable numbers of young men returning from the cities, midwestern farmers dissatisfied with high rents and taxes, and people unhappy with the uncertainties of urban life were finding locations in its territory. The Milwaukee claimed that settlers were buying land even in the dark days of 1932–1934 and that interest increased later. The Missouri Pacific placed several families in southwestern Louisiana in 1933, for a time employing a special agent for that work, and later a number of farmers were located in southeastern Missouri. More indicative of trends, however, was the retirement of the last Missouri Pacific colonization agent in 1934.[24]

Even after World War II some roads still talked of the possibility of land settlement. In the course of the war the Milwaukee reported that it was receiving "thousands" of inquiries and in 1945 it distributed over 10,000 pieces of literature to persons asking for information. Meanwhile the Northern Pacific and the Santa Fe announced in 1946 that they were attempting to locate settlers, the latter road professing to believe that large numbers of returning veterans would be interested in settling on the land. In the early 1950s such roads as the Northern Pacific, Great Northern, Santa Fe, Southern Pacific, and Burlington had promotional literature available, and the Union Pacific issued a revised version of its *Farm Seekers' Guide* in 1957.[25]

Nor were western roads the only carriers to devote some attention to land settlement in the post–World War II period. In 1946 the New York Central thought it was worthwhile to issue a 42-page promotional pamphlet "to help those who are truly fitted and equipped for the land to find the farms they want. . . ." The publication warned prospective homeseekers that life on the farm called for many skills, that few farmers became rich, and that cash returns were moderate. "However, if you and your family really love the land . . . like to make things grow . . . enjoy simple pleasures . . . and prize the health that goes with physical activity and outdoor life . . . then, truly, farming can be for you the most deeply satisfying of all professions." New York Central territory, the pamphlet claimed, could produce all crops except cotton and citrus fruits. Lands were described as highly productive, the living conditions comfortable, and markets large and convenient. The pamphlet did not list lands available along the company's lines, but the railroad pledged its help to persons wishing to locate in its territory.

Still there could be no denying that the post–World War II years witnessed the end of a century of railway colonization work. Perhaps symbolic was the closing of the Santa Fe's Land Department on 1 April 1956. Since 1897 that office had been concerned with the disposal of the fourteen million acres of land in Arizona and New Mexico that had come with the acquisition of the Atlantic and Pacific Railway Company.[26] Most roads, of course, had no granted lands and their colonization efforts had been directed toward other properties. But those too were gone by the 1950s, if not earlier, and an age in railroad history had come to an end.

CHAPTER SIX

Agricultural Development Work at High Tide, 1920–1930

THE PROSPERITY DECADE saw railway companies resume their development work in agriculture. Activities and expenditures reached new highs, although objectives and general patterns indicated a return to "normalcy." Since railroad managers continued to believe that the "welfare of the agricultural people . . . and the welfare of the railroads are parallel," agricultural development departments set out to "bring about better agricultural conditions generally." That statement of goals would have been equally appropriate in the years before World War I.

Still, railway development men soon found that they were facing new conditions. In contrast to the decade and a half before 1917, the 1920s were not prosperous years for farmers. Low prices for farm commodities resulted in part from overproduction of staples, and railroadmen recognized that they could not strive simply to increase output. The character of railway development work was altered also by the growth of governmental activity in agriculture. The appointment of county agents in most agricultural counties and of Smith-Hughes teachers in many high schools meant that these individuals now assumed some of the tasks that might have been performed by railway agricultural agents. Moreover public agencies now tended to formulate general policies and to initiate programs, leaving railroads to take supportive or supplementary roles. The appearance of trucks on the nation's highways in some instances gave a new urgency to railroad efforts; in other situations it caused top management to question development programs that promised to generate traffic susceptible to truck competition.[1]

The central thrust of agricultural development programs in the 1920s continued to be the improvement of farming methods, but the objective was not simply to increase aggregate output. One answer to the dilemma of overproduction seemed to be an even greater emphasis on diversification, almost a magic word among businessmen and their spokesmen in the 1920s. Advocates of diversification believed that a shift from those crops produced in superabundance to a wider range of farm commodities would help to shield farmers from the full impact of low prices, give rural dwellers steadier incomes, and reduce their dependence on costly credit. Related to the businessmen's advocacy of diversification was an effort to encourage farmers to "live at home." If farmers produced more of the food and feedstuffs consumed on their farms, their costs would be lower and they would be less adversely affected by the prevailing trends in prices of farm products.[2]

Railroadmen in the 1920s were even more alert to the public relations aspect of their work than they had been in the Progressive period. Although top executives viewed with some suspicion the political attitudes of farmers in the mass, they believed that it would be beneficial to the industry to maintain good relations with those men who were considered to be leaders in the rural community. These included farm bureau and grange officers, members of breeders' and growers' associations, a number of progressive farmers in almost every neighborhood, and especially personnel of the agricultural extension service. The establishment of good relations with such men, in fact, might be the most rewarding kind of development work.[3]

Promotional Techniques in the 1920s

Railroads in the 1920s employed a remarkable variety of old and new methods to reach and influence farmers. By means of the printed word, exhibits, radio, educational trains, and a multitude of other techniques, the carriers poured so much information into the countryside that few rural residents failed to come into contact with at least some of it.

Railroads continued to distribute huge amounts of literature. Some of it was produced by the U.S. Department of Agriculture, the agricultural extension service, and such private groups as the Southern Fertilizer Association, but many roads were still turning out their own literature. The number of development magazines, for example, increased until most major carriers had publications of that nature, and the colonization periodicals that remained gradually shifted their purposes to agricultural development.

These increasingly sophisticated periodicals were designed in part to sell "the development department to the patrons of the road." According to officials of the Burlington, the magazines should be "sane, conservative and regular" and they should be written in language that could be understood by the ordinary farmer. The periodicals proved to be especially useful in distilling material presented in the more technical experiment station bulletins. Many railroads sent their development magazines to country editors, thereby gaining a wider circulation of the information contained in them and at the same time earning the good will of rural newspapermen.

One of the new development magazines that was fairly typical of the group was the Atlanta and West Point's *Agricultural Bulletin.* First issued in 1924 as a monthly, the periodical was distributed free to a select list of farmers, merchants, and bankers. Circulation exceeded 10,000 by 1927. The first issue discussed methods of controlling the boll weevil; subsequent issues dealt with poultry raising, soil improvement, and other farm topics, generally taking them up in season.[4]

Several railroads turned quickly to the new marvel of the decade, the radio. The Burlington was one of the pioneers, sponsoring a series of broadcasts over an Omaha station from 1924 to 1926. The program was inaugurated to encourage seed corn testing, following a poor crop year in 1923, but later speakers discussed methods for controlling smut in wheat and diseases in hogs, the value of purebred sires, and other topics. Edith Fullerton, who for twenty years had been her husband's co-worker on the Long Island and who succeeded him when he retired, gave a series of radio talks in the fall of 1928 on the marketing of farm crops and related matters. Beginning that year the Chicago and Illinois Midland sponsored a fifteen-minute program from Chicago each weekday. E. D. "Farmer" Rusk, a well-known personality, conducted the program, which featured grain and livestock prices, short talks by a variety of speakers, and music by a country trio. For a time a St. Louis station carried each Monday during the noon hour a talk on "Timely Soil and Crop Topics" by a development agent of the Wabash railroad.[5]

Several railroads continued the ancient policy of offering reduced fares to farmers attending agricultural meetings, awarding prizes to farmers who excelled, and placing exhibits at agricultural fairs and elsewhere. The Missouri Pacific was especially active in the latter area, maintaining for years displays at the American Royal Livestock Show at Kansas City and at state and county fairs throughout its territory.[6]

Although farmers' institutes were of declining importance after World War I, some railroads, including the Rock Island and the Gulf, Mobile and Northern, sponsored meetings that resembled the old affairs. T. A. Hoverstad, a recognized authority in agricultural education then employed by the Chicago Great Western, held forty-five sessions in the winter of 1921–1922, and the work continued at least until 1929, attracting as many as 18,000 people a year. According to Hoverstad, the meetings were "public forums" where participants discussed any topic of interest, including not only agricultural matters but also problems of railroad operations and service.[7]

The growth of the county agent system meant that railroads in the main could abandon direct, personal work with individual farmers, but a few carriers still offered such services. In 1921 the Chicago Great Western launched its "personal service campaign" in which a representative of the road visited farmers and discussed their problems with them. A decade later the Lackawanna reported that its "trained agriculturist" was available for consultation on all matters related to farm operation.[8]

Many of the railway demonstration farms that had existed before World War I were converted to other purposes during that struggle, and in the 1920s a majority of railway executives believed that company-owned farms would only duplicate the work of the agricultural colleges and other public agencies. The Long Island sold its two farms in the 1920s, and late in the decade a survey showed that only nine carriers maintained anything that resembled demonstration farms. One of the few new ones established in the 1920s was the Chicago and Illinois Midland's Cimco Farm, a 240-acre property near Havana, Illinois, that the railroad acquired in 1928.[9]

The Central of Georgia used demonstration plots in a pasture improvement program that continued throughout the 1920s. Knowing that better pastures were a prerequisite to the development of a viable livestock industry, the company set out to establish a test pasture in every county in Georgia and Alabama served by its line. The railroad paid half of the costs associated with each plot and provided supervision based on plans developed by the University of Georgia. Contracts were first signed with farmers in the spring of 1921.[10]

In terms of numbers and degree of sophistication, the decade of the 1920s was the golden age of educational train operation. However the goals and relationships with other groups and educational agencies had undergone changes. To a greater degree than earlier, the trains were coordinated with or were parts of agricultural extension programs; quite often they were the important, opening step to be followed by extension personnel using other methods. Many railroads refused to operate a train unless the subject matter had been approved by the extension service in the states concerned, and there were greater efforts to insure that information presented from the trains squared with the views of recognized agricultural authorities. Commercial firms and groups were still allowed to participate in educational train work, but many carriers screened them closely and required that all exhibits and other educational materials be approved by appropriate extension officials.[11]

Educational trains appeared in all sections of the United States, but they were most numerous in the heartland of the country, from Ohio westward to the prairie and plains states and from Texas northward to the Dakotas and Montana. Some trains operated in the lower Mississippi Valley and in the Southeast. They were less common in the Northeast and on the Pacific Coast. Among railroad companies operating educational trains, the Missouri Pacific was perhaps the leader; it sent a total of twenty-five over its lines from 1923 to 1930.

Some of the trains presented programs that were especially noteworthy. A feature of a crop diversification train that appeared in Arkansas in 1927 was the presentation at each stop of a drama entitled "The Problems of James Staples." In the play, James Staples, a poor cotton farmer, called on his banker to ask for an extension of his loan. Staples was also in debt to Fred B. Furnish, a local merchant. The farmer's methods compared poorly with those of John B. Thrifty, who raised less cotton but did it well, who had a dozen dairy cows and a drove of hogs, and who was a thoroughly diversified operator. After a full examination of Staples' faults and problems, the banker and merchant agreed to carry him another year, provided he obtained some livestock, planted a garden, reduced his cotton acreage, and used good seed and fertilizer, all under the direction of the county agent.[12]

Several other trains were unique or carried particular messages that made them stand out. A Missouri Pacific dairy train in 1928 carried for demonstration purposes some purebred cattle as well as "Leaping Lena," a cow of questionable ancestry whose "annual board exceeds her production by $20." Southern Pacific trains seemed to be especially impressive; an eleven-car train appeared in Texas in 1922, and a fifteen-car special toured company lines in California in 1928. An Illinois Central "agricultural college on wheels" took the message of diversification to Mississippi and Louisiana farmers in 1927. A farm convenience train operated by the New York Central sought to convince farmers that their wives needed modern equipment as much as they did. Its speakers pointed out that "a woman rubs clothes 52 times a year to save an expenditure of about $100, while the man spends $300 to $400 for a piece of machinery (which must have a seat) to be used only a few days each year during harvest."[13]

Since railroads had helped to establish rural youth clubs before 1914, they were enthusiastic supporters of the 4-H movement, and later the Future Farmers of America organization, in the 1920s. When the Great Northern's Ralph Budd observed that "One of the most constructive movements for the upbuilding of the Northwest is the boys' and girls' clubs," he was thinking of both improved farming and good will.

Some roads awarded prizes to 4-H club members, and a number of carriers participated directly in club programs. Development men often joined with agricultural extension personnel in staging club encampments, short courses, and demonstrations at state fairs. Company development magazines extolled club work and encouraged others to support it.[14]

Several roads offered agricultural scholarships to outstanding rural youths. The Union Pacific, under the leadership of President Carl R. Gray, reportedly had the largest scholarship program in the industry. At first limited to 4-H club members in Nebraska, the program was later extended to the entire Union Pacific system and to vocational agricultural students. As the program evolved, scholarships of $75 (later raised to $100) and free transportation to and from the appropriate institutions were given to one 4-H member and one vocational agricultural student from each Union Pacific county. Recipients were chosen on the basis of their project work, scholastic standing, character, and leadership qualities. Winners might elect to use their scholarships to attend a college short course, but management hoped that most would enroll in the regular four-year courses in agriculture. Similar if less extensive were the scholarship programs of a number of other lines, including the Baltimore and Ohio and the Louisville and Nashville.[15]

One of the most popular forms of aid to rural youth groups was free transportation for state club winners attending various kinds of meetings. The idea of sending outstanding club boys to the International Live Stock Show originated in 1918 when Cully A. Cobb, Mississippi state club agent, arranged for 9 boys to make the trip. The next year some 150 boys from several states appeared in Chicago, and from those beginnings came the National 4-H Club Congress, held annually in conjunction with the International. Later the Wabash, Kansas City Southern, and Missouri Pacific were leaders in sending Future Farmers of America members to the American Royal Livestock Show in Kansas City, while the Atlantic Coast Line and other carriers made it possible for prize-winning boys and girls to attend the National 4-H Club Camp in Washington. Railroads also provided funds for youths to attend the National Dairy Exposition, as well as a multitude of state and regional fairs and meetings.[16]

Better Livestock and Crops

Railway development work in the 1920s touched every facet of agriculture, but its central thrust was toward diversification and lowered unit costs of production. With those goals in mind, railway development men sought to promote the raising of more and better livestock and poultry and the growing of a wider range of high-yielding crops.

To encourage the raising of better livestock and the building of more productive dairy herds, railroads embarked upon a variety of programs, including the old technique of distributing better grades of breeding stock. The usual procedure was for a railroad company to purchase high-grade bulls and boars and then lend them to farmers, sometimes taking scrubs in trade. Some carriers offered prizes for the best offspring of the animals that they distributed. Several carriers gave purebred calves to 4-H club members. The Baltimore and Ohio used the standard methods to improve the production of sheep in southern Ohio and West Virginia. In the course of distributing purebred bulls in Colorado and Nebraska, the Burlington staged mock trials at which farmers were convicted of "harboring scrub bulls." Some of the cattle distributed by the Great Northern had been purchased from the famous Carnation Stock Farm near Seattle.[17]

More important in the aggregate were railway efforts to help farmers locate the breeding and feeding stock they needed. Fairly typical was the program of the Katy. Its agricultural agents sought to drum up interest in livestock raising or dairying by means of public lectures, displays of exhibits and demonstration materials, and personal visits with farmers. When farmers decided to buy stock, company men acted as agents for them, sometimes buying in carload lots at lowered prices. A number of other roads functioned in a similar manner.[18]

As part of their livestock promotion campaigns, northwestern roads participated in the efforts of the Agricultural Credit Corporation to diversify agriculture in the area from Michigan to Montana. Created in 1924 as a privately financed nonprofit concern to lend money to hard-pressed country banks, the Mineapolis-based corporation soon shifted to the lending of funds to farmers who wished to acquire livestock. Loans might be for as much as $1,000, carried 6 percent interest, and were secured by a mortgage on the stock. The first cattle purchased under the plan arrived on North Dakota farms in June 1924, and by the end of 1930 a total of 13,929 farmers in six states had purchased 356,000 head of sheep and 36,000 head of cattle with $6.7 million borrowed from the Agricultural Credit Corporation. Several major carriers, including the Great Northern and the Northern Pacific, were large subscribers to the corporation's bonds, and after the concern shifted its purposes to agricultural diversification, railway agents urged farmers to take advantage of the opportunities offered, helped to locate animals available for purchase, and instructed purchasers in the proper handling of their stock.[19]

In a variety of other ways railroads did what they could to promote livestock raising and dairying. In 1921 in Mississippi's Attala County, the Illinois Central conducted a series of three-day programs to show depressed cotton growers the potential in dairy farming. The Burlington, in common with most western railroads, held meetings to encourage farmers to build silos, one agent attending seventy such gatherings in a single year. That carrier was one of the promoters of the Nebraska Dairy Development Association, formed in 1924, and was a financial contributor to it. Southern roads cooperated with state departments of agriculture and other agencies in the war on the Texas tick and helped to enforce quarantine regulations.[20]

Since the raising of poultry squared well with the carriers' interest in diversification, that farm enterprise received a great deal more attention than earlier. The business required little capital and generated a steady income for farmers, thereby reducing their need for credit and increasing the purchasing power of whole communities. Some railroadmen believed that the generation of poultry and egg traffic along branch lines would help to compensate for the loss of short-haul passenger business to automobiles and buses.

Development agents spent considerable time holding meetings where they gave illustrated talks on the care of poultry, selection of breeds, and control of diseases. Exhibits at fairs were another common technique, the Illinois Central claiming that in one year 400,000 people saw its poultry exhibits at five fairs in Mississippi. Such roads as the Missouri Pacific sponsored innumerable poultry shows and helped organize county poultry associations. That road also gave awards to boys and girls exhibiting the best birds at state fairs. The Baltimore and Ohio established poultry clubs among rural youths, beginning in Illinois in 1922 and later in other states. Members were provided with high quality eggs, and after chicks reached maturity the company staged local poultry shows and awarded prizes to winners.[21]

The Burlington was one of several roads that sought to put turkey production on a commercial basis. Procedures were in the main those used with chickens. One of the Burlington's special trains devoted considerable attention to the raising of turkeys, and before the decade was out the company was able to report sizable gains in production in such states as Colorado, Wyoming, and Nebraska.[22]

In addition to encouraging farmers to turn to livestock and poultry production, railroads promoted the growing of new crops. Soybeans, for example, attracted the attention of railroaders. Later known as the "wonder crop" of American agriculture, soybeans were generally ignored by agricultural scientists and farmers alike until the 1920s. During that decade it was discovered that the crop grew well in the heartland of the country, that soybeans benefited the soil, and that they were an excellent feed for livestock. In addition, increased soybean production would mean that fewer acres would be planted in corn, a crop that was being grown in overabundance.

The Illinois Central and the Missouri Pacific especially did much to popularize the new crop. The former company used a special train in 1927 to arouse interest among Illinois farmers. Later it distributed seed among growers and helped to arrange at Stoneville, Mississippi, one of the pioneer meetings of the American Soybean Association. The Missouri Pacific sent a soybean special through four states in 1930, attracting some 20,000 people. Exhibits showed different varieties of soybeans, demonstrated approved cultural methods, and suggested the advantages of growing the crop.[23]

Interest in livestock production and an awareness of the need to rebuild soil fertility caused railroads to continue their interest in the growing of alfalfa and various kinds of clovers. The Chicago and Illinois Midland leased to farmers portions of its right-of-way for alfalfa demonstrations. Agents of the Illinois Central suggested to Mississippi Delta planters that they meet some of their needs for feedstuffs by growing alfalfa and other forage crops. The Burlington used field demonstrations to promote the growing of sweet clover in Wyoming's Big Horn Basin, and it cooperated with the Missouri agricultural extension service in a statewide "Clover and Prosperity" campaign that urged farmers to adopt a four-year crop rotation system with one-fourth of their tillable land in legumes.[24]

Fruit growing interested railroaders because those crops often complemented existing agriculture or utilized marginal land. An example was provided by the Crowley's Ridge area of Arkansas. That geological formation extending southeastward from the Missouri border to the Mississippi River near Helena, Arkansas, was a cotton-growing section in 1924 when the Missouri Pacific undertook to develop a peach industry there. The soil and climate were favorable, and the harvest season for peaches fell conveniently between the time that cotton was laid by and before picking began. In the course of its campaign the railroad held a number of meetings with farmers in the area, helped to organize the Crowley's Ridge Development Association, and hired a former county agent to work directly with growers who in time established some 5,000 acres of peach orchards.[25]

Arkansas and the Ozarks region of Missouri, in fact, were areas in which railroads were most deeply involved in the promotion of fruit growing. The Frisco, for example, believed that opportunities for the development of a grape industry were especially promising in northwest Arkansas where twenty years earlier it had settled an Italian community. A promotional campaign begun in 1921 succeeded in increasing acreage from 150 to 5,000, and in time the Welch Grape Juice Company installed a plant at Springdale, Arkansas, to use the crop. Meanwhile the Frisco devoted attention to other fruit, issued its *Fruit Growing in the Ozarks,* and was gratified to see its strawberry traffic increase some ten-fold between 1918 and 1928. The Rock Island conducted strawberry experiments near Hodge, Arkansas, and the Kansas City Southern circulated among growers in western Missouri and Arkansas an educational bulletin on fruit spraying.[26]

Elsewhere, similar work went on. In the Pacific Northwest the Great Northern and Northern Pacific continued work begun earlier to stimulate the development of the apple industry in the Wenatchee and Yakima valleys of Washington, while in the East the Chesapeake and Ohio joined in an advertising campaign to increase consumption of Virginia-grown apples. The Seaboard Air Line cooperated with a Georgia plantation owner in experiments with Satsuma oranges, while the Central of Georgia, which years earlier had helped to establish the Georgia peach industry, turned its attention to the utilization of low-grade peach pulp as a base for jams and jellies. The San Antonio and Aransas Pass conducted a series of schools in south Texas to instruct citrus growers in the proper selection of rootstocks for particular soils and climates, the approved methods for caring for young trees, and related topics.[27]

Truck crops were as attractive to railroadmen as fruit and were promoted by similar methods. For a time the Missouri and North Arkansas Railroad had on its payroll an agent who devoted his full time to the development of a tomato industry in the area between Joplin, Missouri, and Helena, Arkansas, and the Missouri Pacific hired a plant breeder who was responsible for the introduction of a new variety of Bermuda onions in the area near Laredo, Texas. Meanwhile, near Crystal City in the same state, the Missouri Pacific worked to induce growers to produce green beans, and the Texas and Pacific sought to demonstrate to sugar cane growers that their land would produce spinach and carrots.[28]

Potatoes, a crop that yielded a heavy tonnage per acre, especially interested railroadmen, and many carriers were active in promoting that crop. The Michigan Central was a prime mover in the Top O'Michigan Potato Show, and it distributed northern-grown certified seed potatoes among 4-H club members in the southern part of the state. The Burlington set out to expand potato growing in its territory, operating demonstration trains in Nebraska and Wyoming in 1920 and 1921, distributing high quality seed, and educating farmers in proper handling and marketing practices.[29]

Like potatoes, sugar beets produced heavy tonnage and in addition fit in well with desirable crop rotation systems in such areas as the Red River valley and on a number of irrigation projects. Beet tops could be used as livestock feed. The Great Northern pushed beet production in Minnesota, North Dakota, and Montana, while the Burlington joined with sugar companies to conduct in its western territories educational campaigns in which farmers were urged to use better seed and improved tillage methods and to provide more adequate supervision of labor.[30]

Nor did railroads ignore the nation's more traditional crops. Their general better farming campaigns were directed in part toward corn, cotton, wheat, and tobacco, and special efforts were made to increase the quality of output of those crops, to meet certain problems encountered in producing them, and to introduce them in areas where previously they had not been grown. For example, roads serving southern Georgia and Alabama and northern Florida tried to induce farmers there to grow bright leaf tobacco, and the Missouri Pacific worked to promote the production of burley tobacco in the White River area of Missouri and Arkansas.

Although cotton was produced in overabundance, some railroads devoted attention to that staple. In 1922 the Rock Island issued *Cotton — The Great Cash Crop of the South,* an educational pamphlet discussing practices that were expected to make growing of the crop more profitable. In the hill areas of Mississippi and Louisiana the Illinois Central established a number of demonstration plots to show that cotton could be grown on marginal land if farmers used proper seed, tillage methods, and fertilizer. The road furnished the usual fertilizer and supervision for the cooperating farmers, and the results were given wide distribution in the company-issued *Cotton Demonstration Work.* The boll weevil was a major concern of cotton growers, so a number of roads turned their attention to that pest. The campaign for diversification in the southern states, of course, was given greater urgency by the dangers of weevil infestations, but several roads instructed farmers in methods of controlling boll weevils, generally by dusting or spraying with various poisons.[31]

Even corn and wheat came in for attention. During the early years of the decade the Burlington undertook to introduce corn in Wyoming's Big Horn Basin by distributing early-maturing varieties of seed, organizing a corn-growing contest, and helping to stage the state's first corn show in 1923. The Southern's corn cup contest was a means of encouraging corn production in the Southeast. In the wheat country of eastern Colorado and in Nebraska, where twenty years earlier the Burlington had worked to hasten the demise of cattle grazing, the railroad conducted a wheat smut prevention campaign.[32]

Miscellaneous Activities

Aid extended to farmers, of course, did not end with the planting and the harvesting of crops or with programs that increased the number and quality of livestock on farms. Railroadmen recognized that farmers needed help in marketing, that the building of soil fertility was basic to any improvement in farming, and that irrigated agriculture needed strengthening. Finally, railway development men in the 1920s found that certain sections of the country suffered from unique problems.

Marketing work took various forms. Most roads were eager to provide space along their lines for shipping facilities, and some built them for the use of their customers. A number of roads continued to encourage producers of fruit and vegetables to establish growers' associations to help with production and marketing problems. For a time the Rock Island assigned one man to the watermelon-producing districts of Oklahoma where he busied himself with the establishment of local growers' assocations. In the lower Rio Grande valley men representing the roads there helped to attract canning and quick-freeze firms in order to create local markets for produce. Other roads cooperated in short courses for persons engaged in the marketing of perishables.

Standardization was a key word in the railroads' marketing efforts. Everywhere railway agents preached that only through the adoption of high standards of quality could growers receive highest prices for their produce. Standardization of containers, too, was important. The Frisco, for example, was largely responsible for the adoption in its territory of the use of the 24-quart ventilated crate for the shipment of strawberries.

The search for new markets received high priority. Many roads produced lists of producers and buyers of specific commodities and gave them wide circulation. Others attempted to deal with specific marketing problems. When the Frisco found that apples produced in the Ozarks could not compete in the St. Louis market with those from Calhoun County, Illinois, the railroad located new markets in the oil-producing districts of east Texas and Oklahoma. The Seaboard Air Line instituted carload poultry sales in the Southeast to free poultrymen from reliance on local markets, which were often glutted and characterized by depressed prices.[33]

Some roads undertook or sponsored sophisticated surveys to provide growers with detailed marketing information. As early as 1916 the New York Central made a study of peach growing in New York State that led to the opening of broader markets; in the 1920s a survey of the New York milk shed included a detailed analysis of existing supplies of fluid milk and suggested ways by which demand could be increased. Later in the decade the Lackawanna made a study of the use of fluid milk in its territory that led to an educational campaign among farmers to encourage them to adjust production to fit changing seasonal demand.[34]

The maintenance or improvement of soil fertility, of course, was central to any successful agricultural development program. "The more productive the soil . . . the more prosperous the people in the country," the Illinois Central's H. J. Schwietert wrote in the 1920s. Increased production of livestock and the growing of legumes were expected to improve soil fertility, but other practices were necessary as well. Railroads made a major effort to increase the use of limestone. Many soils were highly acidic, soil scientists knew, and for years authorities had been urging farmers to apply limestone. Even while the roads were in the hands of the Railroad Administration, some lines were at work spreading the gospel. Illinois Central agents held educational meetings in southern Illinois, while the Chesapeake and Ohio leased at nominal rates to newly formed community lime clubs sites along its line for the storage of cooperatively purchased lime.[35]

As the 1920s progressed, carriers developed new methods to increase the use of lime. In 1921 the Baltimore and Ohio began a series of limestone demonstrations in Ohio, Indiana, and Illinois. Farmers in eighteen counties were induced to apply lime, county agents joined in the work, and the program culminated with farmers' meetings where the results were discussed. The New York Central had a similar but more extensive program. The Wabash agreed to deliver lime at points between stations, using work trains for the purpose, thereby reducing expensive wagon hauls. In 1929 the Chicago and Illinois Midland organized its Cimco Development Company that used trucks to haul lime from stations to farmers' fields, charging only actual cost for the service.[36]

Related to the use of lime and to the broader topic of soil fertility was the operation of soil-testing trains by several railroads. In 1929 the Chicago and Eastern Illinois and Purdue University sent a train into Indiana that made soil tests for 2,300 farmers and reportedly helped to swell the carrier's limestone traffic by 50 percent. The Baltimore and Ohio, the Erie, and the Missouri Pacific also operated soil-testing trains in their territories in the 1920s.[37]

In the West railroads retained their long-term interest in irrigation. By 1930 the railroads aggregated 2,360 miles on the Bureau of Reclamation projects, and other trackage served the Carey Act, Indian Service, and other districts, giving the carriers a substantial stake in irrigated farming. Moreover, irrigated agriculture was intensive and diversified, the type of farming that generated heavy tonnage. Most western carriers devoted a considerable part of their efforts to the promotion of farming on the projects served by their lines. One Missouri Pacific agent, for example, was assigned to the irrigation districts of Colorado, where he promoted the growing of fruit and truck crops. In Montana the Great Northern was a leading advocate of the growing of sugar beets on the Milk River, Sun River, and Lower Yellowstone projects, and the establishment of refineries at Chinook and Sidney was viewed as a major triumph.

A significant part of railway work with irrigation dealt with the retention of settlers on irrigated acreage. Not all farmers wanted to irrigate their crops, and some who tried to do so lacked the necessary skill or capital. The result was many failures among settlers, a loss of population, and the threatened financial collapse of several irrigation projects. Railroad managements recognized clearly the dangers that such problems presented, and they did much to solve them. The Union Pacific was credited with saving one project by its energetic efforts to recruit settlers to replace those who had decamped and to help new arrivals adjust to their new environment. The Great Northern functioned in roughly the same manner with some projects in Montana and Washington, while on more than one occasion Burlington men went to Washington where they conferred with authorities concerning the renegotiation of contracts covering repayment and operating costs.[38]

Despite the commonly expressed view of many authorities that new irrigated acreage would only compound the overproduction problem, western roads were active in the planning of new projects and the expansion of existing ones. The Milwaukee and the Great Northern were enthusiastic supporters of those groups calling for the development of a giant project in the Columbia Basin, and the Burlington helped at almost every step in the creation of the Central Nebraska Public Power and Irrigation Project. That road and the Union Pacific urged the federal government to make a feasibility study in the 1920s, and a Burlington special train transported a group of congressmen on a tour of the proposed project. In the next decade a railroad agent was a prominent participant in the organization of the district under state law, and he visited Washington to talk with authorities there on behalf of the district. When the first water became available in the late 1930s, it was as much a triumph for the railroad as it was for farmers and users of electricity.[39]

Roads serving such areas as northern Montana found it necessary to help residents solve problems that in some instances had been created by the carriers themselves. Prior to World War I the Great Northern and other roads had been major forces in the rush of settlers to the bench lands of eastern and northern Montana, only to discover later that the country was not suited to the type and size of farms being created. The miscalculation led to severe hardship among the settlers, a heavy loss of population, and a sharp decline in rail traffic.

Railway executives recognized clearly that the roads would have to do what they could to help agriculture make the necessary adjustments in such areas. Preliminary studies by Montana State College's M. L. Wilson pointed the way, and in 1923 an educational train toured the region to spread the gospel of better tillage methods and low cost production through the use of larger and more efficient machinery. Later Wilson's "Fairway Farms" project cast still more light on the needs of Montana agriculture, and in 1929 and 1930 other demonstration trains popularized the new findings.[40]

Impact of Depression, Drought, and War

Shaping agricultural development work in the 1930s and later were conditions of depression and war, droughts, and the New Deal programs in agriculture. Franklin D. Roosevelt's innovations produced mixed reactions among railroadmen. At the outset, they greeted the new departures with considerable enthusiasm, seeing in them means by which farming might be lifted from depression. Some New Deal programs, such as those in soil conservation, earned the warm praise of industry spokesmen, and agricultural agents were eager to help in the rehabilitation of erosion-damaged lands in the West and the South. Roads there cooperated with the federal government in programs to retire marginal land, worked with relief agencies and the Resettlement Administration, and helped in the establishment of at least one subsistence homestead.[2]

On the other hand, production restrictions went counter to the carriers' historic objectives, while any number of other New Deal innovations ultimately outraged the railroadmen. As the industry recovered from the initial shocks engendered by the economic collapse, many spokesmen became loud in their criticism of Roosevelt and his policies. The Farm Security Administration, for example, was labeled as wasteful, paternalistic, and un-American, and New Deal philosophies in general were denounced as counter to American principles. In the late 1930s the Northern Pacific's John W. Haw claimed that he could not "conceive of a man whom I think has done as much harm" as Henry A. Wallace, and Earle E. Reed of the Union Pacific declared that in total the New Deal had been detrimental to farmers and to the country as a whole.

Although railway development men denounced some New Deal programs as wasteful or worse, they were perfectly willing for the government to spend money in certain ways. For example, railroadmen argued against cuts in expenditures for agricultural research and for the agricultural extension service. They urged counties to continue their contributions to the maintenance of county agents, fought those groups that considered agricultural extension to be an unnecessary luxury, and carried their appeal to congressmen and senators and to President Roosevelt. Western railroads enthusiastically greeted announcements from Washington concerning irrigation developments, such as the construction of the Grand Coulee Dam on the Columbia River, and denounced vigorously those who opposed expansion of irrigated acreage because of overproduction in agriculture.[3]

If the reaction of railroadmen to the New Deal was mixed, the carriers displayed no such ambivalence in helping farmers meet the problems of the 1903s. Historically, railroads had extended aid to hard-pressed farmers, and their reaction in the 1930s was prompt. The drought and dust bowl conditions of that decade, with resulting crop failures, depletion of pastures and herds, and grasshopper plagues, brought railroadmen out in force.

Some forms of aid to drought victims became so common as to be standard operating procedures. Railway agents were conspicuous members of numerous relief committees established to coordinate state and local efforts. More important, every major carrier serving the drought-stricken states gave reduced rates on inbound feedstuffs in an effort to save foundation herds and grazing stock in their territories. Where conditions had so deteriorated that inbound feed could not save livestock, or where farmers could not afford to buy feed, railroadmen sought other alternatives. At different times during the decade, but especially in the terrible years of 1934 and 1936, railroads granted grazing-in-transit privileges on stock bound for market and agreed to handle free of charge breeding stock returning to those areas. They also slashed rates on livestock moving from drought areas to better grazing lands, and railroad agents sought out farmers farther east and in the South who had pastures and feed supplies adequate to finish animals and were willing to do it on a share basis. In 1934 alone the Louisville and Nashville handled 4,200 cars of western cattle bound for the Southeast. Hogs and sheep were also shipped to eastern and southern farmers for finishing.[4]

When drought conditions produced grasshopper plagues, railroadmen were ready to fight the infestations. They offered reduced rates on bran, Paris Green, and oils – the ingredients of a recommended bait and poison mixture – and held innumerable meetings to instruct farmers in its use. Many railroads also spread bait along their tracks and elsewhere to eliminate breeding places and as examples to farmers.

In a number of other ways, too, railroads helped farmers survive the depression. Many company agents thought that prevailing economic conditions gave a new urgency to their historic interest in diversification. Throughout the Cotton Belt, railroadmen urged farmers to shift to the production of food and feedstuffs and emphasized that dairy cows, other livestock, and poultry would shield growers from ruinously low prices of cotton and other staples. In a few instances aid was more direct. In 1931 and 1932, for example, the Hill roads helped sugar beet growers obtain loans for seed and other expenses by depositing company funds in country banks serving beet growing districts.[5] Everywhere railroad agents participated in meetings where various governmental programs were explained. Usually railroadmen urged farmers in their territories to take advantage of the opportunities made available to them.

When World War II erupted, railroad development men found themselves involved in the war effort as they had a quarter of a century earlier. The goal was now to maximize production, an objective that railway men found more congenial than those of the preceding decade. Drawing upon its World War I experience, the Baltimore and Ohio compiled lists of people willing to help farmers harvest crops and offered free transportation to waiting jobs. Val Kuska of the Burlington busied himself with various wartime committees that sought to increase food production, while the Milwaukee told its stockholders that its agricultural men were devoting all of their energies to the war effort. Several roads directed their agricultural agents to do whatever they could to aid governmental agencies to locate sites for military installations, shipyards, and war industries.

As part of their wartime work, many railroads again became promoters of gardening. Some cooperated with the National Victory Garden Institute, while others and the Association of American Railroads produced and distributed literature on the growing of vegetables. Several companies allowed their employees to plant gardens on company property, and the Illinois Central conducted a garden contest among its employees and awarded prizes to those who excelled.[6]

Procedures and Methods

Regardless of changing conditions after 1930, until they finally disappeared from the scene agricultural development men functioned much as they had earlier. Some of the methods they used to reach and influence farmers were as old as development work itself; others were innovative, taking advantage of new communications technology.

Railway development periodicals were still published, but most were ultimately terminated and others were changed to reflect new goals. The Missouri Pacific discontinued its *Agricultural Development Bulletin* in 1930; the Santa Fe's *Earth* ended its long career in 1938; and the Chicago and Illinois Midland's *Cimco Fortnightly,* launched in 1932, survived until 1953. Meanwhile, the Northern Pacific changed the *Northwest* to bring it more into accord with the new thrust of the company's development program, industrial location.[7]

Railroads continued to produce literature for distribution to farmers, even if economic conditions curtailed volume. During the Depression Decade and later the Great Northern issued several items that dealt with methods to control soil blowing and to conserve moisture, and the Atlantic Coast Line prepared weekly agricultural news articles that went to agricultural college personnel, extension workers, vocational teachers, and editors of newspapers and farm periodicals. Even after World War II the Union Pacific had available for distribution at least seven different booklets dealing with irrigation, dairying, and truck farming.[8]

The radio remained an effective means to reach farmers, and carriers turned quickly to television. The railroads in New York state, Cornell

University, and the Grange combined in 1950 to present a series of farm-related programs on radio, and as late as 1968 Illinois Central agents conducted more than 700 radio programs, consisting of timely tips and useful information for farmers, and made twenty-two television appearances.[9]

Motion pictures were used in railway development work as late as the 1960s. The Union Pacific's "Along the Milky Way" was released in 1943; by 1965 the company had a total of eighteen films that were shown before audiences of farmers and other agribusinessmen and offered to colleges in the states served by the railroad. In the same decade the Southern Railway used its "Opportunity . . . on the Hoof" to promote livestock production.[10]

Demonstration farms were rare in the 1930s and later, although the Chicago and Illinois Midland maintained its Cimco Farm into the 1950s, and in the 1960s two roads put the ancient teaching device to use. In 1962 the Detroit and Mackinac had under way in Michigan a cattle feeding operation to demonstrate the usefulness of low-priced land in such enterprises. More like the demonstration farms of the past was a 300-acre property near Kodak, Tennessee, that the Southern Railway purchased in 1964 to show the feasibility of producing prime beef and pork in that region.[11]

Educational trains practically disappeared until the later years of the 1930s when improving economic conditions inspired railroad companies to resume their use. In 1937 the Pennsylvania operated a soybean car over its lines from New Jersey to Illinois, a livestock train of the Atlantic Coast Line attracted 28,000 people in Georgia, and the Santa Fe, in cooperation with Kansas State College, used an educational train to show Kansas farmers and their wives how rural homes could be improved. Activity increased in 1938 and continued until wartime conditions prohibited it. The Pennsylvania, the Great Northern, the Burlington, and the Illinois Central were particularly busy. A "veritable short course on wheels" toured the latter company's main line from Chicago to New Orleans in 1940.[12]

Educational trains underwent a brief revival after World War II, but they were few in number and soon disappeared from the scene. Among companies operating educational trains in the late 1940s were the New York Central, the Katy, and the Illinois Central, which used a train to popularize the work of 4-H club members in Mississippi and Louisiana. One of the last educational trains of the traditional type was operated by the Georgia and Florida railroad in 1955. The venture was inspired by a severe drought the previous year that stirred interest in supplementary irrigation. The University of Georgia and the Southeastern Sprinkler Irrigation Association joined the railroad in the project. Finally for fifteen years after World War II the Union Pacific maintained an agricultural car. A theater on wheels with projection and sound equipment, the car was used in meetings arranged by the company's agricultural agents, usually in cooperation with the agricultural colleges. During its first ten years the car was put to use in almost seven hundred communities.[13]

Other practices of the past that were used to some extent in the 1930s and later were the arranging of educational meetings, the offering of reduced rates for persons attending agricultural meetings, and the awarding of prizes to members of farm families who excelled. In the late 1930s the Chicago and Illinois Midland held annual field days on its Cimco Farm that attracted almost 15,000 people a year. Many roads continued to offer rate concessions to persons attending the International Live Stock Show as well as numerous less well known affairs. After World War II the Gulf, Mobile and Ohio inaugurated its "Farm Family of the Year Award," in which winners were given a trip to the Mississippi Gulf Coast and New Orleans.[14]

Railroads also continued to contribute to rural youth groups. Several railroads made sizable annual donations to national youth organizations, the Santa Fe giving $3,000 to the National Future Farmers of America (FFA) Foundation in 1958. That railroad in 1951 sent seventy winners to the National 4-H Club Congress and an equal number to the National Vocational Congress for Future Farmers of America members. The National Dairy show and the National 4-H Camp were two other meetings to which railroads continued to send rural youth, 1941 marking the fourteenth year that the Atlantic Coast Line had provided funds for such purposes.[15]

Many more boys and girls were reached through work at the local level. Agricultural agents of many lines cooperated with others in arranging various kinds of local contests and shows, assisted in judging contests, and helped members obtain livestock for their projects. They also showed company films to youth groups, staged banquets for local winners, and in some areas helped in the organization of new groups. The Gulf, Mobile and Ohio seemed to be especially active. It maintained for years in Missouri a FFA achievement awards program, sponsored in its southern territory a better living contest for Negro girls, and conducted in Illinois a rural youth community service program.[16]

Livestock, Poultry, and Crop Promotion

Although railway development work in agriculture declined during the decade of the Great Depression and for all practical purposes had been abandoned by the early 1970s, the carriers' programs during those decades had many similarities to those of the past, especially in terms of objectives. Railroads were still interested in improving and increasing livestock raising, some of them continued to be promoters of expanded poultry production, and practically all carriers were prepared to devote time and energy to the improvement of existing crops and to the introduction of new ones.

Livestock promotion took a variety of forms. The sponsoring of tours and shows of different kinds remained popular. Some railroadmen helped to organize local breeders' associations, while others helped to establish cooperative milk plants, urged the construction of silos, and made detailed studies of production and demand for livestock and livestock products.[17] Some railroads promoted the use of new feeds. In the late 1940s, for instance, the Missouri Pacific urged the feeding of sweet potatoes to livestock, and in the next decade the Atlantic Coast Line advocated the use of fruit pulp resulting from the production of frozen juices as feed for cattle and hogs.[18]

The Illinois Central played an important role in the development of a mechanical pasture renovator in the 1950s. Company men discovered that southern farmers needed an implement that would fertilize and reseed old pastures without plowing or discing the soil, steps that inevitably left the land susceptible to water erosion. Acting upon suggestions by the railroadmen, International Harvester Company produced three experimental machines and turned them over to the Illinois Central for testing. Use brought changes and improvements, and by 1954 the machines were available throughout the country.[19]

In the 1960s the Southern Railway used a combination of rate innovations and traditional techniques to spur cattle feeding in the South. For years, southern land-grant colleges, noting that the region was a net importer of red meat, had been encouraging cattlemen to produce grain-fed cattle. Early in the decade the Southern Railway instituted its so-called "Big John" rates on grain, using high capacity cars, heavy loading, and multiple car shipments, an innovation that reduced rates and made the finishing of cattle more attractive to farmers. Related to the railroad's program was the establishment of the demonstration farm in east Tennessee and the production of a promotional film on cattle feeding.[20]

The distribution of purebred livestock, one of the oldest development techniques, was limited after 1930. Still as late as 1940 the Illinois Central placed a carload of Jersey and Holstein bulls in its southern territory under arrangements much like those used in the 1920s. But more important in the long run was its work with artificial insemination.

Carriers in Wisconsin and elsewhere ultimately promoted artificial insemination as a means of improving livestock raising and dairying, but the Illinois Central appears to have been the pioneer and most active in the work. The first step came in 1945 when the railroad loaned a purebred Shorthorn bull to the Crawford County, Iowa, Breeders' Association for aritificial insemination purposes and promptly followed that with the loaning of three Jersey bulls to a newly established artificial insemination association in Yorkville, Tennessee. By the fall of 1946 the railroad was furnishing bulls to associations as far south and west as Ruston, Louisiana. Twenty years later, according to the Illinois Central, "more than a million cows are bred artificially by the associations that we started."[21]

Increased turkey production attracted many railroad development men, especially in the 1930s and 1940s. The Missouri Pacific undertook to develop a commercial turkey industry in Colorado and Texas. According to company spokesmen, turkeys were "not the mortgage lifters of Eastern Colorado, but . . . they have been the grocery-bill-payers when all else failed." In Illinois and Indiana agents of the Chicago and Illinois Midland and the Baltimore and Ohio had turkey projects underway.[22]

Aid to crop production in the 1930s and afterwards was of different kinds, some of which had been in use for decades. As late as 1937 the Burlington distributed grain sorghum seed in western Nebraska and continued on its right-of-way alfalfa leases that had been arranged years earlier. Throughout the 1930s Milwaukee agricultural men held in Minnesota, South Dakota, and Iowa typical "schools" where they urged farmers to shift some of their tillable land to malting barley. Hybrid corn received a great deal of attention. Railroads were also ready when crop farmers had specific problems. Several roads, for example, were active participants in a long-term campaign against wheat rust, contributing in the aggregate a substantial sum to the Rust Prevention Association and waging war on the barberry bush. After World War II the Great Northern played a major role in the introduction into Montana of a variety of wheat resistant to stem sawfly disease.[23]

Soybeans remained the miracle crop to many railroadmen. The Baltimore and Ohio, the Burlington, and the Milwaukee were among those roads that had active soybean development programs in the 1930s and later. The most common technique in use was the staging in cooperation with extension personnel of innumerable meetings where farmers, processors, and local dealers learned of the different varieties of beans and were instructed in proper methods of raising, storing, and marketing the crop. On its Cimco Farm the Chicago and Illinois Midland tested more than twenty varieties to determine those most suited to central Illinois.[24]

Western roads continued their interest in sugar beets and potatoes, partly because those crops yielded heavy tonnages. As late as 1942 the Milwaukee was still working directly with sugar beet growers on Montana irrigation projects, the Union Pacific was still involved in promoting the potato industry in Idaho, where it had been active for decades, and a number of roads continued their work in the production of certified seed potatoes and the expansion of the southern potato industry using north-ern-grown seed.[25]

The Illinois Central retained its historic interest in truck crop pro-duction throughout its southern territory. As late as 1968 company agents were at work, trying to interest landowners in the Mississippi Delta in the commercial production of vegetables. Programs of numerous other roads differed only in location. The Louisville and Nashville claimed credit for strawberry industries in Henry and Blount counties, Tennessee, and in 1932 an agent stationed in Knoxville scored a success when he induced Stokely Brothers to accept Tennessee-grown carrots. In the 1930s the Missouri Pacific helped to develop a "green wrap" tomato industry in Louisiana, the Seaboard Air Line introduced the growing of iceberg let-tuce in Florida, and the Baltimore and Ohio undertook to develop garden truck production in the muckland areas of northern Indiana.[26]

Two decades later, in a typical case, Baltimore and Ohio men deter-mined that Garrett County, Maryland, had the proper climate and soils to produce different garden crops in August and September, following the California harvest but preceding the Long Island season. In the first step a company representative and the county agent induced two farmers to plant test plots of vegetables, the company providing plants as well as growing and marketing suggestions. When the experiment proved successful and other farmers took up the crops, the railroad organized a growers' cooperative, with a company agent serving temporarily as its first manager.[27]

In a number of instances, railroads took action to aid growers of truck crops who were encountering problems. In Mississippi's Copiah and Hinds counties, where the Illinois Central had established a tomato in-dustry as early as the 1880s, declining quality was causing northern markets to reject the product by the 1930s. Company agents ascertained that the soil had become deficient in organic matter and was highly acidic. To point out these problems to growers and to demonstrate reme-dies, the company established thirteen 1-acre test plots scattered throughout the district and applied limestone and planted soybeans to rejuvenate the soil. It also introduced a variety of tomatoes more resistant to disease and better able to withstand handling to distant markets. Simi-lar programs helped to rejuvenate strawberry industries in eastern Loui-siana and in McCracken County, Kentucky.[28]

Among the new crops promoted by railroaders were tung nuts, sun-flowers, and safflowers. Tung nuts, useful for their oil which was an ingredient of many paints, varnishes, and lacquers, were in the 1930s mainly imported from China. In that decade the Illinois Central helped to introduce the crop into Mississippi where it remained important for more than thirty years. Meanwhile officials of the Northern Pacific and the Great Northern were enthusiastic advocates of sunflowers and safflowers, believing that they were well suited to the Northern Plains where they could be a second cash crop for wheat farmers.[29]

Other Programs, Old and New

Despite innovations in governmental policies and difficult economic conditions in the 1930s, railroadmen continued to devote attention to the promotion of irrigation, soil fertility and conservation, and marketing. The overproduction of agricultural commodities that led to governmental programs to control output caused some to question the wisdom of launching new irrigation projects, an attitude to which western railroads objected. When in 1934 Secretary of the Interior Harold L. Ickes appointed a committee to study the question, the Northern Pacific's John W. Haw was named to serve on it. He used his position to champion vigorously the idea that because of the isolation of the West and its distance from sources of food supply, expansion of reclamation was fully justified.

Western railroadmen spent a great deal of time in the 1930s in gathering data and appearing before congressional committees on behalf of proposed projects or expansion of existing ones in their companies' territories. The Burlington and the Union Pacific helped to organize in 1934 at Greeley, Colorado, the Northern Colorado Water Users' Association to mobilize support for the Colorado-Big Thompson Project. The Great Northern, Northern Pacific, Santa Fe, and Milwaukee were among the other railroads engaged in similar activities.[30]

Nor did the role of railroads in irrigation promotion change markedly in the immediate post-World War II period. As late as 1958 the Union Pacific told its stockholders that it was still promoting irrigation development through cooperation with local groups and national officials. A Burlington publication, *Irrigation: A National Asset,* sought to show eastern interests that western irrigation was a sound government investment. Those roads serving central Washington watched with approval as the Columbia Basin Project took shape and did what they could to speed completion.[31]

Interest in soil conservation was stimulated by the appearance of dust bowl conditions in the plains states and by the establishment of the Soil Conservation Service. Major carriers in the West advocated strip farming, listing, and the use of cover crops to protect the soil. Articles dealing with these procedures were prepared for newspapers and magazines circulating in the plains area, and several carriers produced educational brochures that were distributed widely. In Nebraska the Burlington undertook a pasture rejuvenation program to show landowners how previously tilled land could be returned to a use that would limit soil blowing in the future.

Railroads cooperated enthusiastically with the Soil Conservation Service. Throughout the country railway agents went to work, explaining the program to farmers and helping to organize conservation districts. Railroadmen also joined with public and private agencies to urge the improvement of river valleys, including those of the Tennessee and the Missouri, with better control of erosion being one of the major goals.[32]

All major railroads having agricultural development offices continued to be interested in soil fertility. They promoted the use of limestone, encouraged in part by New Deal programs that gave added incentives to farmers, and later took up as well the use of commercial fertilizers. Work in these areas led to the operation of soil-testing trains, but according to railroadmen these trains did not reach the small farmer living some distance from the tracks, the individual most in need of soil analysis. The result was the introduction by the Illinois Central of mobile soil-testing laboratories capable of going directly to any farmer needing their services. First used in 1952, these mobile units mounted on trucks made it possible for the company to serve almost any farmer who asked for aid. In 1963 agents made 22,000 separate tests for 3,600 farmers. Most of these were typical small landowners, but officials of Mississippi's giant Delta and Pine Land Company attributed a sizable jump in cotton yields in 1964 to tests performed by Illinois Central men. Meanwhile as late as the 1960s the Gulf, Mobile and Ohio had underway in several central Missouri counties a crop fertilization contest for adult farmers.[33]

Marketing of agricultural products remained an important concern of railway development agents in the 1930s and later. In 1949 one southern railroad claimed to have marketing agents stationed in ten states to put the producer of any farm commodity in contact with buyers. The Santa Fe worked closely with agricultural colleges and producers' associations to achieve better marketing of citrus fruits and vegetables, while the Northern Pacific played an important role in the establishment at East Grand Forks, Minnesota, of a potato research center charged with the task of expanding markets for potatoes grown in the Red River valley.[34]

Agricultural development men still found one of their primary responsibilities in the area of public relations. Farmers were still viewed as natural allies of business, and railway executives believed that their agricultural agents could ask "farm folks to help us save their country and themselves from socialism or worse." Such work was considered to be especially effective on the state level since most of the state legislatures "are still predominantly rural in make-up." Agricultural development men made every effort to maintain their contacts with individuals believed to be influential with farmers, and they often were active members of such groups as the Grange and the Farm Bureau.[35]

As agricultural development work of the traditional sort declined in the 1930s and later, agricultural development men found new tasks. Probably most important was the discovery that their knowledge and talents were of use in their companies' industrial development programs. For some men, their careers changed in midstream; agricultural development agents at the outset, they became involved in the promotion of industrial location. This change came most easily to those men whose companies' industrial development programs were primarily with the location of firms using farm commodities or supplying farm needs.

Such new developments as the appearance of chemurgy facilitated the change in duties of some agents. After world War II several railroads developed active programs in the new area. In 1946 the Great Northern hired a chemical engineer, and the Louisville and Nashville was one of several roads whose development men devoted much of their time to chemurgy.[36]

The gradual absorption of agricultural development men by their companies' industrial promotion programs was illustrated by innovations on the Southern Railway. In the 1960s that company established a department of agribusiness, headed at the outset by a former president of the Georgia farm bureau. The new office prepared a monthly *Agri-Business Newsletter* and spent a great deal of its time explaining how the company's "Big John" rates on grain would contribute not only to further diversification of agriculture but also to the location of industries to process feeds as well as to a larger number of livestock.[37]

Some agricultural development men proved to be useful in helping to keep top management informed concerning developments in the countryside that influenced operations and revenues. Men knowledgeable in agriculture, quite obviously, could best determine when crops might be expected to move, enabling operating men to mobilize the needed rolling stock. They could also provide informed estimates of the aggregate volume of shipments of agricultural commodities, allowing top management to project future earnings and plan capital expenditures.

A number of agricultural departments produced crop reports for the use of company executives and others. On the Santa Fe this work originated in 1938 when the public relations department began to prepare a mimeographed crop report for distribution among top company officials. In time the circulation list was enlarged to include interested persons outside the company, and in 1953 responsibility for compiling a printed report was given to the agricultural department. By 1962 circulation was some 9,000 and included grain men throughout the United States and abroad. Using data from the U.S. Department of Agriculture, the Weather Bureau, state agricultural agencies, and cooperating farmers and ranchers as well as information gathered by the company's agents, the Santa Fe's crop reports were often more accurate than those issued by public authority.[38]

Agricultural departments also found that they could provide significant services to other railroad departments and offices. Northern Pacific agricultural men often helped the passenger department by working out itineraries for tourists, escorting groups visiting the Northwest, and providing information for advertising and public address announcements on passenger trains. For the freight traffic department, agricultural men provided information in rate making and studied the movement of agricultural commodities by competing modes of transportation. Because of their knowledge of soils, they were consulted by engineers planning line extensions or relocations, and they were helpful in the purchase, sale, and leasing of real estate.

Agricultural departments were called upon to help reduce loss and damage on shipments of agricultural commodities and to aid in the settlement of claims against their companies, especially those involving farmers. Historically railroads had made a great deal of "pure bred stock out of scrub and grade cattle," and some railroadmen noted that the "best way to increase the value of a cow was to cross it with a locomotive." Agricultural men were better able to appraise the value of livestock killed on the tracks, forests destroyed by fire, and crops damaged by weed sprays, and in contrast to other railroad officers, they were able to talk to farmers presenting claims in language that the latter understood.[39]

It was development men's interest in loss and damage prevention that in the post-World War II period inspired the American Railway Development Association to arrange for the holding of an annual short course on the topic. The first short course on Transportation Losses of Fruits and Vegetables was held at Purdue University in 1947, attracting fifty participants. According to its promoters the meeting was the first attempt to unite railroadmen, county agents, agricultural college personnel, and farmers in an effort to reduce the waste that inevitably occurred when fruit and vegetables were handled improperly. Later the programs were enlarged to include meats and the shipment of perishables by piggyback service.

The Purdue short course spawned a number of regional gatherings having the same purpose. In 1950 such courses were offered at Cornell University, Texas Agricultural and Mechanical College, the University of Florida, and Yakima Junior College, where the land-grant colleges of Washington, Oregon, and Idaho joined in sponsoring the meeting. The program at Yakima became an annual affair, continuing until 1960.[40]

The rise of damaging truck competition in agricultural commodities called into question the value of much of the agricultural development work of traditional kinds, but it also gave railway development men new tasks. No longer was it adequate to generate new business; development men were expected to do all they could to insure that it did not move by truck. Accordingly they joined in the vigorous demand in the 1930s for truck inspection and regulation, served as watchdogs to insure that existing laws were obeyed, and organized meetings where opposition to truckers and their practices were aired. The agricultural exemptions embodied in the Motor Carrier Act were denounced vigorously. Finally agricultural development men seized every opportunity to point out to farmers certain adverse effects of truckers and their operations. Much was made of the fact that itinerant truckers often had a disturbing impact on prices of some farm commodities.[41]

Despite all such innovations in responsibilities and tasks, agricultural development work declined rapidly in importance after 1945 and, for all practical purposes, had disappeared by the early 1970s. The termination of agricultural development work, however, did not mean that railroad managements considered their programs to have been failures. In the early 1950s President Wayne A. Johnston of the Illinois Central stated that the "large sums which we have spent over the years to develop agriculture . . . have not been a donation of pure charity. The Illinois Central had a long-range motive in all of these activities."[42] That "long-range motive," very obviously, was the generation of traffic through the strengthening of the rural economy of Illinois Central territory. The same goal had motivated other carriers for almost a century, but by the 1970s the need for railroad promotional programs no longer existed. Typical of developments were those on the Illinois Central. Its agricultural development department was abolished in 1970, and when the Illinois Central merged with the Gulf, Mobile and Ohio to form the Illinois Central Gulf, the new giant railroad company had only one agricultural agent on its payroll. That individual was awaiting retirement. A phase of agricultural and railroad history was at an end.

Promotion of Forest and Mineral Resources

RAILROAD PROMOTERS AND MANAGERS have been interested in the utilization of forest and mineral resources since the appearance of the railroad industry in the United States. In the nineteenth and early twentieth centuries, construction of much new line was inspired by a desire to reach stands of virgin timber or to serve newly opened mineral deposits. Later products of mines and forests represented sizable portions of many carriers' freight traffic, and railroads were themselves heavy users of coal, ballasting materials, and a variety of wood products. A few carriers owned substantial mineral and forestry properties. For these and other considerations, in the nineteenth century some railroads employed at different times and often on a temporary or consulting basis men who were knowledgeable in geology. In the twentieth century, as distinct development functions and departments emerged, many major carriers added to their staffs professional geologists and foresters and gave them the specific task of generating new business in mineral and timber products.

Forestry Development Work

Railway forestry programs fall into three clearly defined historical stages. The first, which came in the late nineteenth century, was a part of the carriers' colonization programs and involved those roads serving the trans-Mississippi prairie states. A second stage came in the first decades of the twentieth century when railroadmen, influenced by progressivism and convinced that the industry faced a serious shortage of timber products, were swept into a conservation movement. A third stage began in the 1930s. It involved especially the roads in the Southeast, although carriers in the Northwest and elsewhere were not disinterested, and its objective was the traditional one of development programs, the generation of freight traffic in both the short and the long run.

The trans-Mississippi carriers took up forestry promotion in the late nineteenth century as part of their efforts to make the prairies more attractive to settlers. In the early 1870s, for example, the Burlington and Missouri River Railroad spent $14,000 in setting out in Nebraska willow, cottonwood, and other trees that were expected to form effective snow fences and windbreaks and to serve as examples to farmers. Later the Kansas City, Fort Scott and Memphis set out black walnut, osage orange, and catalpa trees on two sections of land in Kansas; the project was a demonstration, but in addition management hoped that it would ultimately provide a supply of ties. Among several other railroads that used tree plantings to enhance the attractiveness of the West were the St. Paul and Pacific and the Kansas Pacific. Some of their work was inspired by the notion that vegetation would increase precipitation, but out of the St. Paul and Pacific's experience came a manual for prairie tree planting that enjoyed substantial circulation.[1]

Influential, perhaps, in launching the railroads into the second stage of their forestry work was a stirring speech before the New York Railroad Club in 1903 by Herman von Schrenk of the U.S. Bureau of Plant Industry. He informed the railroaders that the nation's forests were being rapidly depleted, that a severe shortage of timber was inevitable, and that railroads, as users of large quantities of wood products, should take positive steps toward meeting their future needs. Aware that prices of timber products were rising and moved to some degree by Progressive sentiments, railroaders embraced what one scholar has called the depletion myth and embarked upon a conservation program.[2]

Individual railroads responded in different ways to the expected crisis. Always concerned about fires set by their engines, railroaders redoubled their efforts to clear trees and brush from their right-of-ways and from strips of adjoining land. In the Northwest some roads contributed financially to protective forest fire associations, one railroad donating $14,000 in 1911 alone. Others encouraged the work of the U.S. Bureau of Forestry, and in 1904 the Northern Pacific asked the bureau to formulate forest management policies for the company's extensive timber properties in Washington and Idaho. Finally railroads embarked upon a new wave of tree plantings and related activities.

Some of the new plantings differed little from those of thirty years earlier. In 1902, for example, the Fort Worth and Denver City was still planting trees in Texas to form windbreaks that would reduce wind velocity and evaporation and thereby improve the prospects of agriculture in the area. The Boston and Maine purchased several small demonstration plots adjoining its right-of-way and applied approved methods of forest management to them. Other plantings by such lines as the Boston and Maine and the Pennsylvania were parts of beautification programs then in vogue.[3]

However, most of the new plantings were made at least in part to supply the carriers' future needs for ties and other items. In this work the roads experimented with a wide variety of trees, but catalpas were apparently the most common, the carriers having been swept up into what was one of the crazes of the time. Reportedly catalpas could be grown cheaply and rapidly, and the timber from mature trees was resistant to wear and rot, desirable characteristics in tie materials. Between 1906 and 1921 the Burlington planted some 176,000 trees, mostly catalpas, on test plots scattered throughout the system. The production of ties was the primary objective. In 1902 and 1903 the Illinois Central planted catalpa trees on 250 acres at Harahan, Louisiana, and on 200 acres at DeSoto, Illinois. The Louisville and Nashville had catalpa plantings on 1,000 acres near Mobile, Alabama, and on a small plot at Pensacola, Florida. It also had black locust plantings near East St. Louis, Illinois, and Newport, Kentucky. In 1906 and 1907 the Lackawanna planted 94,000 yellow locust trees. Near Ivor, Virginia, in 1905 the Norfolk and Western cleared 16 acres of loblolly pine and planted catalpas. Going far afield, the Santa Fe in 1906 and 1907 imported some six million seeds of exotic varieties from the Far East and elsewhere. Near Del Mar, California, the company planted eucalyptus trees on almost 9,000 acres with the hopes of harvesting posts and cord wood after six years and as many as 200 ties per acre after a quarter of a century.[4]

The Pennsylvania had an extensive program that combined the objectives of tie production, control of soil erosion, and reforestation. Between 1902 and 1906 the company set out 2 million seedlings, mainly black locust, and later it planted an additional 3.5 million seedlings, primarily red oak. Meanwhile, on lands held chiefly by subsidiaries, the company undertook a scientific forest management program, making selective cuttings of hardwoods on 100,000 acres. The Pennsylvania was the first railroad to employ a professional forester to manage its forestry program. On 1 March 1907 E. A. Sterling, formerly assistant forester in the U.S. Department of Agriculture, joined the staff. A couple of months later John Foley was hired as Sterling's assistant. Foley stayed with the Pennsylvania until his retirement in 1946.[5]

The Delaware and Hudson also carried on forestry work with multiple goals. Between 1911 and 1917 the company set out on its right-of-way almost a million trees, mostly to form snow fences. The work was resumed in the late 1920s, using pine and spruce seedlings supplied by the New York Conservation Commission. More extensive was a major reforestation project in the Plattsburg-Lake Placid region of upstate New

York. After federal foresters made a survey of the company property, the railroad sold the marketable timber and then began a reforestation program, in part in the hope of providing a supply of ties. To provide seedlings, the company established nurseries at Wolf Pond and Bluff Point. This work continued into the late 1920s and in time encompassed some 150,000 acres on the east and north slopes of the Adirondacks.[6]

Despite high hopes, railroad efforts to assure the companies of adequate supplies of timber products proved to be less than successful. Railroaders found that it was more difficult to grow usable timber than they had supposed. Some of the plantings had been undertaken by men who were little more than enthusiastic amateurs and who were unable to cope with disease and adverse weather. Rates of returns on investments in almost every case proved to be inadequate. Finally by the 1920s the carriers were using increasingly effective methods for preserving wood, so their approach to the problem of forest depletion came to be not the growing of more wood but the consuming of less. When railroadmen concluded that it was better to leave the growing of timber to others, a stage in the history of railroads and forestry came to an end.[7]

Nevertheless some railroads retained in the 1920s their interest in conservation. Carriers in the South and such states as Michigan, especially, turned their attention to reforestation and to the control of such dangers as forest fires. In the South, for instance, there were in 1921 as many as 156 million acres of cutover land, according to an official of one railroad. Since much of that land was clearly unsuited to agriculture, by even the most optimistic estimates, reforestation was a necessity if a viable economy were to be retained.

With such views in mind, a number of roads embarked upon notable programs. The New Orleans and Great Northern claimed to be a pioneer when in the early 1920s it arranged for a series of forestry schools at points along its line. A typical "chautauqua" at Bogalusa, Louisiana, featured lectures by noted foresters who discussed the natural seeding of trees and the supression of the three archenemies of reforestation, razorback hogs, bark beetles, and forest fires. In 1925 when President Coolidge proclaimed American Forest Week, the Southern Railway devoted a special edition of its *Southern Field* to forestry. Articles dealt with equitable taxation of timber lands, protection against fire, methods of preserving timber, reforestation, and scientific forest management practices. Other roads also put forestry materials in their agricultural magazines, and many industry leaders called for larger appropriations for federal forestry programs.

To promote reforestation and to show that trees might be grown as a crop in the South, the Southern Railway in 1925 set aside 12,000 acres of standing pine in Dorchester County, South Carolina, as a demonstration farm. A forester and three assistants were assigned the task of managing the property, which was named for Lincoln Green, assistant to the president of the Southern and a prime mover in the project.[8]

The control of forest fires was one of the primary objectives of forestry programs in the 1920s. In 1921 alone railroads in Pennsylvania burned some 1,200 miles of safety strips along their tracks to keep right-of-way fires from spreading to adjacent woodlands. The Seaboard Air Line distributed posters urging landowners and others to take steps to prevent fires and argued against the practice, common in some areas, of setting fires in order to get a better stand of grass.[9]

Given the popularity of educational trains in the 1920s, it was understandable that railroads would put that technique to use in their forestry programs. In 1926, for example, a special toured lines of the Michigan Central. The prevention of forest fires was the primary objective of the train; "Keep Michigan Green" was the slogan; and a placard in one car read, "This is God's country—Don't set it on fire and make it look like Hell." Reforestation was the objective of a New York Central train that appeared in Indiana in 1929; the almost 9,000 people who visited the train received pine or spruce seedlings. The next year the Pennsylvania sent a train into Michigan that used lectures, exhibits, and the distribution of seedlings to arouse interest among landowners.[10]

In the 1930s and later, during the third phase of railway forestry programs, rail carriers continued to have at least a twofold interest in timber and timber products. They continued to use huge quantities of wood in different forms, even if technological change had in several cases reduced the amounts. More important to their development function, however, was the fact that timber products constituted a sizable part of the traffic in some regions of the United States. In the late 1940s for Class I railroads lumber products amounted to more than 8 percent of all carload freight and more than 10 percent of all revenues from carload traffic. But 58 percent of the tonnage originating in Washington and Oregon, one third of the tonnage leaving Mississippi and Louisiana on the Illinois Central, and 28 percent of the Seaboard's total freight volume was lumber. To southern roads as a group, only cotton was more important.[11]

Nowhere in the country was railway interest in forestry more intense than it was in the South. Railroadmen there had witnessed the rise, fall, and rebirth of the southern lumber industry, and they were determined to do what they could to encourage the latter stage. The cutting of the region's "first forest" had reached a peak in 1909 when 20 billion board feet, 45 percent of the nation's production, had been harvested. The demands of World War I kept the southern industry alive, but by the 1920s production was falling, and across the South only stumps and blackened ruins stood where the virgin pine forests had been. The tax base contracted, towns disappeared, and railroad traffic declined precipitously.

The rebirth of southern forestry was closely related to the rise of the pulp and paper industry. Studies in the 1920s showed that because southern pine reached pulpwood size in from fifteen to twenty years, the region possessed great potential. Meanwhile, Charles H. Herty had demonstrated that southern pine could be utilized in the manufacture of a wide variety of papers. The result was a move of the pulp and paper industry into the South, breaking the hold that the Northeast, Canada, and Scandinavian countries had previously enjoyed. From 1935 to 1940 fifteen mills were built in the Southeast, and by 1962 some sixty mills were scattered from Virginia to Texas. This new development might well have launched another wave of disorderly and wasteful exploitation of southern forest resources, but now greater insight prevailed among public agencies, mill operators, and landowners. The result was the establishment by the 1950s of the South's "third forest." With proper management, it would become a permanent one.[12] Between the 1930s and the 1960s southern railroads played a not unimportant role in that evolution.

By the 1930s railroads had employed professional foresters for a quarter of a century or more, primarily for the acquisition or production of forest products for the use of the carriers employing them. In the Depression Decade, however, railway foresters came to be development men, charged with the single task of retaining or generating timber traffic for their companies.

The Seaboard Air Line claimed to be the first railroad to employ a full-time forester in this new role. In 1937 the company hired A. E. Wackerman and instructed him to do "everything you can to grow more trees in the territory served by the Seaboard." The establishment of several pulp and paper mills on the Seaboard during the preceding years and the desire to work toward insuring a continuing supply of pulpwood were important in the Seaboard's decision to create a forestry department at that time. Wackerman resigned in 1939 to accept a position in Duke University's forestry school. His successor served until 1944, when Robert N. Hoskins began a long career as the Seaboard's forestry director.

Inspired by the same concern that had stirred the Seaboard to action, the Illinois Central created its forestry department in 1945. Two men were appointed that year, one being assigned to Mississippi and the other to Louisiana. They were expected to improve marketing methods of small landowners, reduce destruction by forest fires, sell better forest management to all concerned, and generally rehabilitate the cutover longleaf pine belt. By 1954 the company had four foresters on its payroll, a number that, according to Illinois Central spokesmen, gave the railroad the distinction of having the largest railway forestry department in the country.

In 1949 fourteen railroads employed twenty-four foresters, and the number increased in the 1950s. The group of railroads using foresters included six in the Southeast and four in the Northeast. Others were the Southern Pacific, Northern Pacific, Soo, and Chicago and North Western. In addition, subsidiaries of some carriers employed foresters. For example, the Milwaukee Land Company, wholly owned by the Milwaukee, placed a forester on its payroll in 1948, stationed him at Centralia, Washington, and gave him the supervision of some 60,000 acres of company lands.[13]

Regardless of their location or company affiliation, railway foresters saw their task as primarily educational. They were eager to cooperate with other agencies and groups, both public and private, and with the major firms engaged in lumbering, paper making, and related enterprises. In fact, when A. E. Wackerman first went to work for the Seaboard Air Line, he spent most of his time working in conjunction with paper companies and other large landowners in the South. Railway foresters, however, soon learned that it was the small farmer who most needed help in protecting his woodlands from fire, harvesting his crop efficiently, and managing his property in ways calculated to insure a continuing output.

To reach that small farmer, railway foresters displayed the same ingenuity that agricultural agents had employed earlier. The Illinois Central, for example, used short courses held in rural neighborhoods and aimed at typical Mississippi and Louisiana farmers. Included in the instruction were field demonstrations in timber estimating, timber marking, fire prevention, and tree planting.[14]

Railway-issued literature played the same role in forestry work that it did in other development activities. In 1943 the Seaboard Air Line launched its *Forestry Bulletin,* reportedly the first such railroad publication in the United States. Issued periodically, the *Bulletin* went to timberland owners, wood products industries, and others in Seaboard territory having an interest in forestry. Circulation was 13,000 in 1950. The Baltimore and Ohio's *Balancing the Budget,* issued in the late 1940s, contained general information on forestry as an adjunct to agriculture in the "Bumper Belt." The Illinois Central had its *Timber,* which it distributed to Boy Scouts, college students, foresters, 4-H members, and others.[15]

As part of its forestry work, the Seaboard Air Line in 1941 resorted to a typical educational train. The three-car affair spent fifty-nine days touring company lines from Virginia to Florida, making fifty stops enroute. Cooperating in the project was the U.S. Forest Service and the different state forestry agencies. Exhibits demonstrated the importance of forest resources to a wide spectrum of the southern population and depicted the approved methods of fire prevention and management of forest lands.[16]

A wide variety of other educational techniques was also used by the forestry men. Demonstrations large and small were common. As early as 1934, a decade before the Illinois Central hired its first professional forester, the company's agricultural men staged more than twenty tree planting demonstrations throughout the South. The Chicago and North Western's forestry agent spent a great deal of time speaking to forestry groups and landowners, advocating selective logging and reforestation using desirable species. Several railroads with forestry programs were active supporters of the Keep America Green campaign, which in 1950 was being carried on under the sponsorship of the American Forest Products Industries.[17]

A few companies acquired mechanical tree planters which were used in demonstrations or loaned to landowners. The Chicago and North Western and the Seaboard acquired such machines in the late 1940s and used them in tree planting demonstrations each spring and fall for several years. By 1951 the Seaboard was making mechanical planters available to landowners in its territory, and in 1954 another road claimed that in a six-year period it had planted over 2.5 million seedlings on privately owned land and on its own property.[18]

The Illinois Central made a contribution to forestry in the South through the development and use of a lightweight tree planter that could be handled by the type of small tractors found on typical southern farms. After a search, such a machine was found at Purdue University. The Illinois Central took the implement to Mississippi and in the winter of 1948 conducted tests with it, using pine seedlings supplied by the Mississippi Forestry Commission. The machine planted 1,000 seedlings an hour, but company officials decided that it needed alterations to make it more useful. Subsequently the machine was modified in the company's McComb, Mississippi, shops, and two other machines were built there.

With the three machines, Illinois Central's forestry agents began a systematic program of planting seedlings for small farmers who asked for their aid. By 1959 company officials figured that the agents had staged 1,441 demonstrations with the machines, attracted 48,000 people, and planted over 10.5 million trees on 12,000 acres of land. The work continued in the 1960s.

Meanwhile the company helped to make similar machines available to others. After the company constructed its planters in McComb, it offered to provide blueprints to anyone wanting them and estimated the cost of constructing the machines at $250 each. Soon a tractor dealer in Hattiesburg, Mississippi, began producing the implements commercially, and later a firm in Wisconsin turned them out. By 1956 about 500 of the machines were in use.[19]

Some companies used demonstration forests as educational tools. Probably as well known as any was the Southern's Lincoln Green Demonstration Forest, a 14,000-acre "classroom" that served as a laboratory for foresters and forestry students. Among the experiments being conducted by the managers in the early 1950s were tests of controlled or prescribed burning, a procedure by which foresters removed the accumulation of litter on the forest floor during damp seasons and thereby lessened the danger of fire under dry, windy conditions. In 1953 the St. Louis Southwestern converted its forty-year old farm near Alto, Texas, into a reforestation project, planting the entire tract in pine seedlings. Meanwhile in the post-World War II years the Atlantic Coast Line leased free of charge to the Valdosta, Georgia, chamber of commerce a 465-acre tract that was converted into a demonstration property, showing farmers how pine trees might become a money crop. The Central of Georgia, in conjunction with Auburn University, maintained a timber tract for demonstration purposes. As late as 1950 the Chicago and North Western had shelter belt demonstration plantings throughout its western territory, and in 1947 it planted 12 acres of jack pine on railroad land near Spooner, Wisconsin, hoping to encourage small landowners in the area to devote more attention to reforestation.[20]

A number of carriers, especially the great transcontinentals, had large timber holdings which after World War II they undertook to manage scientifically. In 1950, for instance, the Southern Pacific's Land Company employed five foresters to oversee the 690,000 acres, including 420,000 acres of virgin timber, that it owned. In the years after World War II the Milwaukee began a massive reforestation program on timber lands in three western states that it had acquired in 1907 to provide traffic for its newly constructed Pacific Extension. Until 1940 the company had sold land to lumber companies as they required it, but in that decade the company decided to retain title to its property, selling only the timber. As logs were cut from a tract, the Milwaukee reseeded it, in 1950 becoming the first railroad to use aerial reseeding. Douglas fir, western red cedar, and hemlock were the most common varieties used. By 1958, of the 236,000 acres held by the company in those three states, over 21,000 acres had been seeded.[21]

Some railroad forest lands became "tree farms." The tree farm movement originated in 1940 when the Weyerhaeuser Timber Company designated one of its reforestation projects as a "tree farm." Later the American Forest Products Industries took responsibility for inspecting and certifying tracts of timberlands upon which modern methods of forest protection, harvesting, artificial reforestation, and wood utilization were being used. The Southern's Lincoln Green property received such certification as South Carolina Tree Farm 30, but the Northern Pacific was most active in obtaining such designations for its timber properties. That carrier, with some 1.4 million acres of timber lands, had five certified tree farms with a total acreage of more than 300,000 acres by 1951. The number was later increased to 14 consisting of 691,000 acres in Montana, Idaho, and Washington.[22]

The Illinois Central joined with others in Illinois and Kentucky to institute reforestation work on lands that had been strip-mined. In 1948, in cooperation with others, the Illinois Central planted evergreens on stripped land. In half a dozen years, some were marketable as Christmas trees. In 1960 the company planted loblolly and shortleaf pines on more than 300 acres near Carterville, Illinois, owned by the Madison Coal Company, a subsidiary. The company expected to be harvesting pulpwood from the plot in fifteen years. More important was a reclamation project undertaken in the early 1960s by the company and the Kentucky Reclamation Association, an organization of eighty-one coal firms. To provide the necessary seedlings, the promoters of the enterprise established an 8-acre nursery at Earlington, Kentucky.[23]

Since forestry work was primarily educational in nature, all railway forestry men spent a great deal of their time in meetings of groups interested in forestry industries. Notable, however, was an annual outdoor conservation meeting that the Seaboard Air Line inaugurated in 1945 and that in time became one of the premier events in the forest industry in the South. The 1962 conclave, held near Chester, Virginia, attracted some 750 persons, including federal and state officials, industry leaders, and other dignitaries. Among other features were demonstrations of the use of airplanes in controlling forest fires and of a machine owned by the International Paper Company that harvested pulpwood. A decade later visitors at the affair held at Sumter, South Carolina, saw an exhibition of fertilization of woodlands using helicopters and displays depicting recent developments in forestry, air and water quality, recycling, pesticides and herbicides, wild life, and housing and rural development.[24]

As in the case of agricultural development, railway foresters soon discovered that by working through rural youth groups they could influence farmers and other small landowners to adopt better forestry practices and at the same time educate those who would be the landowners of the future. In 1945, for example, the Seaboard Air Line launched its Farm Youth Forestry Program in which the railroad, in cooperation with state forestry agencies and paper mill interests, urged members of the FFA in its territory to undertake woodland projects. The first year participants planted 1.5 million pine seedlings, and the number grew to 6 million by the end of the fifth year. A quarter of a century after the program was inaugurated, it was still in operation. The Seaboard also sponsored forestry training camps—really short courses—in which older boys were taken into the woods to learn about conservation, tree planting methods, and other aspects of modern forestry practice.[25]

Similar were the programs of the Illinois Central and the Gulf, Mobile and Ohio. The former road introduced its forestry short courses for high school students in 1946. Within a decade 8,000 boys in Louisiana and Mississippi had attended the courses, and in 1960 the company presented a certificate to the 14,000th youth to participate in the program, which consisted of six hours of lecture and classroom work, followed by three hours in the woods. The Gulf, Mobile and Ohio's woodland improvement project also involved the organizing of farm youth, primarily 4-H and FFA members, in those communities in the South where civic and other groups were willing to match railroad contributions. Some 5,000 boys participated in 1961.[26]

Despite the obvious value of the forestry programs in the years after 1945, activity was declining in the 1960s. As early as 1955 an official of the Frisco pointed out that "there are at least 5,000 experts from paper mills and the lumbering industry doing forestry development work today," and he might have added that others from forestry schools, the experiment stations, and federal and state governments were also in the woods, doing what they could to improve and strengthen the forest industries.[27] To top management of many railroads, any forestry development work was becoming largely superfluous, and by the early 1970s even the Illinois Central Gulf apparently had reached that conclusion; at any rate, it was soon to retire its last forestry agent.

Mineral Promotion

The employment of geologists by railroads had much in common with that of foresters. Few matters were of more importance to railroad builders in the nineteenth century than the exploitation of mineral deposits along their lines, and senior officers actively sought to attract the attention of entrepreneurs to mineral resources found in their companies' territories. Many of the early industrial men devoted much of their time to the promotion of minerals. In time, however, it became apparent that the work required expertise that the ordinary executive or industrial man did not possess. The result was the hiring of professionally trained geologists, in some cases on a temporary or consulting basis, and the ultimate evolution of mineral development offices. These were at the outset often attached to agricultural development departments, but by the 1940s the common practice was to unite in one office the geologists and industrial development men.

Some instances of promotion of mineral resources by pioneer railroads are well known. As early as 1854 the Illinois Central began explorations for coal in north-central Illinois, and soon the company employed men to sink a number of mine shafts in the southern part of the state. It also commissioned a former government geologist to conduct a thorough mineralogical survey, a project which resulted in the publication in 1856 of a *Report upon the Mineral Resources of the Illinois Central Railroad.* Any number of other roads participated in one way or the other in the development of mineral resources in their territories. The Louisville and Nashville, for example, actively promoted the use of mineral resources of Alabama, Tennessee, and Kentucky in the late nineteenth century.[28]

By the first years of the twentieth century a few railroads employed geologists in clearly defined development roles. From 1897 to 1918 the Southern Pacific maintained a geological department staffed by professionals, in 1905 the Delaware and Hudson hired a geologist to make a survey of the mineral resources along that line, and in the years before 1917 the Southern had on its payroll an "expert" who studied mineral deposits in the Southeast. The Santa Fe maintained in its industrial department a bureau of mineral resources which, in addition to other accomplishments, located near San Diego a supply of kelp, used in the production of potash, and attracted steel manufacturers to manganese and magnesite deposits in Arizona and New Mexico.[29]

Geologists in railway employ became more common in the 1920s. The Baltimore and Ohio reported in 1923 that its geologist was busily surveying the mineral resources along that line and compiling pamphlets for the information of prospective customers. As early as 1908 the Missouri Pacific had employed on a temporary basis an expert to examine iron ore deposits in Missouri, but in 1927 it hired a full time "mineral technologist." The new agent was a graduate of Missouri School of Mines who had taught at Pennsylvania State College and served in the U.S. Bureau of Mines before joining the Missouri Pacific. Henry M. Payne, formerly associated with the American Mining Congress, joined the Gulf, Mobile and Northern as a geologist in 1926, and among other roads employing such men by 1930 were the Southern Pacific, Northern Pacific, Union Pacific, Central of Georgia, and Atlanta, Birmingham and Coast.

In some instances, railroads needing the services of geologists in the 1920s worked out consulting arrangements with professionals holding positions with other companies or institutions. The Seaboard's F. H. H. Calhoun, for example, was a faculty member at South Carolina's Clemson College.[30]

The Great Depression curtailed the employment of geologists, but with the new emphasis on industrial development that came in the 1940s and later many major carriers added geologists to their staffs. The Milwaukee and Great Northern hired such men in 1941, and other roads were not far behind, especially as it became clear that the continued economic growth of the United States would demand the discovery and utilization of new deposits of minerals to replace those being rapidly depleted in the war effort. The recognition that dwindling supplies of some minerals would force users to develop new technologies to permit the utilization of substandard ores was another catalyst leading railroads to employ geologists.[31]

The duties of railway geologists varied from line to line, but in general their tasks fell into four or five broad categories. First and most important, railroad geologists were expected to become fully informed concerning the location, extent, and character of mineral deposits in their companies' territories. Toward that goal they conducted their own field studies, perused relevant literature, and established contact with public agencies and other individuals who were informed concerning mineral deposits.

Railway geologists, however, could not be mere "rock hounds"; they also had to be industrial economists. To function satisfactorily, they had to understand thoroughly the economics involved in the utilization of minerals and have at their fingertips information concerning market conditions, aggregate production and consumption, and the specific requirements of different firms and industries.

In company with all development men, mineral agents publicized resources existing in their companies' territories. Data gathered by various means were compiled in forms that facilitated its use, and mineral men employed it and a variety of other techniques to attract the attention of businessmen.

At times railway mineral men encouraged others to undertake research looking to the further utilization of minerals. In this line they cooperated with state agencies and in some instances contributed funds to universities and other research agencies that might be expected to turn their expertise to the solution of problems involving minerals.

Finally, like the later agricultural agents, geologists often provided valuable services to other railroad departments. Most important, no doubt, was the information they contributed to industrial departments that helped the latter locate industries along company lines. Geologists were consulted by traffic department personnel concerning the proper classification of mineral and chemical commodities, sources of minerals which competed with those in their railroads' territories, and the value and physical condition of various minerals and chemicals. The specialized knowledge of geologists was useful when engineering departments were considering line extensions or relocations, especially where tunnels or major bridges were involved. In searching for sources of water, ballasting materials, and similar items, geologists often proved their value. By the

1970s they could at times add something to discussions of environmental problems.[32]

Surveying and mapping the mineral resources of a railroad's territory required the greatest part of a geologist's time. According to one of the railway geologists of the 1920s, he was "primarily interested in . . . mapping undeveloped mineral resources and also developed deposits in the territory" of his railroad. Resulting maps showed not only the location and scope of deposits but also their relationship to transportation, power, and other materials needed in their utilization. Reports on undeveloped mineral deposits also had to contain sufficient information on their physical and chemical characteristics so that potential users could better estimate their value.[33]

The scope and nature of surveying and mapping work by railway geologists varied over time and from line to line. The Baltimore and Ohio, for example, undertook to study its entire territory prior to World War I and as early as 1917 it told its stockholders that it had available for distribution maps showing the location and extent of major deposits. Members of the Milwaukee's agricultural and colonization department began in the 1930s to search the company's territory for minerals. Among their discoveries were bentonite in South Dakota and Wyoming, ornamental stone in Wisconsin and Montana, and kaolin in Montana. After the United States entered World War II the company's geologists turned their attention to minerals needed in the war effort. By 1950 the Milwaukee claimed that for all practical purposes it had mapped all known deposits in its territory.[34]

The Union Pacific began a sophisticated mineral inventory survey of its territory in 1946 that was still in progress twenty years later. By the early 1950s the company's geologists had discovered by exploratory drilling deposits of titanium that perhaps were the largest in the United States. Low-grade beryllium and low-grade iron ores were found in Utah and Montana, respectively. In 1962 company men scoured Colorado, Wyoming, and Utah for silica sand deposits with the hope of locating a glass factory in the intermountain region. The next year large sources of feldspar were found in five mountain states, and the survey work continued in later years.[35]

In other instances, surveys were directed toward specific areas or specific resources. In the 1920s, for instance, the Seaboard Air Line directed its consulting geologist to make a detailed study of Marion County, Florida. A quarter of a century later, recognizing that Georgia's glass and ceramic industries were handicapped by the fact that the nearest feldspar was located some 200 miles away in North Carolina, the Central of Georgia conducted a survey and discovered substantial deposits of feldspar near Monticello. The opening of the atomic age inspired some railroad geologists to conduct searches for radioactive materials. Spokesmen claimed that development agents of the Chicago and North Western carried Geiger counters as they traveled about the company's territory in the early 1950s. Later in that decade geologists of the Baltimore and Ohio made a systemwide survey looking specifically for radioactive materials.[36]

While railway geologists generally searched for minerals, some of them used their expertise in surveys for other items. In 1957 geologists of the Chicago and North Western completed a study of hot and cold water in the Black Hills and produced a prospectus containing the results of their work. In the same decade the Southern joined with the U.S. Geological Survey in a study of underground water supplies in the Carolinas.

In some instances railway geologists were inspired by specific operating problems to seek sources of new mineral traffic. The Chicago and North Western, for example, suffered from low traffic density on its western lines, due to sparse population and truck competition, so in 1940 its executives directed its geologists to turn their attention to the problem. A diligent search turned up substantial deposits of bentonite. By 1953 the company was hauling 10,000 carloads a year, much of it long-haul business to Chicago.

In gathering data and mapping mineral deposits, railway geologists relied in the main upon their own explorations and the published work of others, but in some instances they joined in cooperative projects. In 1958 the Great Northern combined with the Pacific Power and Light Company to finance a five-year program by the Montana Bureau of Mines to survey mineral resources in the western portion of that state.[37]

More so than in agricultural or industrial development, mineral promotion required research of a relatively high order. Railway geologists were themselves scientists, professionally trained, and they maintained close contact with their colleagues in universities and elsewhere. Some railway geologists were provided with sophisticated laboratories in which they conducted what could only be described as research, while other companies were prepared to spend sizable sums of money to support research by others.

In the 1920s the Central of Georgia encouraged research on the value and usefulness of Alabama and Georgia clays. The two states had tremendous deposits of various kinds of clays, but little use had been made of them by the ceramics industry. The railroad joined in an agreement with the U. S. Bureau of Mines for a joint study, the railroad paying half of the costs. Later, the Central of Georgia urged Georgia Tech to establish a course in ceramic engineering and a research laboratory to study Georgia clays and played some role in inducing the state legislature to provide necessary funds.[38]

A later example of a railroad's role in the stimulation of research on mineral resource problems is provided by projects undertaken by the Great Northern in the 1950s and 1960s. That company served areas of North Dakota that were underlaid with tremendous deposits of lignite, low-grade coal whose BTU values were such that the fuel could be consumed economically only near the mines. At the same time, because of the rapid depletion of iron ores shipped directly from the Mesabi Range, the company faced the loss of traffic that since the 1890s had been an important source of revenue. In the mid-1940s authorities had pointed out that the future of the Mesabi Range rested on the ability of scientists to develop techniques by which the vast amounts of taconite – low-grade iron ore – remaining in the Superior-Duluth area might be utilized. By 1954 the steel companies and university scientists had shown that magnetic taconite could be beneficiated by crushing, separating the ore from the waste magnetically, and concentrating the residue in pellets that could be fed directly into blast furances. Unfortunately this innovation promised little to the Great Northern, since its tracks served areas of the Iron Range in which the bulk of the taconite was of a nonmagnetic variety.

To attack this complex of problems the Great Northern and fifteen other companies in 1952 raised $130,000 to finance a study by Arthur D. Little of the possible uses of North Dakota lignite. Four years later the company's directors approved the expenditure of up to a quarter of a million dollars to support university research on beneficiation techniques for nonmagnetic ores and on the possible use of lignite in the process. The work was to explore the possibility that nonmagnetic ores could be converted to magnetic type through a roasting process using carbon gases produced from North Dakota lignite. By 1964 some $175,000 of company funds had been spent on the project, which had shown conclusively that the procedure was technically successful, even if it was not yet clear that it was economically feasible.

The next year the Great Northern set aside funds for research on other possible uses of lignite. The primary objective was to investigate the possibilities of extracting from lignite a liquid that might be used as a fuel or for chemical purposes.[39]

Some roads, heavily dependent upon a particular mineral, sought to increase utilization of that resource. Coal-carrying roads especially were engaged in such work. In the 1920s the Norfolk and Western recognized that customers were beginning to buy coal on the basis of its chemical content and its suitability to their particular needs, a development that made necessary the use of new merchandising techniques. The railroad became a leader in research to determine the best use of particular types of coal and in presenting that information to customers. It conducted studies in its own laboratory in Roanoke and in 1929 it opened a coal bureau in Chicago, subsequently establishing similar promotional agencies in five other cities. The company also published booklets giving the results of its research, issued more than 350,000 pieces of promotional literature, and advertised widely in coal trade magazines.

The Chicago and Eastern Illinois and the Chesapeake and Ohio were two other carriers that sought to help the coal industry meet its problems. In 1938 the former road established its combusion engineering department. Headed by a fuel service engineer, the department offered an advisory service to both producers and users of coal with a view toward increasing the consumption of coal. In the 1950s the Chesapeake and Ohio maintained a coal traffic and development department. A company official was chairman of the mining development committee of Bituminous Coal Research. One of the projects of the time was perfection of a machine that would cut and load coal in one continuous operation. Another committee, on which Chesapeake and Ohio men served, was seeking entirely new uses for bituminous coal.[40]

One result of the Union Pacific's mineral work was the development of a trona mining and refining operation near Green River, Wyoming, in the early 1960s. Substantial amounts of trona, a form of sodium carbonate convertible to soda ash, were found on Union Pacific and other lands in the area. To process the material, the Union Pacific joined with the Stauffer Chemical Company to create a new firm, Stauffer Chemical Company of Wyoming, the railroad holding 49 percent of the capital stock. Operation began in 1962 and by the end of the first year almost 150,000 tons of soda ash had been produced. Growing demand induced the company to add a second refinery in 1963 and to plan for a third, with a total projected output of 500,000 tons annually, a business that not only produced satisfactory earnings for its owners but also gave substantial new traffic to the Union Pacific.

Meanwhile the Union Pacific financed research on titaniferous iron ore found in its territory. Results at a plant at Niagara Falls, Canada, which performed the work, showed that, properly handled, the material would yield a high-grade iron ore as well as a slag from which titanium and vanadium could be extracted.[41]

The surveying and mapping of mineral resources and the promotion of research on the uses of minerals meant little unless businessmen were informed of these findings and developments, so a primary function of railway geologists was to disseminate as widely as possible information concerning the resources of their companies' territories. This task was pursued vigorously, and the techniques employed were limited only by the ingenuity of the men involved.

Probably personal contact was the most widely used and productive method for getting information to potential users of resources. Company executives had historically sought to establish contact with entrepreneurs, and they continued this role in the twentieth century. When railroads hired geologists, they functioned in the same manner, their expertise making them more effective in negotiations with businessmen.[42]

Railway exhibits were used to advertise mineral resources in much the same way as they were utilized in colonization and agricultural development programs. In fact, many of the land shows and similar affairs that were so common before World War I often included displays of minerals, while the governors' special, an eleven-car exhibit train sent East in the fall of 1911 by the Northwest Development League, carried displays of minerals. The National Exposition of Chemical Industries, held annually in New York City from 1915 through the 1920s, attracted numerous railroad exhibits, especially from the South. In 1917, for example, five southeastern roads had exhibits of ores from their territories, but in 1927 one of the largest displays was that of the Southern Pacific.

A quarter of a century later, the Baltimore and Ohio used a "traveling coal exhibit" in an effort to increase the consumption of bituminous coal as a fuel for home heating and to counteract the inroads of oil and gas. The exhibit included several types of furnaces and heaters for homes, a diorama of a coal mine and a huge map showing coal-producing areas along the Baltimore and Ohio. The exhibit was shown to 300 retail coal dealers and members of the press in Chicago in February 1950 and later it was displayed in other cities. Presumably the exhibit gave the retail men "sale ammunition" for expanding their markets.[43]

Tours of businessmen also served the same purpose in mineral promotion as they did in other development work. In 1899 the Union Pacific's passenger department used the technique to create an interest in fossil fields in Wyoming, and ten years later it issued a descriptive pamphlet. More common were tours such as those conducted in the late 1940s by roads in Oklahoma in which businessmen and newspapermen were escorted through parts of the state containing important mineral resources.

Finally and widely used as a promotional tool was railway-issued literature. All railway geologists produced brochures and pamphlets describing resources along their lines. The items ranged widely in quality and content, but as a generalization they tended to become more detailed and useful as the twentieth century progressed.

Remarkably thorough for a pioneer effort was a study of the mineral resources of east Texas that was produced by the Southern Pacific in 1918 after almost twenty years of work. According to the report, "the Geological Department of the Southern Pacific Lines in Texas and Louisiana, within the course of its work on the oil conditions and mineral resources of the territory tributary to its lines in southeastern Texas, has made detailed investigations of a portion of the area and the general results are deemed of sufficient interest to warrant publication by the University of Texas."

More typical of the early mineral literature was the Chicago, Burlington and Quincy's *Mines and Mining in the Black Hills.* The pamphlet discussed in general terms the minerals found in the region, outlined the major producing areas, and listed the mining companies in operation there. All in all, the pamphlet probably was of little value to men conversant with the realities of Black Hills mining and perhaps was most useful in building passenger traffic.[44]

Many of the general promotional pamphlets issued before World War I contained information on mineral resources. The Missouri Pacific's *Resources on the Missouri Pacific Railway,* a 350-page booklet issued in 1905, not only discussed business conditions and opportunities and social and educational advantages of some 600 localities reached by the railroad but it also listed the known deposits of minerals. Similarly an *Official Guide for the Use of the Company's Patrons* turned out by the Norfolk and Western the same year used ten pages to discuss mineral resources, material which presumably satisfied the book's promise to "furnish facts pertaining to natural resources that may enable prospective investors and manufacturers to form an intelligent opinion of opportunities. . . ."

With the employment of professionally trained geologists in the 1920s roads produced literature on mineral wealth that was of higher quality than those appearing earlier. The Central of Georgia put its geologist to work examining mineral resources along its line and compiling reports which were placed on file in the company's industrial department. Subsequently the company issued its *Directory of Commercial Minerals,* which contained brief descriptions of the commercial deposits in the sections of Alabama and Georgia served by the road. Harris County, Georgia, for example, contained deposits of mica, pyrite, road materials, sand, gravel, granite, talc, soapstone, and asbestos, according to the booklet.[45]

A number of other roads produced similar items. The Seaboard Air Line issued its 51-page *Geological Resources: Seaboard Air Line Railway Territory* in 1925. The publication was intended to be both an inventory of and a directory to all known deposits in the carrier's territory. The Baltimore and Ohio's geological engineer was putting in bulletin form the results of his explorations as early as 1923. By 1928 "quite a number" had been issued. According to a company spokesman, the pamphlets did not "tell the entire story by any means, but we think we have shown enough . . . to show that we know what we are talking about, and will open up contacts, which they have already done." Earlier the company geologist had prepared a mineral map of the system that was given wide circulation. The first of a projected series of booklets discussing mineral resources along the Missouri Pacific was issued in 1928. The Delaware

company with other Americans, railroadmen were surprised to learn that inflation and recession could exist at the same time.

Any number of new issues complicated the lives of industrial development men, not the least of these were those generated by the ecology movement and the energy crisis. Railroaders knew that there was a shortage of natural gas long before most Americans realized that a problem existed. Ecologists and railroad industrial men had little in common, but in time the latter learned that they needed to know about the Environmental Protection Agency and a few of them even decided that membership in the Sierra Club was worthwhile.[1]

Of major significance to industrial development work after 1945 was a strong decentralization trend and a marked regional shift in industrial activities. Increasingly businesses moved from the cities of the East to smaller communities in the West and South. Many firms established branch plants and distribution centers, others sought more favorable labor conditions, and still others were encouraged to migrate because of the obsolescence of existing installations. The revolution in technology that came after 1945 created a multitude of new businesses, many of which sought locations in the West or in the South. Especially important were electronic, chemical, aircraft, plastics, and aluminum industries and the expansion of hydroelectric power in the Pacific Northwest. Significant, too, was the growing concern with the quality of life, which presumably was better in areas removed from the historic industrial centers. Finally World War II and the Cold War contributed to the geographical shift in industry. As soon as the national defense effort began, a surge of manufacturing plants and military installations into the West and South ensued, highlighted perhaps by the creation of Los Alamos in the Santa Fe's New Mexico territory. After 1945 some officials advocated the placing of new industry in the nation's interior on the grounds that such locations would be less vulnerable to enemy attack.[2]

These developments had important implications for railroads. Territorial shifts in industry gave eastern roads strong incentives to strengthen their industrial development programs and were unmixed blessings to carriers in the West and South. Having spent large sums for improvements to handle wartime traffic, western and southern roads were eager to do what they could to insure that the war-created population centers would not become the ghost towns of the future. Meanwhile southern railroadmen watched with anticipation as the states of the old Confederacy went through a boom that for the first time made the term "New South" reasonably descriptive. By the early 1960s the South had "turned the corner in its effort to move from its old position as an economic problem area." While its historic attractions to industry – lower wages, weaker labor unions, and the character of southern workers – remained, the South was now able to serve "as its own market for the goods it produces," a development that opened the way for new types of businesses and marked a significant step in the evolution of its economy.[3]

The merger movement that transformed the railroad system after 1955 had a significant impact on industrial development work. Combinations that produced stronger roads generally had a beneficial effect. Mergers often allowed roads to gain greater expertise, which helped to make development efforts more sophisticated, provided improved service and transit times, and strengthened in interregional competition the territories they served, thereby enhancing attractions to industry. Communities previously served by weak roads benefited, since firms were understandably hesitant to go to locations where carriers could not guarantee good service and an adequate car supply. Finally a merged road generally had stronger financial resources that permitted it to purchase industrial lands, increasingly a major prerequisite of successful industrial development work.[4]

While railroads continued to be by far the most important mode of transportation in the promotion of industrial development, they had both more assistance and more competition in the work after 1945. In 1971 one authority estimated that there were some 16,000 industrial development organizations in the United States. Such groups as chambers of commerce and regional and state development commissions aided railway efforts when their goals coincided, but the number of such agencies also increased the competition for industries. Meanwhile power companies were now assuming a developmental role, and in some instances they were the first source of information for firms seeking new locations. Barge operators devoted some attention to the placing of industries, although their role was minor in comparison to that of the railroads. Trucking companies and airlines did little.[5]

During the years after 1945, primary locational factors — availability of markets, labor, and raw materials — remained, but other factors gained in importance. As G. F. Defiel of the Northern Pacific observed, the "trend is definitely toward more sophistication" in choosing sites. Prominent among new factors were those that dealt with conditions within communities, such as the prevalent attitude toward industry, zoning ordinances, tax structures, recreational, educational, and medical facilities, community law enforcement and political atmosphere, and the general quality of life. When DuPont located a Dacron plant in North Carolina in the 1950s, for example, it weighed eighty-three separate factors.[6]

The new complexities of industrial location made the role of industrial agents both more essential and more difficult. In theory a concern seeking a new location should be able to ascertain with precision the spot best suited to its needs, but in practice the selection of a site remained a series of compromises based on a combination of available data, intuition, and salesmanship. Nevertheless railway development men had to become more sophisticated. "Thirty years ago our industrial salesmen went out with a lot of pizzazz, personality, and a fistful of cigars," a veteran in the work reported in 1971, but today "they must be highly trained professionals. Industry wants to know all there is to know. . . . If you can't produce that kind of package, somebody else will." Industrial departments found it necessary to upgrade the knowledge and skill of their personnel, to employ men with more specialized abilities, and generally to provide "a highly competent professional plant location service." Market research, planning, and team effort became key items.

The new conditions also caused development departments to become more selective in choosing industries to be located. There was "a lot of difference between 300 carloads of sand and 300 carloads of TV sets," so industrial men concentrated more of their attention on the "location of industries which would be the most lucrative." Meanwhile some railroads were willing to locate industries that shipped by truck, since their executives recognized that inbound shipments would rise as the prosperity of a community increased. Any "new industry adds fresh blood and both the community and the Frisco will ultimately benefit from it," observed an official of that line in 1955. The appearance of trailer-on-flatcar service added another dimension to industrial development work by giving railroads access to off-line locations and enhancing the significance of their trucking subsidiaries. According to a spokesman for the Union Pacific in the 1960s, customers' truck docks were "as frequent as rail sidings" in his company's territory.[7]

By contrast, basic motives for industrial development work changed little after 1945. "No railroad can be content with merely handling traffic already existing on its lines. New sources of revenue must continually be sought," the Erie-Lackawanna informed its stockholders in 1961 in a statement that would have been equally appropriate forty years earlier or twenty years later, and an official of the Chesapeake and Ohio–Baltimore and Ohio noted that "the best way to lock in future transportation business is to help an industry . . . locate a site on your line. . . ." The old goal of a diversified traffic flow continued to be very much in the minds of company officers. The "location of . . . different types of industry . . . is the best insurance" against economic fluctuations, one executive pointed out.[8]

Perhaps more so than earlier, railroad men after 1945 viewed industrial development as a tool to protect their companies against anticipated declines in traffic. In the 1960s coal-carrying roads in the East hoped that the location of new industries would at least balance the loss of coal traffic, and railway executives generally believed that the distressing shift of high-rated goods to trucks was a problem that could be met in part by a successful industrial development program.[9]

At least one new motive for industrial development work appeared after 1945. Railroadmen became more interested in the rent that might be earned by the location of industry. "Potential traffic, while highly important," said an official of the Norfolk and Western in the early 1970s, "is no longer the overriding consideration. What we are after is revenue for the railroad, but at the same time we intend to make money on the real estate." The merging of industrial development and real estate offices on some lines was a step toward that goal; so too was the use of computers as analytical tools to determine with a high degree of precision the maximum returns that might be expected from a given piece of industrial property.

In total the importance of industrial development work increased markedly after 1945. An official of the Western Pacific put the matter plainly in 1962 when he stated that "any railroad which fails to replace lost industries will wither and die. Any company which fails to attract new industries will stagnate." According to President William N. Deramus of the Katy in 1958, "Today, more than ever, the future of a railroad lies in the availability of volume and diversified traffic. . . . A strong industrial department is, therefore, essential and performs a vital function in assuring the future of any railroad." Nor was there likely to be any change in the need of such services in the future. Indeed, it was expected to continue as long as "scientific research discovers new industrial . . . methods and products, and so long as a growing, progressive nation voices a demand for those products."[10]

Practices and Procedures

The basic techniques employed by railway industrial men changed little after 1945. As the Chicago and North Western expressed it, "The Industrial Development Department . . . shall use every means at its disposal to foster and promote the location of new and the growth of existing industry, by pointing the way to the soundest, most economical locations on its system. . . ." These goals, of course, led to others. Industrial development men were expected to process tips and data received from a variety of sources, promote the development of new sites, correlate the requirements of an industry with sites that were available, and handle at least preliminary negotiations for the land sales or leases and for side track arrangements.

The first task, as earlier, was to contact businessmen and arouse their interest in the opportunities in a railroad's service area. Some roads used extensive advertising campaigns, while others, especially those with only limited funds available for the work, tended to rely on personal contacts. Probably most roads used a combination of these approaches. Top executives used their contacts to learn of a firm's plans to relocate. All industrial development men watched business magazines for tips and maintained close contact with bankers, state and local promotional agencies, key personnel in the different industries and individual firms, and others likely to be informed concerning plans, proposals, and possibilities.[11]

Advertising of the traditional sort remained important, not only to attract attention to the industrial potential of an area but also to give a railroad a favorable "image." According to the Rock Island in 1964, it devoted 25 percent of its advertising budget to industrial development. In the 1950s the Central of Georgia had underway a major advertising campaign which, according to company spokesmen, produced "excellent results" in the form of 254 serious inquiries in a single year at a cost of less than $50,000. Many roads advertised in *Fortune, Business Week, Traffic World,* and *Railway Freight Traffic* as well as in the leading national news magazines and the financial dailies. In the late 1940s the Southern Railway used 400 newspapers to carry its theme, "Look Ahead—Look South."[12]

Company-issued periodicals apparently were less important in industrial work after 1945 than they had been in agricultural promotion earlier, but still a few were in use. In the early 1950s the Reading sent its quarterly *Industrial News Bulletin* to industrial realtors, businessmen, builders, and engineers. Great Northern's *Great Resources,* a monthly, went to 23,000 business leaders in 1960; the Northern Pacific's the *Northwest* served essentially the same clientele.[13]

Industrial brochures were produced in huge numbers. Some were general in nature, surveying a railroad's entire territory, while others described in detail a single community or even a single industrial park or site.

Illustrative of the broad coverage, general industrial brochure was the Nashville, Chattanooga and St. Louis's *Central South Where Industry Goes to Work,* a pamphlet in use in the early 1950s. Fifteen years later the Seaboard Coast Line's the *Industrial Southeast* described the attractions of six states. The Milwaukee's general pamphlet in the late 1940s was *How to Find a Home for Your Business,* while the Norfolk and Western had its *Industrial Opportunities in the Land of Plenty.* Also general in scope was *Here's Help in Finding a "Central" Location for Your Plant,* issued by the New York Central, and the Louisville and Nashville's *Full Throttle* and *Focus on the South.*

Among brochures that covered a single state or smaller area was *Southern Pacific Guide to Sites for Industry in Northern California* and the

Nickel Plate's *Along the Line* books, each of which described the attractions of a state served by that carrier. The Santa Fe's *North Texas Industrial Empire,* issued in a 10,000-copy edition in 1955, was devoted to the area in five counties that had been made more accessible by the opening of 49 miles of new line north of Dallas-Fort Worth.

Other brochures discussed specific cities or individual industrial districts. In the late 1950s the Santa Fe had available glossy pamphlets on many of the cities it served, and most other major lines were equally well prepared. Typical of industrial district literature was a brochure issued by the Nashville, Chattanooga and St. Louis to promote its Southland Industrial Center at Atlanta. "Immediately outside the city limits, only four miles from the heart of the downtown district, 170 acres of ideal plant locations are being shaped," the publication proclaimed. "With no further work being required, construction on building sites can begin at once. All utilities . . . are . . . ready for instant connection. Purchasers of sites . . . need only to choose their location, unroll their blueprints, and start construction."[14]

These types of literature were used in different ways. Some roads mailed them wholesale to industrial firms, engineering companies, and contractors interested in plant construction and to state and local industrial promotion groups. Other carriers were more selective; in the early 1970s the Burlington Northern distributed its literature to a select list of companies and executives whose interests suggested that they might be attracted to the railroad's territory.

As the economic condition of some carriers deteriorated in the 1960s and later, there was a tendency to reduce the number of industrial publications. The Reading, for example, reported that it had only one brochure, choosing instead to make a custom-made presentation when a customer revealed his interest and needs. Similarly by 1973 the Rock Island had no general brochures available for distribution. When contact was made with a firm, the company ascertained the prospect's needs and then prepared a package of data.[15]

Motion pictures in sound and color were much in use after 1945. Representative was the Seaboard Air Line's "New Horizons," a 16mm film that described the development taking place in the company's territory. Presenting the film before a variety of groups and organizations as well as on television, Seaboard spokesmen claimed a total audience of 1.5 million people in five years. Meanwhile the Rock Island had its "Wheels of Progress" and the Illinois Central its "Gold Mine on Main Street." The Union Pacific, Frisco, Boston and Maine, and Southern Pacific were other carriers that used films in their industrial development work.

Advertising also took the form of for sale or lease signs that were erected on industrial properties. The Chesapeake and Ohio believed that the method was useful, citing the wholesale use of outdoor signs by other industries.[16]

Industrial tours remained a widely used method of advertising a region's industrial potential. Special trains or buses transported groups of industrial realtors, engineers, architects, financial and newspaper men, and others on inspection trips of industrial sites and buildings in a given district; in a few instances, the tours covered broader territories.[17]

After a railroad learned that a particular firm was considering the location of a new facility, its industrial development personnel contacted appropriate executives of the firm to determine specific requirements. With these in hand, development men examined sites on their road and attempted to match them with the customer's needs. Packages of data on a number of sites were assembled for presentation. As an official of the Milwaukee described the work in 1954, "For a company requiring a site, we pick out several that could meet the needs and submit a complete study showing water, power, gas, sewage, drainage, . . . labor by skills and community sentiment." Procedure was the same on the Chesapeake and Ohio in 1981. For industries requiring them, railroads made detailed studies of specific factors. Throughout the negotiations, railroadmen maintained confidentiality, if the prospect so desired, and most roads were willing to represent the customer to forestall premature release of plans. In short, as President Edd H. Bailey of the Union Pacific noted in 1967, railroads were prepared to "provide freight-producing industries with every possible . . . aid in locating. . . ."[18]

A prime prerequisite for the providing of such service, of course, was the accumulation of sophisticated files on the different communities along the line and on industrial properties available for sale or lease. Railroadmen spent a great deal of time gaining such information, but as competition for industries became more severe many carriers found that it was useful to employ outside experts to gather and compile the data.

Soon after World War II, for example, the Chicago and Eastern Illinois retained the economist Arthur Longini and placed him in charge of producing a number of volumes dealing with the industrial potential of the road's territory. Among the first to appear was a 159-page *Industrial Potentialities of Southern Illinois,* a volume that told "of the manifold opportunities and advantages to be found in this area." Reportedly it was the "most detailed site survey ever prepared by a railroad." Later studies dealt with the Evansville, Indiana, area, the lower Wabash Valley, and the Chicago-Chicago Heights area.

One of the more comprehensive industrial surveys was made by Fantus Area Research for the Norfolk and Western. Dividing the railroad's territory into five districts, Fantus produced a huge volume on each, the first appearing in 1962. According to high company officials, the studies represented "an entirely new type of industrial survey which explores specific potentials at each site in great depth."[19]

Among the important new tools in industrial development work were electronic computers. The remarkable capabilities of the new marvels made their use inevitable, given the growing complexities of industrial development work. By the mid-1960s the Chicago and North Western was using computers to determine the size of markets and labor supply, and other companies were employing the machines to "take the needle out of the haystack of industrial site selection." The Milwaukee claimed to be the first in the industry to computerize its site data, doing so in 1968. Soon it was able to provide almost instantly information on some 300 towns and communities as well as on more than 600 individual industrial sites. On the other hand, site data on the Chesapeake and Ohio were manually retrieved as late as 1981.[20]

Some roads took to the air to show sites to prospective customers or make easier visits to sites in remote areas. The Western Pacific claimed to be a pioneer when in the 1950s it began to use helicopters. The Atlantic Coast Line found that its DC-3 purchased in 1965 was useful in industrial development work. Site seekers appreciated seeing sites and adjacent country from the air, and the flight characteristics of the DC-3 made it ideal for visiting out-of-the-way towns. The Burlington was more modern, buying a Grumman Gulfstream in 1966, and in the early 1970s the Burlington Northern was using a jet to fly customers about the system.[21]

More common was the use of aerial maps and photographs. The Missouri Pacific employed them in the selected cases in the early 1940s, but their use became more sophisticated later in the decade. In 1957 the Milwaukee began a thorough aerial survey of its industrial properties and other available sites in its territory, producing both black and white photographs and color slides. The Chesapeake and Ohio, Seaboard Air Line, and the Santa Fe also used aerial maps and photographs extensively in their industrial work.[22]

Certainly industrial development work remained "everybody's business" after 1945. All employees, from the chairman of the board down to station agents, were still supposed to be aware of the importance of industrial work and to participate in it. If performance was less than industrial men wanted, it was still substantial. On the Burlington in the 1960s, for example, from 75 to 80 percent of the tips received by the industrial department came from freight traffic agents scattered throughout the nation. On-line traffic men helped to keep industrial development personnel informed concerning plant and warehouse vacancies in their territories.

Some roads instituted programs to improve the cooperation between industrial development departments and other company offices. In the late 1940s the Union Pacific began circularizing its traffic representatives and general agents to keep them informed concerning available industrial properties so that they might be better prepared to advise prospects. Other roads held seminars to instruct traffic department personnel in the character of industrial development work and the role that they could play. As Santa Fe employees progressed through that company's training programs, they learned that every "Santa Fe employee is a possible ID person if he'll just keep his ears open."[23]

Railroadmen maintained after 1945 that they were still the "professors emeriti of industrial development," but they found that industrial promotion was more of a cooperative work than earlier. Railroads were eager to work with such highly successful development organizations as the Detroit Metropolitan Area Regional Planning Commission; the Michigan Department of Economic Development; the Arkansas Industrial Development Commission, headed at one time by Winthrop Rockefeller; and the New England Council. In the aggregate, however, cooperation with a multitude of local chambers of commerce and comparable groups was more important. Many of these agencies admittedly had little to offer except their enthusiasm, but their limitations gave the carriers with their greater expertise opportunity to be of substantial service.

Aid to local promotional groups took different forms. Railroadmen helped them plan and develop industrial sites, then made the availability of those sites known to potential users. Company men encouraged local groups to become more aggressive and sophisticated in their search for industry. The Santa Fe's film, "Blueprint for Progress," was used to inspire local civic groups to greater or more realistic efforts, and in the 1950s that company had on its payroll men trained in the mechanics of community development. Meanwhile the Illinois Central and most other major carriers were eager to furnish engineering assistance to small communities wanting to make a start toward industrial development.

Where local promotional groups did not exist, railroads encouraged their establishment. The Cotton Belt, for example, was an early and enthusiastic promoter of the Tyler, Texas, Industrial Foundation, created in 1945 to help the community compensate for the loss of Camp Fannin, an important World War II training base. The Nashville, Chattanooga and St. Louis played a similar role in the establishment of the Huntsville, Alabama, Industrial Expansion Committee, and other roads were equally busy.[24]

Railroadmen also sponsored or helped to arrange meetings at which the problems of industrial development were discussed. The American Railway Development Association and the Stanford University Research Institute were cosponsors of a Western Area Development Conference in San Francisco in 1954 where businessmen and professional leaders from throughout the region exchanged ideas. Ten railroads held an industrial development conference in southern Illinois in 1961, and beginning in 1963 a bank in Memphis held an annual Mid-South Industrial Development Conference in which railroadmen were prominent participants.[25]

Despite the multiplication of agencies and groups promoting industrial development and the assumption of promotional responsibilities by power companies, railroadmen claimed that they enjoyed certain advantages that helped them retain a primary role in the work. They had been active in the field longer than others, and so perhaps their men were more experienced. If an industry required a rail siding, it was logical for it to turn to a railroad for assistance. Railway development men were also in a strategic position to help a shipper with his transportation and rate problems. Finally railroadmen enjoyed an excellent reputation for protecting the identity of their clients.

On the other hand, according to some observers, railroads had certain limitations as sources of site information. They tended to provide a narrow geographical coverage, since they were concerned primarily with sites that could be reached from their tracks. Critics claimed that some railroads tried to steer concerns away from communities having competing carriers. Others complained that railroadmen ignored small companies and tried to preserve choice sites for those firms that promised to give a railroad a heavy volume of traffic, a practice that allegedly became more common as prime land came to be in shorter supply. Railroaders denied at least the latter charge. According to an official of the Norfolk and Western, "We extend the same courtesy and assistance to every industry, regardless of size. . . ."[26]

Modern Industrial Property Management

A necessary prerequisite to a successful development program after 1945 was an adequate supply of industrial property. Traditionally, railroads had located firms on tracts of company land not needed for railway operations and on privately owned land reached by their tracks. These practices continued, but after World War II carriers had to take steps to increase their inventories of attractive properties. Quite obviously railroads having abundant supplies of industrial lands had important advantages in the competition for new traffic-generating enterprises. Railroad ownership eliminated the middleman who at times complicated negotiations, expedited arrangements so that construction could begin "the next morning," and made it easier to preserve and protect land having industrial potential.

The growing pressure on the supply of land caused railroad companies to examine carefully their properties to identify land and buildings that could be converted to industrial use. Technological change in the railroad industry and the decline of passenger operations made some locomotive and car repair shops, roundhouses, and passenger stations and passenger car storage yards available for sale or lease. Relocation of lines also occasionally opened to industrial use valuable parcels of land.

Some industrial land was literally created. The New York, Susquehanna and Western took silt from the Hudson River to fill swampy "meadows" in New Jersey, while in Seattle, where piers for James J. Hill's Far Eastern trade once stood, the Great Northern used fill to create 35 acres of prime industrial land.[27]

A major new departure was the large-scale purchase of industrial land by railroads. As T. T. Martin of the Gulf, Mobile and Ohio explained, "For the past fifty years we have been literally living off our fat by locating people on bits and pieces of railroad . . . real estate. At the same time, almost without notice, land along the railroad has been almost exhausted." The answer was to buy "industrial land so that we can have some goods on the shelf in future years." A report released in 1959 by the prestigious Committee for Economic Development showed that 57 percent of railroads studied were spending money for industrial land, and a majority of the carriers indicated that their acquisitions were limited only by the funds that could be allocated to that purpose. Land purchases continued throughout the 1960s and the next decade, although the deteriorating financial condition of some carriers severely restricted their activities.[28]

The generally prosperous Union Pacific had one of the more aggressive land-buying programs. In 1953 the company owned industrial acreages in all of the principal cities along the line, but during the decade the company made steady purchases. In 1954 it reported the acquisition of 73 acres at Fremont, Nebraska; in 1955, 188 acres at East Portland, Oregon, and 90 acres at Topeka, Kansas; and in 1956 another 50 acres at East Portland. This level of purchases continued into the 1960s, but in 1965 the company greatly expanded its buying program, acquiring that year 3,270 acres at a total cost of $17 million.[29]

Purchases of a few other carriers were on a par. In the 1950s the Western Pacific reportedly spent $11 million to strengthen itself in the San Francisco area. One tract of land near Milpitas aggregated 1,000 acres. In the course of three years — 1965–1967 — the Milwaukee purchased 2,345 acres, including a 610-acre tract at Schaumburg, Illinois, some 25 miles west of Chicago. In 1965 alone the Southern laid out $9 million for 4,740 acres at Greenville, South Carolina; Charlotte, North Carolina; and Atlanta.

Other roads purchased smaller amounts of land. In the 1940s and 1950s the Gulf, Mobile and Ohio bought "fair sized" tracts at Mobile,

Alabama; various Mississippi towns; Alton, Illinois; and Independence, Missouri. Throughout the post-World War II period the Northern Pacific purchased industrial land near the Twin Cities, in the Red River valley, at different towns in Montana, and in the Columbia Basin, where irrigation was expected to lead to industrial development. The Illinois Central told its stockholders in 1958 that it was embarking upon a land-buying program, especially in the Memphis and Baton Rouge-New Orleans areas. The Rock Island was actively buying land in the 1940s and the 1950s, but by the 1960s the road's financial condition brought the program to an end. In 1964, in fact, the Rock Island reported that it held only 1,100 acres of industrial land, and its holdings had declined to 530 acres by 1970.[30]

In their efforts to build up their inventories of industrial land, some railroads made unusual acquisitions. In 1960 the Milwaukee bought a 150-acre golf course near Chicago's O'Hare Field. The Burlington and the Southern added to their inventories by buying abandoned airports at Denver, Lincoln, and Raleigh. Even more unusual was the Burlington's use of caves as underground warehouses. Near Kansas City, Missouri, the company improved a cave underlying 225 acres, at a cost comparable to that of building traditional warehouses, and leased the space to firms handling sugar, canned and frozen foods, and other items requiring close control of humidity and temperature. The company expected to use two caves near Quincy, Illinois, in the same manner.[31]

Stronger roads were able to report substantial holdings of industrial land by the 1960s and later. The Penn Central counted more than 18,000 acres in its inventory in the early 1970s, but in 1973 the bankrupt road was no longer buying industrial land. In that period both the Burlington Northern and the Southern owned over 20,000 acres of prime industrial land, the Union Pacific 17,000 acres, and the Southern Pacific 38,000 acres. The Santa Fe, which earlier had described itself as "land poor," had 22,000 acres in 1970 and claimed that another 26,000 acres could be turned to industrial use when the need arose. The Norfolk and Western reported ownership of 12,000 acres in 43 towns and cities in 1971. A couple of years later, the total in the company's "land bank" had fallen to 11,000 acres, and an official stated that the company had stopped buying land except in those instances where prompt utilization was assured.[32]

All railroads, regardless of whether they held substantial amounts of industrial land, worked with other owners to make property available to firms seeking sites. A common practice was to encourage businessmen in a community to create a public industrial site organization to purchase land and hold it for future industrial use. This insured a community that it would have sites to offer some years ahead, permitted the acquisition of land at prevailing prices, and eliminated the tax burden on the property during the interim period. Railroads also helped local investors accumulate land for industrial location by acting as a "straw-party" to preserve the identity of their clients. In other cases railroad companies approached owners of potential industrial lands with the proposition that, if the owner would guarantee to maintain a fixed price for his land, the carrier involved would promote utilization of the land and provide the needed trackage to reach it.[33]

A major development that came in industrial land management policies after 1945 was the vastly increased importance of industrial parks or districts. A variety of factors contributed to the new popularity of these "planned industrial communities." American working men now wanted to drive to their jobs, a fact that dictated the location of many new businesses outside the core cities and in reasonable proximity to adequate highways. The almost uniform use of the single-story, straight-plant layout, combined with the high cost of land in the cities, also forced businessmen into more open country. A well planned industrial park gave occupants good security against neighborhood deterioration, a desirable location in an attractive setting, and community facilities and services at reasonable cost. For railroads, the establishment of industrial parks constituted one means of obtaining control of land and protecting it for industrial uses. Moreover enterprises that located in industrial parks, such as warehouses and light manufacturing, were likely to ship by truck, a tendency that perhaps could be minimized by locating them in an industrial park well supplied with railroad connections.

In terms of ownership, industrial parks fell into three categories. Some were established by municipalities or local community development groups. Others were created by private investors. Most desirable from the railroad point of view, assuming that a carrier had funds to invest, were those industrial districts developed and controlled exclusively by a railroad. Private developers, municipalities, and local community development groups, understandably enough, were not guided in their managerial decisions by the volume of traffic that might be generated or by the mode of transportation likely to be used by occupants.[34]

The Santa Fe, one of the pioneers in the industrial park field, became much more active after 1945. In the early 1960s the road was developing near Chicago three new districts aggregating over 2,000 acres of prime land and costing about $10 million without improvements. Later the railroad completed the acquisition of land that became the 1,500-acre Argonne Industrial District located some 25 miles southwest of Chicago. The Santa Fe also had important industrial districts near other major cities, including the Central Industrial Park at Houston and the Camelback Industrial District at Phoenix.[35]

The prosperous Union Pacific, another of the early leaders in industrial park work, also expanded its activities after 1945. Its pioneer Fairfax

Industrial District at Kansas City, Kansas, had grown to 2,300 acres with more than 100 industries employing 25,000 workers by 1958, and the company was in the process of creating others. In the mid-1950s the Union Pacific purchased 90 acres at Topeka, installed the usual facilities, and labeled the new project the West Topeka Industrial District. An East Denver Industrial District was enlarged more than once. The Muncie Industrial District, located 8 miles west of Kansas City, was opened in the 1960s to provide new space in that metropolitan area. Other Union Pacific parks were located at Omaha, Los Angeles, Portland, Salt Lake City, Spokane, and Seattle.[36]

In some instances major carriers established railroad-owned parks in the 1950s using land acquired years earlier. The Texas and Pacific's Eagle Ford District at Dallas, for example, had been purchased in 1922, but it flourished only after World War II when it was annexed by the city and provided with water and sewage facilities. In 1937 the Piedmont and Northern bought a 121-acre tract near Charlotte, North Carolina, and began to improve it. Business came with a rush after World War II, and by 1964 the property was occupied by over 50 traffic-generating industries.[37]

Fairly typical of railroad-owned industrial parks was the Wabash's Hazelwood-Berkeley Industrial District, located some 10 miles northwest of St. Louis. Consisting of more than 700 acres assembled by the railroad over a dozen years, the district contained 16 industries representing an investment of more than $60 million in 1957. Among the tenants were Kroger, International Harvester, and Rexall Drug Company warehouses, an assembly plant of Ford Motor Company's Lincoln-Mercury Division, an office building belonging to McDonnell Aircraft Corporation, and a Crown-Zellerbach facility manufacturing paper products.[38]

Meanwhile most railroads cooperated with private or public developers in the establishment of industrial districts. Roads lacking adequate financial resources were forced to do so, if they were to have desirable sites to offer customers, and even strong carriers could not afford to establish their own industrial districts in every community they served. In the mid-1960s, for example, the Frisco held through ownership or lease 19 industrial districts but, in addition, it encouraged "private developers and local communities to take steps to insure the availability of attractive industrial sites." By working with private developers, the company helped to establish the South Perkins and Airport industrial parks in Memphis and it participated in similar projects elsewhere. During the immediate post-World War II years the Rock Island created its own industrial parks in a number of its major cities, but later as its financial position deteriorated the road "worked with others which have taken the investor role. All of our efforts have been to encourage privately owned parks and public industrial foundations to improve land adjacent to our railroad."[39]

Policies with industrial park developers varied from road to road, but some were sufficiently common to be standard operating procedure. Practically all roads were willing to provide engineering aid in laying out industrial parks and in solving track design and other problems, particularly to insure that curvature and grade standards were met. Railway personnel also could make suggestions concerning clearances, length of spurs, and heights of loading docks. Generally, railroads were willing to advise developers on financing problems, to join in sales and marketing programs, and to promote favorable legislative and community relationships.

A prime example of railroad cooperation with private developers was afforded by the Brook Hollow Industrial District at Dallas. Billed as the "largest and most modern of its kind in the nation" when it opened in 1953, the 1,200-acre project was owned by a prominent Texas family and served by the Rock Island and the Katy, which together spent some $500,000 in putting rail facilities in the park. According to the owner the role of the railroads "has been extremely helpful, not only during the district's formative stages, when they provided primary guidance and counsel . . ., but up to the present in practically every phase of its growth."[40]

In addition to providing sites for the location of industries, many railroads acquired or constructed buildings for use by traffic-producing firms. In some instances carriers were willing to put up a building for a specific customer. Prosperous roads, of course, were most active in this type of work, and there is evidence that competitive pressures forced other carriers into it when they would have preferred to have used their funds for other purposes.

The Union Pacific seems to have been one of the more active roads in this area. Between 1946 and 1952 that carrier or its subsidiaries built twenty-seven warehouses at such cities as Kansas City, Topeka, Omaha, Cheyenne, Denver, Boise, Spokane, Seattle, Portland, and Los Angeles. They also purchased at least one and enlarged nine others during the same period of time.

Among other roads willing to construct buildings to strengthen their industrial development programs were the Northern Pacific and the Atlantic Coast Line. In 1959 the Northern Pacific's Northwestern Improvement Company built a $1.3 million grocery distributing warehouse in Fargo, North Dakota. Some $800,000 of the cost was borrowed from an insurance company, but Northern Pacific stockholders were informed that the rent was adequate to cover mortgage payments. In the early 1950s, as part of its effort to attract industry to Atlanta, the Atlantic

Coast Line joined with a warehouse company to spend $7 million over a two-year period in constructing several warehouses in the city.[41]

By the early 1960s some railroads offered "one package jobs" in which all financing was arranged and structures were built to the specifications of a specific tenant. The New York Central labeled its program "Operation-Turn-key." In it, the railroad offered partial or complete financing of all costs of a new installation and coordinated the work of architects, engineers, and contractors to produce a completed facility. The customer could obtain the installation by long-term lease or by purchase, but he paid nothing until the property was ready for occupancy. The Southern Pacific provided a similar service in the late 1970s.[42]

Railroads were willing to sell industrial property to firms promising substantial volumes of traffic, but generally they preferred to lease it. By so doing they were able to exercise some control over future use, avoid the payment of heavy capital gains taxes on property often acquired years earlier, and maintain their industrial property inventories without having to enter the market at a time when prices were rising rapidly. Apparently most businesses also preferred to lease industrial property. Exceptions were those concerns with special requirements necessitating substantial improvements or that wanted to mortgage the property and use funds thus raised for other purposes.

When railroad industrial property was sold, some carriers wrote into sales contracts provisions that allowed them to retain some control over future use. So-called "trucking clauses" sought to insure that property would be used in a manner that would generate tonnage or that permitted roads to reclaim property at the selling price. In other cases, recapture clauses covered misuse of property or failure of a buyer to put property to use within a reasonable period of time.[43]

The Interstate Commerce Act and its amendments continued to provide imperfect guidelines for the sale or lease of industrial property. The dictum that, in relations with shippers, railroads must show no "favoritism by any means or device whatsoever" left many questions unresolved. A fair return on the cost of a property, plus maintenance, depreciation, and taxes, presumably constituted an acceptable basis for determining sale price and rent, but costs of a property often bore little relationship to its market value. Nor was the determination of market value a simple task, influenced as it was by numerous factors difficult to assess. Some authorities advocated the use of cost of reproduction or capitalization of income to determine rent or selling price of a property, but others rejected those measures. A question also existed as to whether the same standards should be applied to excess railroad property and to lands and buildings acquired specifically for industrial development purposes.

In practice, no answer served in all circumstances. The common procedure in establishing rents was to aim for some percent of the cost or market value, plus another 2 to 4 percent to cover taxes, insurance, and related items. Sale prices were generally set by market value as determined by sales of comparable properties in the area. In any case there was always pressure to keep rents or sale prices low in order to win customers. As an official of the Santa Fe expressed it, "We try to get a fair price without driving anybody away." It was this situation that caused every railroad industrial development man to be deeply suspicious of his competitors and that occasionally forced railroad companies into court to defend themselves against charges of violating the Elkins Act.[44]

Similar problems arose when a prospective customer needed financial assistance. Railway development men maintained contact with investors, mortgage bankers, and insurance companies so that when an industry required external financing they were able to provide guidance, but some firms asked for aid of a more concrete nature. Arrangements were occasionally worked out by which a railroad company either directly or indirectly guaranteed a mortgage loan of a customer; in other instances, railroads were asked to provide financing. These situations placed carriers on the horns of a dilemma. If aid were refused, the prospective customer might well have better luck with a competing carrier. On the other hand, direct financial aid by a railroad exposed the carrier to legal problems if the aid were extended under terms that were easier than were granted to other customers, while at the same time it absorbed company funds that might have been allocated to other purposes. Financially weak roads were at a severe disadvantage in this area of activity. Nevertheless it is apparent that under some circumstances railroads did finance industries, even if they chose to say little about it. The Illinois Central, for example, reported in 1961 that it did not enter directly into the business "to an appreciable extent," but in the early 1950s the Northern Pacific told its stockholders that it had assisted in the financing of several warehouses.[45]

The matter of sidetrack installation also remained one of considerable confusion and controversy. In a general way most carriers continued to follow the outlines of General Order 15, but no policy was used uniformly. Railroads, of course, wanted to minimize outlays for new construction and they had to avoid the appearances of favoritism, but they were prepared to bargain to land an industry. As one senior officer explained it, industrial "side tracks are negotiated on the basis of division of cost determined by economic realities of the proposed facility. . . ." Special arrangements were made "if tonnage justifies" or if the "industry is of sufficient value from a traffic standpoint." Railway development men believed that the establishment of a uniform sidetrack agreement "would surely reduce the number of nervous breakdowns among our ranks," but competitive realities made such an accomplishment impossible.

Some railroads continued the old policy of paying the costs of construction of industrial spurs to the clearance point or to the right-of-way line and requiring the industry to pay for the balance of the track. Growing in popularity after 1945, however, was an arrangement in which an industry paid the entire cost of a spur, and a portion of the outlay was then refunded to the industry at some agreed rate per car handled on the spur. This arrangement freed the railroad from paying for track that might well produce little traffic and at the same time encouraged an industry to maximize its use of the spur and thereby provide the carrier with more business.

In 1961, for example, the Louisville and Nashville required an industry to deposit with the railroad an amount equal to the estimated cost of an entire spur. When the spur was in operation, the carrier refunded the cost of the spur from switch point to clearance point at a predetermined rate per car of revenue freight handled on the spur during a five-year period or until the cost of the track was met. A decade later the Norfolk and Western generally required an industry to build any part of a spur on the industry's property and to advance to the railroad the cost of that portion of the spur that was on the railroad's property. This part of the shipper's outlay was then refunded on a per car basis. But in some instances, advances by the shipper were waived if specific conditions so dictated. On the Boston and Maine the industry paid the entire cost of the spur, but the portion that covered the track from switch point to clearance point was refunded at the rate of $2.00 per car. In some cases, however, the Boston and Maine was willing to meet the cost of that portion of the spur between the switch point and the clearance point.

For the Southern Pacific to advance the cost of the spur from switch point to clearance point, estimated in the late 1960s to cost $5,500 or more, annual gross revenues had to equal at least ten times the cost of the spur. Where estimated revenues were less than that amount, the railroad required the customer to pay all costs of the turnout and then made a refund at a rate of $10 per car. Spur track construction beyond the clearance point was the sole responsibility of the shipper, but the work was subject to the approval of railroad engineers.

In the aggregate, spur track construction involved substantial sums of money, even under these arrangements. Between 1965 and 1969 the Denver and Rio Grande Western built for new industries eighty-five sidetracks. They amounted to twenty-two miles of track and cost $1.4 million. Of the total mileage, about five miles became the property of the carrier, and the cost of that track was refunded to the industries concerned.[46]

Industrial parks required special arrangements. Drill tracks had to be built from main lines to the spurs serving individual industries. Government regulations required that in the building of drill tracks railroads avoid discriminatory practices, but beyond that stipulation arrangements were left to negotiations between the carrier and the developer. In the case of the Southern Pacific, the railroad paid for the drill track from switch point to clearance point and the developer paid for the balance, which was generally subject to a refund agreement. The developer usually transferred title to the drill track right-of-way to the railroad and arranged for construction by a private contractor who worked under railroad supervision. The Southern Pacific was responsible for maintenance. The Illinois Central Gulf adopted a similar arrangement in the case of the Governors Gateway Industrial Park, a 1,200-acre development thirty miles south of Chicago.[47]

Among other problems that complicated the lives of industrial development men after 1945 were those involving zoning ordinances. One railroadman complained in 1952 that development personnel never knew when "some starry-eyed professional 'city planner' is going to come in and destroy, forever, the possibilities of developing a suitable site" for industry. Such enthusiasts were accused of failing to recognize that industry "is a community's principal source of revenue. . . . Parks and green belts are a delight and much to be desired, but a man must work to live and the community needs tax money to keep the grass in the park cut." But in final analysis there was little that railroadmen could do to alter the general trends in zoning. The American Railway Development Association created a zoning committee that worked with other groups interested in the problem, while on the local level development men tried to educate and restrain officials.[48]

New in industrial development work was a greater willingness to work with real estate agents. Traditionally railroads had tried to avoid the use of realtors, but this attitude changed after 1945. Those roads, such as the Chesapeake and Ohio, that had relatively small parcels of industrial land scattered throughout their territories found that it was useful to establish a working arrangement with at least one realtor in each community. Meanwhile several roads established relationships with the Society of Industrial Realtors, an organization formed in 1941 that claimed a membership of 600 by 1954. Some carriers listed their industrial properties with members of the society. Others believed that they could at least make common cause with the organization on such matters as zoning ordinances and land taxes.[49]

As the problems of industrial land management grew more complex, some roads established subsidiaries to handle their industrial properties. According to the Western Pacific, which in 1953 reactivated its Standard Realty and Development Company, the use of a subsidiary produced savings in property taxes, permitted greater freedom in arranging construction contracts and outside financing, and allowed the company to manage its industrial properties with less attention to ICC and other government regulations and to sell lands without having to go through the formality of obtaining a release of mortgage. Inspired by similar reasons, the Denver and Rio Grande organized its Rio Grande Land Company in 1946. Among other roads with landholding subsidiaries were the Gulf, Mobile and Ohio, the Milwaukee, and the New York Central. By the early 1970s responsibility for acquisition and development of real estate on the Union Pacific was vested in its Upland Industries Corporation, while the Southern Pacific Land Company performed that function for its parent concern. On the other hand, in 1956 the Northern Pacific liquidated its sixty-year old Northwestern Improvement Company, claiming that accounting and administrative benefits resulted from the shift of land management to the parent company.

By the 1970s some carriers were moving beyond the traditional goals of industrial development in their land policies. The Southern Pacific Land Company, for example, was charged with the management of 3.9 million acres of agricultural, timber, and desert lands as well as 38,000 acres of industrial and commercial property. Responsibilities were divided into three categories. The industrial development division located industries in Southern Pacific territory; a real estate division managed the company's rail-related properties as well as office buildings in several cities; and a natural resources division handled the bulk of the agricultural and other lands. Meanwhile, the Southern Pacific Development Company developed company-owned land and assumed a dealer role in the sale of property, while Sequoia Pacific, another subsidiary, provided "specialized or complete turnkey services including planning, design, construction, and overall packaging" for industrial and other projects.[50]

New, too, were the roles of certain carriers in the development of air rights. Given the growing pressure on space in the downtown areas of the great cities, railroads were quick to recognize the potential value of the space over their yards, tracks, and terminals. Such space, one authority claimed, was worth from 75 to 80 percent as much as the land beneath it, and in Chicago alone in 1963 air space above railroad properties was estimated to be worth $100 million. In the 1960s the New York Central and the Pennsylvania were involved in the utilization of air space in New York City and Philadelphia, while in Chicago the Illinois Central went to court to defend rights that the carrier believed were worth $50 a share of company stock. Railroads serving Atlanta were also interested in air space utilization, and by the early 1970s the Burlington Northern was participating in air rights development in Seattle.[51]

While attempting in various ways to obtain new earnings from industrial property, many roads tried to increase the income from existing leases and to dispose of any property that had no value for either operating or industrial purposes. In the 1950s and later a number of carriers undertook lease review programs calculated to bring rents into line with current land values. Meanwhile several roads conducted excess property surveys and succeeded in disposing of sizable amounts of surplus land and in reducing their tax bills. In the 1960s the Rock Island launched a land sales program, and the Burlington employed an outside real estate consulting firm to appraise company property. When the survey was completed, the company began a campaign to sell all land not needed for railway operation or having little potential for industrial development.[52]

By such programs and procedures, industrial development men worked to generate new traffic and earnings for their companies. Certainly by the post-World War II years industrial promotion far overshadowed other forms of development work. Land settlement had long ceased to be a significant concern of railway companies, and agricultural and forestry development was soon to follow colonization work into history. But in a very real sense the location of industries along the tracks represented a logical evolution of railway promotion activities that had begun a century earlier. According to *Railway Age,* the leading voice of the industry, "Years ago, western railroads were the colonizers of the territory in bringing people out where the tracks went. And they are still doing the same job—only this time the 'immigrants' are whole companies, whole industries."[53]

CHAPTER TEN

Railway Development Work: An Evaluation

HISTORIANS HAVE GENERALLY AGREED that railroads were a major force in shaping American economic development in the nineteenth century. Leland H. Jenks's famous article written in the 1940s remains a classic, even if some of its conclusions have been challenged, and a number of writers have shown that the transcontinental lines "changed the nature of pioneering" by "outrunning the course of settlement."[1] But the developmental role of railroads did not end with the sale of the land grants, the disappearance of the frontier, or the opening of the twentieth century. Indeed, the era of railway promotion of economic development through creative traffic generation continued in the ninth decade of that century, although the character of the work had changed markedly over time.

Unlike other aspects of railway operation, the impact of most forms of development work was difficult to measure. When a railroad company opened a new line, executives could determine with reasonable accuracy the volume of traffic that the new line provided. An innovation in operating procedures or technology often produced a measurable reduction in operating expenses or a gain in operating revenues that railroadmen hoped could be carried through to net income. In contrast, the result of expenditures and effort in development work was seen only far in the future, and even then it was often impossible to separate the contribution of the railroads from that of other groups and agencies engaged in the same kinds of activity.

All railroad companies produced data purporting to show the results of their development programs, but those statistics demonstrated only imperfectly the role of the carriers. In colonization work, for example, railroadmen reported the numbers of people that poured through the major gateways and counted homeseekers carried, cars of immigrant movables handled, and settlers located in their companies' territories. In February 1906 some 25,000 homeseekers passed through three southwestern gateways in a single day, and as late as 1917 railroadmen claimed that 15,000 people went through St. Paul in a period of six weeks. Individual roads reported handling huge numbers of homeseekers. The Northern Pacific took 1,000 cars of immigrants to the West in the spring of 1907, and in 1906–1908 the Santa Fe hauled 5,228 carloads of immigrants to west Texas and central New Mexico. On the eve of American entry into World War I the Great Northern's E. C. Leedy stated that his road was still handling an average of 200 homeseekers a day.[2]

The volume of immigrant movable traffic was also huge. In the first three months of 1907 the Santa Fe took 1,340 cars to west Texas, and the next year the Texas and Pacific hauled 1,049 cars to points on its Rio Grande division. In March 1917 the Milwaukee took 100 cars to Montana.

Impressive, too, were the numbers of settlers actually placed along railroad lines. The Great Northern figured that in 1901 about 70,000 people settled in its territory. In the spring of 1910 the Hill roads and the Soo reported the location of 6,750 families in Minnesota, North Dakota, and Montana. In the Southwest the Frisco stated that it placed 1,508 farmers along its lines in 1904; a decade later the figure was 2,934, most of whom located in the Ozark region of Missouri.[3]

Results for southern carriers were not comparable to those of western roads, but they were by no means insignificant. The Alabama Great Southern, for example, claimed that in 1900 almost 800 newcomers bought or rented land along its line; two years later, the Southern reported that 583 northern and western farmers purchased land in its territory. During the thirteen years from 1905 through 1917, the Atlantic Coast Line placed in its territory over 27,000 heads of families, the great majority of whom were farmers. In 1907 the Illinois Central's J. F. Merry claimed that in a quarter century of work he had settled 1,500 Italian families in Mississippi alone. Later, when the Gulf and Ship Island was busily at work promoting the settlement of cutover lands in south Mississippi, it attracted 437 families during the years 1912–1915.[4]

All such data, however, left much to be desired, both by railroadmen called upon to justify colonization programs and by historians who later would seek to assess their impact. Numbers of homeseekers and colonists' tickets sold were no certain guide to results, since people who had no intention of becoming settlers took advantage of the reduced rates. Nor were figures on the movement of immigrant movable cars an accurate reflection of the magnitude of the work. As a general rule settlers moving relatively short distances were likely to ship their personal belongings, while those moving longer distances often sold their livestock and equipment, hoping to restock at their new locations. This tendency apparently became stronger in the 1920s, when in addition many settlers moved by truck or shipped their goods as less than carload freight.

Statistics on numbers of new farms established or farms sold along railroad lines, the number of acres homesteaded or purchased, and the increase in population also failed to provide accurate measurements of railroad contributions. A diversity of other individuals and groups were engaged in the same type of promotion work as were the railroads. "It is not . . . possible for an immigration official to measure even approximately how much he had succeeded or failed," noted one authority in 1912, "as so many other factors are working for the settlement of the region to which his attention is devoted."

The role of railroads in agricultural, mineral, and forestry promotion was equally difficult to evaluate. The objectives in brief were to increase output over the long run and to eliminate short-term seasonal or other variations in production. To a degree that made American agriculture the model for much of the remainder of the world, the first goal was reached in the mid-twentieth century, and certainly in large areas of the country the old one-crop economies of an earlier era had disappeared. In like fashion mineral output soared, and in woodlands wasteful and exploitive harvesting practices of the past had been replaced by modern scientific forest management procedures that promised to provide in the future a perpetual supply of lumber products.

Railroad programs certainly contributed to these accomplishments. An official of the U.S. Department of Agriculture acknowledged in 1912 "the great value of the service the railroads are rendering" through their development departments. Fifteen years later, in a study conducted in Kansas, authorities found that one-third of farm families contacted had been exposed to railway development programs and of that number one in seven reported they had benefited from the experience, a result that compared reasonably well with other kinds of extension teaching.

But railway development departments were by no means alone in their efforts to promote agriculture and forestry. The U.S. Department of Agriculture, the land-grant colleges with their experiment stations and extension services, farm machinery manufacturers, bankers, lumber companies, state departments of agriculture, and a multitude of others shared the work and made important contributions. Because of this "complex intermingling" of men and agencies, it was "extremely difficult to evaluate the contribution of each to the sum total. . . ."[5]

Specific examples demonstrated this point clearly. In 1905 the Long Island Railroad employed one of the pioneer agricultural development agents and directed him to improve farming on Long Island. Results were mixed, partly because of the rapid urbanization of the island, but the percentage of farmland in Suffolk County that was improved increased from 47 in 1900 to 90 in 1920. Similarly the Missouri Pacific could point to notable results in its efforts to promote peach production in the Crowley's Ridge area of Arkansas. Between 1919 and 1939 output in a five-county area jumped 600 percent while statewide production fell 32 percent. In the earlier year, growers on Crowley's Ridge produced only 1 percent of the peaches in the state; twenty years later, the percentage was 13; and in the 1970s the area remained important for its output of peaches.[6] But in both instances the state agricultural extension services as well as other agencies were at work, making it impossible to determine the impact of the carrier's activities.

On a larger scale the problem of assessing the contribution of railroad agricultural, forestry, and mineral programs is magnified. Railroads undoubtedly were significant forces in popularizing soybeans and in promoting the growing of alfalfa, sugar beets, and the full range of truck crops and fruit. The Illinois Central certainly contributed over a period of a half century to an expansion and upgrading of dairying and livestock production in the territory served by its southern lines. Such roads as the Burlington, Great Northern, Union Pacific, and Santa Fe played major roles in developing viable systems of agriculture on irrigation projects in their territories and in helping farmers meet the unique problems of High Plains agriculture. Southern roads were important in the shaping of the South's "third forest" which held so much promise for the future of that section. Railroad geologists helped to make available to the nation its mineral resources. But again in every instance other agencies, including publicly supported ones, shared the goals of the railroads and conducted promotional and educational programs that had much in common with those offered by the carriers. Indeed, it was in large measure the growth of publicly supported work that in time induced the railroads to terminate their development programs in agriculture and forestry.

The impact of railway industrial development work is also difficult to measure. Most carriers reported from time to time the number of firms that were located or that expanded their operations along their lines. In some instances the data included the number of jobs created, the investment in new enterprises or in the extension of existing ones, and the volume of traffic that the roads serving the concerns was expected to gain.

According to such reports, railroads located huge numbers of new businesses even during the early years of systematic industrial development work. George C. Power, the pioneer industrial agent of the Illinois Central, claimed to have placed 169 new businesses along his road during the years 1895–1900. These results were quickly overshadowed by those of other carriers. The Southern told its stockholders that from 1900 through 1914 there were 8,337 new firms representing an investment of $500 million established along its lines. Between 1905 and 1915 the Rock Island claimed 1,877 new industries, valued at $78 million and employing 55,900 workers. Atlantic Coast Line locations equalled 2,000 between 1905 and 1914, while the Central of Georgia bagged 1,269 with an aggregate investment of $25 million and a work force of 31,500 in a period of seven years.

Most of these firms were small. The Missouri Pacific reported the location or expansion of 5,027 businesses between 1907 and 1917; the average investment was $36,000. Among 92 industries located by the Norfolk and Western in 1902 were 36 different kinds of businesses. Most common were saw mills, which numbered 22, followed by ice plants, flour mills, canneries, coal mines, cement works, and a chair factory.[7]

Patterns did not change markedly in the 1920s and 1930s, although numbers of firms located by most railroads fell off in the Depression Decade. Between 1921 and 1927, for example, the Chesapeake and Ohio averaged 129 new industries a year; the figure for 1931–1936 was 83. On the other hand, the Illinois Central counted 1,233 new firms between 1929 and 1936, generally favorable results that management attributed in part to the depression itself. Executives of some firms recognized that prevailing low prices for land and materials afforded opportunities that would evaporate later, while lowered profit margins forced other enterprisers to relocate where production and distribution costs were lower. Most firms were still small; average investment in firms located on the Missouri Pacific between 1920 and 1939 was $39,750. Among the 325 industries placed along the Frisco in 1930 were 92 oil distribution plants, 61 coal yards, and 49 warehouses, as well as a number of cotton compresses and gins, canneries, grain elevators, and creameries.[8]

In the post-World War II era railroads continued to report their accomplishments in industrial development work, in general presenting the same kinds of information as earlier. Between 1959 and 1970 the Gulf, Mobile and Ohio located 912 new firms, while 342 existing concerns underwent expansions. The Union Pacific counted 3,883 new industries in 1954–1969, and during the twenty years after 1945 the Atlantic Coast Line averaged 176 new businesses and 54 expansions of existing firms per year. The newly merged Erie-Lackawanna claimed 383 new and expanded firms in 1960–1963; results in 1968–1971, when the company's fortunes had declined sharply, equalled 261. In the decade of the 1970s, the Burlington Northern gained 5,486 new firms, while the Southern Pacific counted 5,222 in the 1970–1978 period.[9]

Small firms still dominated in terms of numbers, but the average investment had jumped sharply. Between 1946 and 1959, for example, the Missouri Pacific reported the location or expansion of 6,263 firms representing a total investment of over $3 billion, giving an average of $483,000, a dramatic increase over the pre-World War II figures. In the 1950s the Southern Railway calculated that 16 percent of the firms located along that line after 1945 represented a capital investment of more than $500,000. Average investment in firms located by the Southern Pacific in the 1970s was over $920,000.[10]

The great prizes in industrial development work were those giant installations of major companies that almost assuredly would provide substantial volumes of traffic over many years. All major roads were able to report such locations from time to time. In the 1920s the Boston and Maine placed at East Somerville, Massachusetts, a Ford Motor Company plant that at the outset turned out 500 automobiles a day. Among the new industries located by the Southern Pacific in 1930 were three that represented investments of more than $5 million each. The Seaboard's prize catch in 1936 was a $4 million paper mill at Savannah.[11]

Giant installations became both larger and more numerous after World War II. In the early 1960s the New York Central was able to report the location of three steel mills; a decade later, despite its many problems, the Penn Central succeeded in attracting a number of major installations of prominent companies; and in 1976 Conrail began to serve a new Miller brewery at Fullerton, New York, that represented an investment of $239 million. In 1967 the Louisville and Nashville located at Louisville, Kentucky, a truck assembly plant of Ford Motor Company that was expected to employ 3,000 workers. One of the largest plants in New Hampshire appeared on the lines of the Boston and Maine when in 1968 Anheuser-Busch started construction of a $40 million brewery at Merrimack. A major development in the Northwest in the 1960s was the location near Bellingham, Washington, on the lines of the Great Northern of a $60 million aluminum reduction plant, a joint project of the American Metal Climax, Howe Sound Company, and Pechiney of France. The Chicago and North Western was able to report in 1973 the location at Norfolk, Nebraska, of the first steel mill in that state.[12]

In contrast to other areas of development work, railroadmen believed that they could estimate promptly and with a reasonable degree of accuracy the new traffic generated by their industrial programs. Indeed, such calculations were often the determining factors in decisions to offer industrial sites to firms and to install industrial sidetracks. The Erie figured that a new Ford assembly plant placed at Mahwah, New Jersey, would generate $9 million in new revenues annually when it went into production in 1955. The Frisco was understandably pleased when in the early 1970s it located a Schlitz brewery on its lines at Memphis; the installation was expected to swell the Frisco's freight revenues by some $3 million each year. Officers of Burlington Northern calculated that the line gained some $644 million in revenues as a result of locations registered in the decade of the 1970s.[13]

Another product of industrial development work—the gain in rents on industrial properties—was measurable. On the Northern Pacific, for example, gross rental income rose from $1.3 million in 1956 to $2.5 million thirteen years later. On the other hand, the Rock Island's rents declined from $1.6 million in 1968 to $1.3 million in 1973, the result of that company's sales of industrial properties to raise funds for other purposes.[14]

Long-term results of industrial development work could be seen in a number of ways. Numerous roads were able to point to increasing diversification in their traffic mixes. Executives of the Missouri Pacific watched with approval as the percentage of agricultural commodities in the road's total freight declined from 23 percent in 1945 to 16 percent a decade later. The Rock Island reported a sizable gain in freight revenues in 1962, despite generally poor crops in its territory, a result that "demonstrates . . . that we are making progress in our continuing efforts to build up non-agricultural business so as to minimize the effects of poor crops on our earnings," the road's president noted. The Chesapeake and Ohio attributed a gain in merchandise tonnage in the early 1950s, when other roads were suffering losses, to its industrial development work. A decade later executives of the Norfolk and Western were pleased with the company's coal traffic, which generated a substantial portion of its total revenues, but at the same time they hoped that the company's industrial development work would reduce its dependence on that "one crop."[15]

Railroadmen could also point to any number of specific areas where industrial development efforts had helped to bring about economic change. The San Leandro, California, area reported the gaining of $64 million in new industry during the years 1947–1952, much of which was due to the work of the Southern Pacific and the Western Pacific. During the decade beginning in 1954 fourteen railroads serving Texas brought in over 4,400 firms worth $2 billion and employing 84,000 persons. The Illinois Central claimed that during the first fifteen years after World War II it helped to attract 500 industries to Mississippi, a state badly in need of industrial development. That carrier also took credit for the location of numerous chemical firms along the lower Mississippi River between Baton Rouge and New Orleans where, by the late 1960s, one of the major industrial-chemical complexes in the nation existed.[16]

Still even these indications of results failed to demonstrate clearly the impact of railway efforts. The location of industry, a highly complex process, involved utility companies and banks, a variety of local promotional groups, state development agencies, and others. A railroad's industrial development department, in final analysis, was only one of several forces involved in the location of a given firm, and its contribution to the end result could not in most instances be isolated from those of other agencies. Indeed, one railroad industrial development man wrote in 1961 that "by the time a decision on a new plant location has been made, there have usually been so 'many fingers in the pie' that no single individual can claim exclusive credit for landing the industry."[17]

That observation would have been equally applicable to all kinds of development work in the twentieth century, but it does not detract from the significance of railway programs. For a century or more, inspired by the recognition that their prosperity has depended upon the prosperity of the country they serve, American railroads have settled land, promoted agricultural, mineral, and forest development, and located industries along their lines. No other institutions have been engaged in the work for that period of time; no other groups have had such diverse programs; certainly no other private enterprises have spent such large sums of money to promote economic development. In short, through their creative traffic generating activities, railroads have contributed much to the growth and configuration of the nation's economy.

NOTES

CHAPTER ONE

1. For a discussion of creative and competitive traffic generation, see Railway Development Association, *Proceedings of the Semi-Annual Meeting,* 1914 (n.p., n.d.), 23; American Railway Development Association, *Proceedings,* 1922 (n.p., n.d.), 26; Ira G. Clark, *Then Came the Railroads: The Century from Steam to Diesel in the Southwest* (Norman, 1958), 275; Henry S. Haines, *Railway Corporations as Public Servants* (New York, 1907), 67.

2. William S. Greever, "A Comparison of Railroad Land-Grant Policies," *Agricultural History* 25(Apr. 1951):84; Ida M. W. Lowe, "The Role of the Railroads in the Settlement of the Texas Panhandle" (M.A. thesis, West Texas State College, Canyon, 1962), 2; Thomas L. Miller, *The Public Lands of Texas, 1819-1970* (Norman, 1971), 101-2; John F. Stover, *The Life and Decline of the American Railroad* (New York, 1970), 60; Lloyd J. Mercer, "Land Grants to American Railroads: Social Costs or Social Benefit?" *Business History Review* 43(Summer 1969):134-35; John S. Cochran, "Economic Importance of Early Transcontinental Railroads: Pacific Northwest," *Oregon Historical Quarterly* 71(Mar. 1970):27-98; Paul W. Gates, "The Railroad Land-Grant Legend," *Journal of Economic History* 14(Spring 1954):143-46; Robert S. Henry, "The Railroad Land Grant Legend in American History Texts," *Mississippi Valley Historical Review* 32(Sept. 1945):171-94; Robert G. Athearn, *Union Pacific Country* (New York, 1971), 378. For the views of one of the leaders in the railroad industry of the time, see Thomas C. Cochran, *Railroad Leaders, 1845-1890: The Business Mind in Action* (Cambridge, 1953), 203-4.

3. Paul W. Gates, *The Farmer's Age: Agriculture, 1815-1860* (New York, 1960), 184-85; George Rogers Taylor, *The Transportation Revolution, 1815-1860* (New York, 1951), 95-96; Frank Andrews, "Railroads and Farming," United States Bureau of Statistics, *Bulletin* 100(Washington, 1912):18. For a critical view of railway promotional work on the western prairies, see David M. Emmons, *Garden in the Grasslands: Boomer Literature of the Central Great Plains* (Lincoln: Univ. of Nebraska Press, 1971), 25-46. Under roughly comparable conditions railroads in Argentina carried on similar colonization work. James R. Scobie, *Argentina: A City and a Nation* (New York, 1964), 113-14.

4. Paul W. Gates, *The Illinois Central Railroad and Its Colonization Work* (Cambridge, 1934), 149-50, 171-81, 332; Gates, "The Promotion of Agriculture by the Illinois Central Railroad, 1855-1870," *Agricultural History* 5(Apr. 1931):57-76; Howard F. Bennett, "The Hannibal and St. Joseph Railroad and the Development of Northern Missouri, 1847-1870: A Study of Land and Colonization Policies" (Ph.D. diss., Harvard University, 1951); Richard C. Overton, *Burlington West: A Colonization History of the Burlington Railroad* (Cambridge, 1941); Ian MacPherson, "Better Britons for the Burlington: A Study of the Selective Ap-

proach of the Chicago, Burlington and Quincy in Great Britain, 1871–1875," *Nebraska History* 50(Winter 1969):373–407; Frederick C. Luebke, *Immigrants and Politics: The Germans of Nebraska, 1880–1900* (Lincoln, 1969), 26–27.

5. Athearn, *Union Pacific*, 148–76; Morris N. Spencer, "The Union Pacific's Utilization of Its Land Grant with Emphasis on Its Colonization Program" (Ph.D. diss., University of Nebraska, 1950), 85–103, 124, 140–47, 184, 189, 197–227; Barry B. Combs, "The Union Pacific Railroad and the Early Settlement of Nebraska, 1868–1880," *Nebraska History* 50(Spring 1969):1–26.

6. James B. Hedges, "The Colonization Work of the Northern Pacific Railroad," *Mississippi Valley Historical Review* 13(Dec. 1926):311–42; Hedges, "Promotion of Immigration to the Pacific Northwest by the Railroads," *Mississippi Valley Historical Review* 15(Sept. 1928):183–203; Stanley N. Murray, *The Valley Comes of Age: A History of Agriculture in the Valley of the Red River of the North, 1812–1920* (Fargo, 1967), 65–68; Murray, "Railroads and the Agricultural Development of the Red River Valley of the North," *Agricultural History* 31(Oct. 1957):59–61; Hiram M. Drache, *The Day of the Bonanza: A History of Bonanza Farming in the Red River Valley of the North* (Fargo, 1964), 42–44; Drache, "The Economic Aspects of the Northern Pacific Railroad in North Dakota," *North Dakota History* 34(Fall 1967):321–72; Ronald H. Ridgley, "Railroads and the Development of the Dakotas, 1872–1914" (Ph.D. diss., Indiana University, 1967), 31.

7. L. L. Waters, *Steel Trails to Santa Fe* (Lawrence, 1950), 221–51; Glenn D. Bradley, *The Story of the Santa Fe* (Boston, 1920), 107, 109–13, 126–37; James Marshall, *Santa Fe: The Railroad that Built an Empire* (New York, 1945), 81–86; Keith L. Bryant, Jr., *History of the Atchison, Topeka and Santa Fe Railway* (New York, 1974), 64–73. The handling of Santa Fe's lands in Arizona and New Mexico is discussed in William S. Greever, *Arid Domain: The Santa Fe Railway and Its Western Land Grant* (Stanford, 1954). See also Kendal Bailes, "The Mennonites Come to Kansas," *American Heritage* 10(Aug. 1959):107, 109–13, 126–37.

8. Edna M. Parker, "The Southern Pacific Railroad and the Settlement of Southern California," *Pacific Historical Review* 6(June 1937):103–19; Neill C. Wilson and Frank J. Taylor, *Southern Pacific: The Roaring Story of a Fighting Railroad* (New York, 1952), 86–87; Walter L. Fleming, "Immigration to the Southern States," *Political Science Quarterly* 20(June 1905):289–90.

9. Robert L. Martin, *The City Moves West: Economic and Industrial Growth in Central West Texas* (Austin, 1969), 20–21; Ralph N. Traxler, Jr., "The Texas and Pacific Railroad Land Grants: A Comparison of Land Grant Policies of the United States and Texas," *Southwestern Historical Quarterly* 61(Jan. 1958):367–69; Kenneth M. Hammer, "Dakota Railroads" (Ph.D. diss., South Dakota State University, 1966), 148, 152; John B. Rae, "The Great Northern's Land Grant," *Journal of Economic History* 12(Spring 1952):140; H. Craig Miner, *The St. Louis-San Francisco Transcontinental Railroad: The Thirty-Fifth Parallel Project, 1853–1890* (Lawrence, 1972), 54–55, 144–46; Richard C. Overton, *Gulf to Rockies: The Heritage of the Fort Worth and Denver-Colorado and Southern Railways, 1861–1898* (Austin, 1953), 212–14; Arlan C. Helgeson, *Farms in the Cutover: Agricultural Settlement in Northern Wisconsin* (Madison, 1962), 4–5; Willis F. Dunbar, *All Aboard! A History of Railroads in Michigan* (Grand Rapids, 1969), 107–8, 114–15.

10. Rowland T. Berthoff, "Southern Attitudes toward Immigration, 1865–1914," *Journal of Southern History* 17(Aug. 1951):333; Bert J. Loewenberg, "Efforts of the South to Encourage Immigration, 1865–1900," *South Atlantic Quarterly* 33(Oct. 1934):374–75, 377–79; Maury Klein, "Southern Railroad Leaders, 1865–1893: Identities and Ideologies," *Business History Review* 42(Autumn 1968):296; William W. Rogers, "Reuben F. Kolb: Agricultural Leader of the New South," *Agricultural History* 32(Apr. 1958):116–17; Robert L. Brandfon, *Cotton*

Kingdom in the New South: A History of the Yazoo Mississippi Delta from Reconstruction to the Twentieth Century (Cambridge, 1967), 99, 103–12; Jonathan J. Wolfe, "Background of German Immigration to Arkansas," *Arkansas Historical Quarterly* 25(1966):161–63, 175, 259–66; Jesse C. Burt, "History of the Nashville, Chattanooga and St. Louis Railway, 1873–1916" (Ph.D. diss., Vanderbilt University, 1950), 179–83; Robert L. Brandfon, "The End of Immigration to the Cotton Fields," *Mississippi Valley Historical Review* 50(Mar. 1964):591–611.

11. Carlton J. Corliss, *Main Line of Mid-America: The Story of the Illinois Central* (New York, 1950), 293–94, 298; James L. McCorkle, Jr., "Nineteenth Century Beginnings of the Commercial Vegetable Industry in Mississippi," *Journal of Mississippi History* 30(Nov. 1968):264; Klein, "Southern Railroad Leaders," 296; Burt, "Nashville, Chattanooga and St. Louis," 184–85.

12. Murray, *Agriculture in the Valley of the Red River*, 155, 161–62, 171, 174; James J. Hill, "Our Wealth in Swamp and Desert," *World's Work* 19(Feb. 1910):12602–4.

13. Athearn, *Union Pacific*, 167; C. Clyde Jones, "A Survey of the Agricultural Development Program of the Chicago, Burlington and Quincy Railroad," *Nebraska History* 30(Sept. 1949):235–36; Overton, *Burlington West*, 486; Lesley M. Heathcoat, "The Montana Arid Land Commission, 1895–1903," *Agricultural History* 38(Apr. 1964):108–9; Murray, *Agriculture in the Valley of the Red River*, 67; Clark, *Then Came the Railroads*, 208; *Oregon Agriculturist* 9(1 Nov. 1899), 50.

14. Athearn, *Union Pacific*, 173–75, 181; Mary W. M. Hargreaves, "Hardy Webster Campbell (1850–1937)," *Agricultural History* 32(Jan. 1958):63; Overton, *Burlington West*, 486; John A. Gjevre, *Saga of the Soo: West from Shoreham* (n.p. 1973), 40.

15. D. J. Crosby to W. H. Boos, 14 Apr. 1913, Agricultural Extension Service Records (National Archives, Washington, D.C.); *Long Island Railroad Information Bulletin* 5(Oct. 1927):79–81; F. B. Mumford to John H. Curran, 12 Mar. 1910, Missouri Agricultural College Papers (University of Missouri Library, Columbia).

16. *Railway Age Gazette* 48(10 June 1910):1428; 52(19 Jan., 14 June 1912):120, 1352; Missouri Pacific-Iron Mountain System, *Home Builder in Arkansas* (St. Louis, 1911), 85; C. Clyde Jones, "The Agricultural Development Program of the Chicago, Burlington and Quincy Railroad" (Ph.D. diss., Northwestern University, 1954), 68–69; *New York Central Lines Magazine* 10(Dec. 1929):66, 106; Southern Railway Company, *Annual Report*, 1912, 10; *Railway World* 58(May 1914):417; Norfolk and Western Railway Company, *Industrial and Shippers' Guide* (Roanoke, 1916), 3; *Progressive Farmer*, 32(8 Dec. 1917):1298.

17. *Railway Review* 55(21 Nov. 1914):636; *Railway and Engineering Review* 40(10 Mar. 1900):134; Francis W. Hoadley, "How Railroads Aid Industrial Development," *Cassier's Magazine* 41(Feb. 1912):189–92; Ira H. Shoemaker, "The Industrial Department of a Railroad," *Independent* 67(15 July 1909):134–35.

18. *Railway Age* 40(14 July 1905):46–47; *Railway Gazette* 39(22 Dec. 1905):586–87; *Chemical and Metallurgical Engineering* 20(1 June 1919):558; Mildred Throne, "Suggested Research on Railroad Aid to the Farmer, with Particular Reference to Iowa and Kansas," *Agricultural History* 31(Oct. 1957):50–56.

19. Railway Development Association, *Proceedings*, 1915, 41–42; Gulf and Ship Island Railroad Company, *Annual Report*, 1912, 6; Delaware and Hudson Company, *A Century of Progress: History of the Delaware and Hudson Company, 1823–1923* (Albany, 1925), 330; Howard D. Dozier, *A History of the Atlantic Coast Line Railroad* (New York, 1971), 155; *American Railroads* 1(12 July 1920):4; Jacob E. Anderson, *80 Years of Transportation Progress: A History of the St. Louis Southwestern Railway* (Tyler, 1957), 61; Baltimore and Ohio Railroad Company, *Annual Report*, 1916, 10.

20. A Century of Agricultural Progress along the Illinois Central Railroad, memo supplied by Paul K. Farlow; Corliss, *Illinois Central,* 293–300; *Illinois Central Employes' Magazine* 2(Mar. 1911):575; *Illinois Central Magazine* 19(Sept. 1930):25; Illinois Central Railroad: Agricultural Development, memo supplied by Paul K. Farlow.

21. Illinois Central Railroad and Yazoo and Mississippi Valley Railroad, *Official Directory of Classified Industries for Buyers and Shippers* (Chicago, 1925), 17; *Illinois Central Magazine* 30(Jan. 1942):9; *Railway Age* 87(20 July 1929):229; R. J. Taylor to author, 16 Jan. 1970.

22. Nick Blazowich to author, 15 Feb. 1970; History of Industrial Development along the Norfolk and Western, memo supplied by Norfolk and Western Railway Company.

23. *Railway Age Gazette* 56(22 May 1914):1131; Railway Development Association, *Proceedings,* 1917, 65–66; New York Central System, *Finding a Farm in the Land of Shorter Hauls to Bigger Markets* (n.p. 1946); Louisville and Nashville Railroad Company, *Directory of Industries* (n.p., n.d.), 13; *Traffic World* 89(3 May 1952):71; R. E. Bisha to author, 6 Mar. 1961; *Industrial Development* 129(Aug. 1960):58, 66–67.

24. Victor H. Schoffelmayer, *Southwest Trails to New Horizons* (San Antonio, 1960), 2, 5; *Railway and Engineering Review* 50(11 June 1910):542.

25. *Railway World* 48(17 Dec. 1904):1425; *Illinois Central Magazine* 19(Sept. 1930):25; *Railway and Engineering Review* 51(11 Nov. 1911):987; Industrial Real Estate, memo supplied by the Norfolk and Western Railroad Company.

26. *Railway Age* 153(6 Aug. 1962):24; *Industrial Development* 135(July 1966):67–70.

27. Railway Development Association, *Proceedings of the Semi-Annual Meeting,* 1915, 77; *Traffic World* 51(11 Mar. 1933):501; *Railway and Engineering Review* 47(12 Jan. 1907):21; American Railway Development Association, Executive Committee, *Proceedings,* 1942, 99–102, 108–10; *Long Island Railroad Information Bulletin* 5(July–Aug. 1928):36.

28. American Railway Development Association, *Proceedings,* 1925, 7; 1946, 4; 1949, 11.

29. *Southern Farm Magazine* 8(15 Apr. 1903), n.p.; *Railway World* 48(19 Nov. 1904):1314; American Railway Development Association, *Proceedings,* 1928, 81; 1929, 147–48; 1931, 103–7; 1932, 136–38; 1953, 22–24; *Manufacturers Record* 77(15 Apr. 1920):117; *Illinois Central Magazine* 12(Feb. 1924):38.

30. *Traffic World* 51(11 Mar. 1933):502.

31. U.S. Interstate Commerce Commission, *Uniform System of Accounts for Railroad Companies,* 1 Jan. 1968 (Washington, n.d.), 62.

32. All statistics taken or compiled from U.S. Interstate Commerce Commission, *Statistics of Railways in the United States,* 1908–1971 (Washington, 1909–1972). Title varies. Figures for 1908–1910 are for "large roads," those with mileage in excess of 250 or annual operating revenues of more than $1 million. Beginning with 1911 all figures are for Class I carriers. Data for districts have been compiled to produce geographical and statistical consistency. The 1967 dollar values have been calculated by using the wholesale price index.

33. Quoted in Jones, "Agricultural Development Program of the Chicago, Burlington and Quincy Railroad," 5, 6; *Sales Management* 71(1 Oct. 1955):28.

CHAPTER TWO

1. Spencer, "Union Pacific's Utilization of Its Land Grant," 10, 293, 363–64; Union Pacific Railroad Company, *Wyoming: Its Resources and Attractions* (Omaha,

1903), 48; Ross R. Cotroneo, "The History of the Northern Pacific Land Grant, 1900–1952" (Ph.D. diss., University of Idaho, 1967), 143, 162; *Railway World* 50(4 May 1906):379; Jones, "Agricultural Development Program of the Chicago, Burlington and Quincy Railroad," 56.

2. Paul W. Gates, *History of Public Land Law Development* (Washington, 1968), 452–54, 464–65, 498–519; *Rock Island Employes' Magazine* 8(Aug. 1914):29; Herbert S. Schell, *History of South Dakota* (Lincoln, 1961), 328–32; *Commercial West* 6(3 Dec. 1904):26; 16(17 July 1909):44, 51; *Railway World* 51(20 Sept. 1907):789.

3. David B. Gracy, *Littlefield Lands: Colonization on the Texas Plains, 1912–1920* (Austin, 1968), 4–10, 99; B. R. Brunson, *The Texas Land and Development Company: A Panhandle Promotion, 1912–1956* (Austin, 1970), 3, 5; *Commercial West* 6(5 Nov. 1904):30; Chicago, Milwaukee and St. Paul Railway Company, *Many Acres Open to Settlers* (n.p. 1907); Chicago, Milwaukee, and St. Paul, Railway Company, *Montana* (Chicago, n.d.).

4. *Railway and Engineering Review* 45(9 Sept. 1905):654–55; Rose M. Boening, "History of Irrigation in the State of Washington," *Washington Historical Quarterly* 10(Jan. 1919):22–24; Calvin B. Coulter, "The Victory of National Irrigation in the Yakima Valley, 1902–1906," *Pacific Northwest Quarterly* 42(Apr. 1951):101; John Fahey, *Inland Empire: D. C. Corbin and Spokane* (Seattle, 1965), 202, 204, 206; E. C. Leedy, "The West Okanogan Irrigation Project," *Western Magazine* 7(Nov. 1915):9–15; *Engineering Record* 74(25 Nov. 1916):640; Mary W. M. Hargreaves, *Dry Farming in the Northern Great Plains, 1900–1925* (Cambridge, 1957), 457.

5. *Railway and Engineering Review* 44(9 Apr. 1904):269; John T. Ganoe, "The Origin of a National Reclamation Policy," *Mississippi Valley Historical Review* 18(June 1931):41; Samuel P. Hays, *Conservation and the Gospel of Efficiency: The Progressive Conservation Movement, 1890–1920* (New York, 1969), 10–11; *Commercial West* 7(2 Sept. 1905):27; Ridgley, "Railroads and the Development of the Dakotas," 128.

6. *Southern Farm Magazine* 9(Aug. 1901):25; 11(Sept. 1903):16; Missouri Pacific-Iron Mountain System, *Home Builder in Arkansas,* 83.

7. Missouri Pacific-Iron Mountain Route, *Louisiana* (St. Louis, n.d.), 15; Burt, "Nashville, Chattanooga and St. Louis Railway," 177; *Railway World* 48(17 Dec 1904):1431–32.

8. *Southern Farm Magazine* 10(Apr. 1902):28; 11(Apr. 1903):26; *Manufacturers Record* 60(21 Dec. 1911):49; Lee A. Dew, *The JLC&E: The History of an Arkansas Railroad* (State University, 1968), 48–49; *Southern Planter* 68(June 1907):561–62.

9. St. Louis Southwestern Railway Company, *Annual Report,* 1906, 53; St. Louis Southwestern Railway, *The St. Francis Country: Southeast Missouri and Northeast Arkansas* (St. Louis, 1906); *Manufacturers Record* 55(1 Apr. 1909):56; 71(31 May 1917):62b.

10. *Railway Gazette* 36(29 Apr. 1904):332; *Railway Review* 59(12 Aug. 1916):202; *Commercial West* 22(24 Aug. 1912):30; Helgeson, *Agricultural Settlement,* 44; *Ohio Farmer* 140(1 Sept. 1917):161. See also James I. Clark's *Farming the Cutover: The Settlement of Northern Wisconsin* (Madison, 1956), and *Cutover Problems: Colonization, Depression, Reforestation* (Madison: 1956).

11. *Commercial West* 17(18 June 1910):49; *Railway Age Gazette* 51(24 Nov. 1911):1071; 55(12 Dec. 1913):1140.

12. John Sebastion to James Wilson, Secretary of Agriculture Records (National Archives, Washington); *Current Events* 1(1 July 1901):3.

13. *Manufacturers Record* 43(19 Feb. 1903):84–85; *Commercial West* 17(22 Jan. 1910):35.

14. Illinois Central Railroad Company, *About the South* (Chicago, 1904); Northern Pacific Railway Company, *Montana: The Treasure State* (n.p. 1913), 53; *Commercial West* 19(28 Jan. 1911):37; Denver and Rio Grande Railroad Company, *The Fertile Lands of Colorado and Northern New Mexico* (n.p. 1912), 3.

15. *Annalist* 3(15 June 1914):746; Illinois Central and Yazoo and Mississippi Valley Railroads, *Southern Homeseekers' Guide* (Louisville, 1898), 3, 4; St. Louis and San Francisco Railway Company, *North and Central Texas along the Frisco Lines* (n.p., n.d.), 3-6, 9-10. See also Patrick J. Brunet "'Can't Hurt, and May Do You Some Good': A Study of the Pamphlets the Southern Pacific Railroad Used to Induce Immigration to Texas," *East Texas Historical Journal* 16(1978):35-45.

16. Chicago, Milwaukee and St. Paul Railway Company, *Montana;* Chicago, Milwaukee and St. Paul, *Many Acres Open to Settlers;* Union Pacific Railroad Company, *Oregon Wheat Lands* (n.p., n.d.), 5; Chicago and North Western Railway Company, *The Black Hills: A Description of a Wonderful and Picturesque Mining Region and Natural Sanitarium* (n.p. 1903), 5; *Commercial West* 16(17 July 1909):51.

17. Illinois Central and Yazoo and Mississippi Valley Railroads, *Southern Homeseekers' Guide*, 3, 10, 11, 66, 97, 135, 164-67; Missouri Pacific Railway Company, *Louisiana* (n.p., n.d.), 15, 57; Louisville and Nashville Railroad Company, *Pass Christian, Mississippi* (Louisville, n.d.), 2.

18. *Railway Age* 33(27 June 1902):955; *Oregon Agriculturist* 1(1 Apr. 1905):210; *Southern Farm Magazine* 2(Jan. 1904):10; Chicago, Milwaukee and St. Paul Railway Company, *Map of South Dakota and Letters from Settlers* (n.p., n.d.); Northern Pacific Railway Company, *What Settlers Say Over Their Own Signatures* (n.p., n.d.), 11; Illinois Central Railroad Company, *About the South*, 52-54, 58.

19. *Commercial West* 2(12 Oct. 1901):26; *Manufacturers Record* 40(19 Sept. 1901):138; 42(25 Sept. 1902):169; 52(5 Sept. 1907):192-93; 60(9 Nov. 1911):62; *Milwaukee Railway System Employes' Magazine* 4(Nov. 1916):15-16; *Railway World* 58(May 1914):416.

20. *Manufacturers Record* 62(21 Nov., 31 Oct. 1912):56, 57; 64(7 Aug. 1913):62.

21. *Railway Age Gazette* 53(30 Aug. 1912):402; *Manufacturers Record* 54(15 Oct. 1908):51; J. C. Clair to J. C. Hardy, 10 Oct. 1911, J. C. Hardy Papers (Mississippi State University Library); Atlantic Coast Line Railroad Company, *Annual Report,* 1912, 10; 1913, 8; 1914, 8; 1917, 7.

22. *Southern Farm Magazine* 9(Oct. 1901):26-27; 11(July 1903):27; 13(July 1905):24; *Manufacturers Record* 43(19 Feb., 4 June 1903):85-86, 395; *Commercial West* 5(5 Dec. 1903):5; 6(17 Sept. 1904):25.

23. *Railway World* 54(3 June 1910):440; *American Fertilizer* 35(7 Oct. 1911):50; *Railway Age Gazette* 54(27 June 1913):1618; *Breeder's Gazette* 57(15 June 1910):1380.

24. Missouri, Kansas and Texas Railway Company, *Annual Report,* 1906, 10; *Railway World* 48(27 Dec. 1914):1426-27; *Manufacturers Record* 40(28 Nov. 1901):332; *Railway Age* 34(19 Dec. 1902):687.

25. *Railway World* 48(17 Dec. 1904):1426-27; *Commercial West* 11(11 May 1907):4; *Manufacturers Record* 43(29 Jan. 1903):30; *Railway Age Gazette* 49(16 Sept. 1910):510; *Southern Farm Magazine* 13(Nov. 1905):30; *Manufacturers Record* 43(25 June, 16 July 1903):458, 515.

26. *Railway Age* 33(24 Jan. 1902):101-2; Atlantic Coast Line Railroad Company, *Annual Report,* 1913, 9.

27. *Railway Age* 37(11 Mar. 1904):392; *Southern Farm Magazine* 12(July 1904):25.

28. Berthoff, "Southern Attitudes toward Immigration," 34; *Manufacturers*

Record 47(4 May 1905):342; *Railway World* 51(4 Jan. 1907):11–12; John V. Baiamonte, Jr., "Immigrants in Rural America: A Study of the Italians of Tangipahoa Parish, Louisiana (Ph.D. diss., Mississippi State University, 1972), 58–61; *Commercial West* 23(1 Mar. 1913):15; Fleming, "Immigration to the Southern States," 288; *Railway World* 57(Mar. 1913):254.

29. Emory R. Johnson and Grover G. Huebner, *Railroad Traffic and Rates* (New York, 1911) 2:117–21; *Railway World* 46(6 Dec. 1902):1370; 48(10 Dec. 1904):1403–5; *Re Transportation of Immigrants from New York,* 10 ICC 13.

30. *Railway and Engineering Review* 52(16 Mar. 1912):209.

31. Andrews, "Railroads and Farming," 24; H. G. Shedd, "Securing Settlers for Private Irrigation Projects," in *Proceedings of the Second Pan American Scientific Congress* (11 vols., Washington, 1917), 3:520; *Commercial West* 10(10 Nov. 1906):55; Railway Development Association, *Proceedings,* 1913, 23; *Railway and Engineering Review* 52(28 Sept. 1912):888.

32. Andrews, "Railroads and Farming," 25; *Railway World* 46(9 Aug. 1902):893; 46(1 Nov. 1902):1230; *Railway Age* 34(25 July 1902):98; *Railway Gazette* 44(21 Feb. 1908):259; *Railway Age Gazette* 55(17 Oct. 1913):717.

33. *Railway World* 48(9 Jan. 1902):892; *Manufacturers Record* 49(1 Mar. 1906):173.

34. Kansas City Southern Railway Company, *The Ozark Region of Western Missouri and Arkansas* (Kansas City, n.d.), 48; Denver and Rio Grande Railroad Company, *Fertile Lands of Colorado and New Mexico,* 3.

35. *Railway Age* 35(6 Feb. 1903):207; Railway Development Association, *Proceedings,* 1913, 23–24; *Proceedings of the Semi-Annual Meeting,* 1914, 10; 1915, 44.

36. Railway Development Association, *Proceedings of the Semi-Annual Meeting,* 1915, 5–6; *Proceedings,* 1917, 50.

37. *Southern Planter* 68(June 1907):562; Atlantic Coast Line Railroad Company, *Annual Report,* 1914, 8–9; Dew, *JLC&E,* 97; *Current Events* 15(Jan. 1916):32–33; 16(Apr. 1917):10; Gulf and Ship Island Railroad Company, *Annual Report,* 1915, 7.

38. *Railway Age* 23(28 Feb. 1902):266; *Commercial West* 6(1 Oct., 26 Nov. 1904):27, 26; *Railway World* 47(27 June 1903):739; 50(27 July 1906):621.

39. *Manufacturers Record* 43(25 June 1903):445; *Commercial West* 29(22 Jan. 1916):35; *Railway World* 48(3 Dec. 1904):1383.

40. Atlantic Coast Line Railroad Company, *Annual Report,* 1905, 10; *Manufacturers Record* 43(22 Jan. 1903):3; Baiamonte, "Immigrants in Rural America," 24; *Railway Age* 42(23 Nov. 1906):660; *World's Work* 27(Nov. 1913):15; Railway Development Association, *Proceedings,* 1916, 7–11; *Breeder's Gazette* 71(26 Apr., 21 June 1917):881, 1245; *Commercial West* 6(3 Dec. 1904):8–9; *Railway and Engineering Review* 52(8 June 1912):501.

41. *Manufacturers Record* 42(25 Sept., 23 Oct. 1902):171, 236–37.

42. Denver and Rio Grande Railroad Company, *Fertile Lands of Colorado and New Mexico,* 9.

43. *Commercial West* 11(9 Feb. 1907):61; 10(18 Aug. 1906):45; 13(4 Apr. 1908):45.

44. Hargreaves, *Dry Farming,* 42–43, 53, 108–9, 145, 148–49, 179–83; Cotroneo, "Northern Pacific Land Grant," 134–39, 143–44; Ridgley, "Railroads and the Development of the Dakotas," 126–28.

45. Howard Elliott, *Montana: An Address Delivered at the Inter-State Fair, Bozeman, Montana, September 1, 1910* (n.p., n.d.); Joseph K. Howard, *Montana, High, Wide, and Handsome* (New Haven, 1943), 168–69; K. Ross Toole, *Montana: An Uncommon Land* (Norman, 1959), 228–41; *Commercial West* 12(23 Nov. 1907):33; 22(23 Nov. 1912):38.

46. *Commercial West* 22(23 Nov. 1912)38; St. Louis and San Francisco Railway Company, *North and Central Texas,* 9-11; *Commercial West* 20(25 Nov. 1911):34-35.

CHAPTER THREE

1. Railway Development Association, *Proceedings,* 1915, 57; 1913, 25.
2. Grant McConnell, *The Decline of Agrarian Democracy* (Berkeley and Los Angeles, 1953), 20; Missouri, Kansas and Texas Railway Company, *Annual Report,* 1905, 12; *Commercial West* 22(26 Oct. 1912):17.
3. Roy V. Scott, *The Reluctant Farmer: The Rise of Agricultural Extension to 1914* (Urbana, 1970), and Roy V. Scott and J. G. Shoalmire, *The Public Career of Cully A. Cobb: A Study in Agricultural Leadership* (Jackson, 1973), discuss these matters in some detail.
4. Frank Anderson to F. B. Mumford, 3 Jan. 1913, Missouri Agricultural College Papers; American Association of Farmers' Institute Workers, "Proceedings, 1902," U.S. Office of Experiment Stations, *Bulletin* 120 (Washington, 1902), 108; J. C. Clair, "The Railroads' Part in the South's Development," Cut-Over Land Conference of the South, *The Dawn of a New Constructive Era* (n.p. 1917), 53.
5. *Railway and Engineering Review* 52(12 Oct. 1912):930; *Illinois Central Magazine* 6(Dec. 1917):33; Railway Development Association, *Proceedings of the Semi-Annual Meeting,* 1914, 35-36.
6. *Railway World* 50(23 Feb. 1906):165; *Railway Age Gazette* 58(12 Feb. 1915):283; Bangor and Aroostook Railway Company, *Annual Report,* 1917, 15; *Railway Age Gazette* 50(2 June 1911):1286.
7. William C. Hunter, *Beacon Across the Prairie: North Dakota's Land-Grant College* (Fargo, 1961), 55; R. C. King to General Passenger Agent, 31 May 1899, R. C. King Letterbooks (Mississippi State University Library); *Railway World* 52(31 July 1908):562; *Book of the Royal Blue* 13(Nov. 1909):3; C. H. Tuck to H. J. Webber, 29 Jan. 1910, Liberty Hyde Bailey Papers (Cornell University Library, Ithaca).
8. O. O. Waggener, *Western Agriculture and the Burlington* (Chicago, 1938), 23; Railway Development Association, *Proceedings of the Semi-Annual Meeting,* 1917, 40; Schoffelmayer, *Southwest Trails,* 17-19; *New England Farms* 1(Jan. 1910):1, 3.
9. *Railway World* 55(21 Apr. 1911):307; *Manufacturers Record* 60(14 Dec. 1911):52; *Railway and Engineering Review* 51(11 Feb. 1911);105; *Railway Age Gazette* 52(5 Jan. 1912):89.
10. *American Fertilizer* 34(11 Feb. 1911):40; Schoffelmayer, *Southwest Trails,* 18; *Southern Farm Magazine* 8(1 Feb. 1903):1.
11. W. B. Kniskner to James Wilson, 1 Dec. 1903, M. V. Richards to Wilson, 1 Feb. 1904, Secretary of Agriculture Records; R. H. Wheeler to L. H. Bailey, 3 Oct. 1911, Bailey Papers; *American Fertilizer* 35(16 Dec. 1911):41; *Breeder's Gazette* 62(28 Aug. 1912):372; F. B. Mumford to C. H. Eckles, 11 Jan. 1913; Mumford to B. W. Redfearn, 28 Oct. 1910, Missouri Agricultural College Papers; *Hoard's Dairyman* 35(6 Jan. 1905):1197.
12. Scott, *Agricultural Extension,* 176-82; *Missouri Pacific Lines Magazine* 8(Sept. 1930):12.
13. *Hoard's Dairyman* 51(12 May, 9 June 1916):661-62, 803; *Breeder's Gazette* 70(20 July, 21 Sept. 1916):91-92, 490; Carl D. Livingston, "Stumps and Their Removal," Cut-Over Land Conference of the South, *The Dawn of a New Constructive Era* (n.p. 1917), 190-91; Marion C. Calkins, "The Cutover Country," *Survey* 45(27 Nov. 1920):303.

14. Oscar O. Winther, *The Transportation Frontier: Trans-Mississippi West, 1865-1890* (New York, 1964), 150-57; Earl Mayo, "The Good Roads Train," *World's Work* 2(July 1901):956-60; J. G. Shoalmire, "The Good Roads Trains, 1901-1902" (graduate seminar paper in possession of the author), 6-31.

15. *Wallaces' Farmer* 30(23 June 1905):802; Henry Wallace, *Uncle Henry's Own Story of His Life*. 3 vols. (Des Moines, 1917-1919) 3:97-99; *Prairie Farmer* 78(16 Nov. 1905):7; *Railway and Engineering Review* 46(20 Jan. 1906); *Southern Planter* 71(June 1910):659-60.

16. *Railway and Engineering Review* 51(21 Oct. 1909):908; Atlantic Coast Line Railroad Company, *Annual Report,* 1912, 9; Southern Railway Company, *Annual Report,* 1912, 8; Worth C. Harder, "For Better Roads: How the Good-Roads Special Is Teaching the Science of Improved Peripateticism," *Harper's Weekly* 56(14 Sept. 1912):15; *Literary Digest* 45(2 Nov. 1912):796; *Missouri Farmer and Breeder* 3(Jan. 1911):13; *Colman's Rural World* 63(12 Oct. 1910):321; Robert Franklin, "Teaching Good Roads by Special Train," *Technical World Magazine* 17(June 1912):448-51; *Railway Age Gazette* 52(22 Mar. 1912):695.

17. *Railway and Engineering Review* 49(18 Sept. 1909):827; *Railway World* 54(10 Feb., 3 June 1910):85, 440; *Commercial West* 16(16 Oct. 1909):17; *Manufacturers Record* 61(14 Mar. 1912):58; Ronald H. Ridgley, "The Railroads and Rural Development in the Dakotas," *North Dakota History* 36(Spring 1969):169-70.

18. Scott, *Agricultural Extension,* 181-83; B. Irby to W. O. Atwater, 8 Jan., 21 Nov. 1890, Office of Experiment Stations Records (National Archives, Washington).

19. Scott, *Agricultural Extension,* 184; Pennsylvania Railroad Company, *How this Railroad Helps the Farmer* (Philadelphia, 1914), n.p.; Long Island Railroad Company, *Annual Report,* 1906, 22; 1909, 24; *Long Island Railroad Information Bulletin,* 5(Feb.–Mar. 1928), 38–39; Robert H. Renehey, "On Long Island's Worst Ten Acres She Runs a Model Farm," *American Magazine* 107(Apr. 1929):73–74.

20. Pennsylvania Railroad Company, *How this Railroad Helps the Farmer,* n.p.; Ivy L. Lee, "The Place of the Interstate Railroad in Reducing Food Distribution Costs," American Academy of Social and Political Science, *Annals* 50(Nov. 1913):17–18; *Railway World* 53(12 Nov. 1909):492; 55(25 Aug. 1911):686; *Railway and Engineering Review* 50(29 Jan. 1910):95.

21. Scott, *Agricultural Extension,* 184-85; *Railway and Engineering Review* 50(22 Oct. 1910):976; *Railway World* 54(28 Oct 1910):863; Clark, *Then Came the Railroads,* 274; *American Fertilizer* 34(8 Apr. 1911):32; Anderson, *St. Louis Southwestern,* 59.

22. Scott, *Agricultural Extension,* 185-86; American Association of Farmers' Institute Managers, *Proceedings,* 1897 (Lincoln, 1898), 34; Donald W. Meinig, *The Great Columbia Plain: A Historical Geography, 1805-1910* (Seattle, 1968), 405n.

23. Corliss, *Illinois Central,* 415; Railway Development Association, *Proceedings,* 1916, 60-61; Scott, *Agricultural Extension,* 186; *Railway World* 57(Mar. 1913):254; John R. Fain, "What Georgia is Doing to Encourage the Utilizing of Cut-Over Lands," Cut-Over Land Conference of the South, *The Dawn of a New Constructive Era* (n.p. 1917), 111.

24. Railway Development Association, *Proceedings of the Semi-Annual Meetings,* 1914, 30-32; Atchison, Topeka and Santa Fe Railway Company, *Diversified Farming in the Panhandle and South Plains of Texas* (Chicago, 1912), 15; Clark, *Then Came the Railroads,* 270; Merle Armitage, *Operations Santa Fe* (New York, 1948), 198-99; Scott, *Agricultural Extension,* 186-87; *Agents' Bulletin* 6(Apr. 1913):8; *Railway and Engineering Review* 53(8 Feb. 1913):114-15; Burt, "Nashville, Chattanooga and St. Louis Railway," 195-96; *Railway Review* 57(25 Sept. 1915):385.

25. Northern Pacific Railway Company, *Report of the Agricultural Extension*

Department, 1913 (St. Paul, 1914), 3-4; 1914, 3-18; 1915, 3, 11, 19; 1916, 2-3, 20-21; Scott, *Agricultural Extension,* 187-88; *Commercial West* 23(15 Mar. 1913):36.

26. Atchison, Topeka and Santa Fe Railway Company, *Diversified Farming,* 3-6; New York Central Lines, *Improving Crop Yields by the Use of Dynamite* (Baltimore, 1911), 104-6; *Commercial West* 6(4 July 1908):8; Railway Development Association, *Proceedings of the Semi-Annual Meeting,* 1914, 19; Clark, *Then Came the Railroads,* 272.

27. Railway Development Association, *Proceedings of the Semi-Annual Meeting,* 1914, 36; *Proceedings,* 1916, 5-6; *Manufacturers Record* 66(12 Nov. 1914):56b; *Railway Review* 58(10 June 1916):806; Corliss, *Illinois Central,* 416.

28. *Commercial West* 5(16 May 1903):7; *Railway Review* 58(10 June 1916):806; *Illinois Central Magazine,* 5(June 1917):79-80; *Frisco-Man* 10(Oct. 1916):4; Railway Development Association, *Proceedings,* 1916, 7; Jones, "Agricultural Development Program of the Chicago, Burlington and Quincy Railroad," 75.

29. *Illinois Central Magazine* 5(Feb., June 1917):66, 80; Corliss, *Illinois Central,* 417; Clair, "Railroads' Part in the South's Development," 51.

30. Jones, "Agricultural Development Program of the Chicago, Burlington and Quincy Railroad," 65, 67; Railway Development Association, *Proceedings of the Semi-Annual Meeting,* 1917, 31; 1914, 28.

31. *Railway Age Gazette* 56(22 May 1914):1130; *Railway Review* 58(10 June 1916):806; *Rock Island Employes' Magazine* 8(Jan. 1915):18-19; Railway Development Association, *Proceedings of the Semi-Annual Meeting,* 1914, 36; *Manufacturers Record* 71(1 Mar. 1917):71; 72(2 Aug. 1917):85.

32. *Railway World* 58(June 1914):447-48; Chicago and North Western Railway Company, *Alfalfa: The Money Crop of the West and Northwest* (Chicago, 1910), 3; *Railway Age Gazette* 56(16 Jan. 1914):134; *Southern Planter* 72(June 1911):703; Jones, "Agricultural Development Program of the Chicago, Burlington and Quincy Railroad," 69-73.

33. Illinois Central Railroad Company, *Organization and Traffic of the Illinois Central System* (Chicago, 1938), 242; Railway Development Association, *Proceedings,* 1915, 23-24; *Railway Age* 85(8 Sept. 1928):449; Anderson, *St. Louis Southwestern,* 59-60; Missouri, Kansas and Texas Railway Company, *Annual Report,* 1908, 14; M. V. Richards to James Wilson, 4 May 1903, Secretary of Agriculture Records; *Manufacturers Record* 62(18 July 1912):50.

34. *World's Work* 24(July 1912):309; Clark, *Then Came the Railroads,* 271-72; *Railway Age* 34(26 Dec. 1902):717; *Southern Farm Magazine* 15(Aug. 1907):24.

35. Ridgley, "Railroads and the Development of the Dakotas," 114; Waggener, *Western Agriculture,* 36; *Railway Age* 32(1 Nov. 1901):496.

36. F. R. Stevens, "What Farmers Can Do to Facilitate the Transportation and Marketing of Produce," American Academy of Political and Social Science, *Annals* 50(Nov. 1913):37-43; Southern Railway Company, *Annual Report,* 1913, 8; T. C. Powell, "The Work of Railroads for Agricultural Development," Conference for Education in the South, *Proceedings,* 1914 (Washington, n.d.), 110-11; *Manufacturers Record* 62(7 Nov. 1912):68-70; *Railway Age Gazette* 56(22 May 1914):1130; Railway Development Association, *Proceedings,* 1917, 77.

37. *Market Growers' Journal* 16(15 Feb. 1916):8; *Manufacturers Record* 62(1 Aug. 1912):65; *Western Fruit Grower* 17(May 1906):240; *Railway Age* 85(8 Sept. 1928):449.

38. Scott, *Agricultural Extension,* 171; Council of North American Grain Exchanges, Crop Improvement Committee, *Proceedings of a Meeting in Chicago, February 8, 1911* (n.p., n.d.), 62; North Carolina Agricultural Extension Service, *Annual Report,* 1916 (Raleigh, 1917), 10.

39. Roy V. Scott, "Railroads and Farmers: Educational Trains in Missouri, 1902–1914," *Agricultural History* 36(Jan. 1962):9; Mississippi Agricultural and Mechanical College, *Biennial Report,* 1912–1913 (Nashville, 1913), 9; *Railway and Engineering Review* 52(20 July 1912):680; *Manufacturers Record* 62(25 July 1912):48; *Progressive Farmer* 31(15 Apr. 1916):550; Gulf and Ship Island Railroad Company, *Annual Report,* 1915, 7; D. E. King to H. J. Waters, 12 Mar. 1907, Missouri Agricultural College Papers.

40. Scott, *Agricultural Extension,* 174–75; Burt, "Nashville, Chattanooga and St. Louis Railway," 197.

41. Corliss, *Illinois Central,* 299; *Southern Farm Magazine* 7(Mar. 1899):16–17; Roy V. Scott, "American Railroads and Agricultural Extension, 1900–1914: A Study in Railway Developmental Techniques," *Business History Review* 39(Spring 1965):78–79, 91–92; Atchison, Topeka and Santa Fe Railway Company, *Diversified Farming,* 16.

42. *Breeder's Gazette* 57(2 Mar. 1910):555; Southern Railway Company, *Annual Report,* 1911, 8–9; 1912, 6; 1913, 7; Alabama Great Southern Railroad Company, *Annual Report,* 1912, 8; Railway Development Association, *Proceedings of the Semi-Annual Meeting,* 1914, 27–28; Fairfax Harrison, *The Relation of Southern Railway to Southern Progress: An Address before the Manufacturers and Merchants of Atlanta, Georgia, June 10, 1914* (n.p., n.d.).

43. Scott, "Railroads and Agricultural Extension," 92–96; George A. Cullen, "The Relation of the Railroad to the Farmer," Massachusetts State Board of Agriculture, *Circular* 82 (Boston, 1918), 10–12; *Railway World* 57(Mar. 1913):254; *Fruit Grower and Farmer* 24(Mar. 1913):227; Railway Development Association, *Proceedings,* 1915, 53.

44. Railway Development Association, *Proceedings,* 1915, 96–97; Corliss, *Illinois Central,* 418–19; Scott and Shoalmire, *Cobb,* 63; Clark, *Then Came the Railroads,* 272–73; Bryant, *Santa Fe,* 245; Montana Farmers' Institutes, *Ninth and Tenth Annual Reports,* 1910–1912 (Bozeman, 1912), 6–7; summary of an article from *Bulletin,* Mississippi Extension Service Records (Mississippi State University Library).

45. Scott, "Railroads and Agricultural Extension," 97–98.

46. *Railway Review* 60(21 Apr. 1917):564; *Railway Age Gazette* 62(11 May 1917):1019; *Reliable Poultry Journal* 24(Aug. 1917):504–5; *Manufacturers Record* 72(9 Aug. 1917):66c.

47. *Railway Age Gazette* 63(24 Aug. 1917):334; Waggener, *Western Agriculture,* 32–33; Railway Development Association, *Proceedings,* 1917, 16–17.

48. Walker D. Hines, *War History of American Railroads* (New Haven, 1928), 22–24, 252; *Railway Age* 64(14 June 1918):1422; U.S. Railroad Administration, Division of Traffic, *Circular* 3, 10 July 1918.

49. *Agricultural and Industrial Service Bulletin* 1(1 July 1918):1–2; *Progressive Farmer* 34(18 Jan. 1919):114; *Frisco-Man* 12(Nov. 1918):14.

50. *Banker-Farmer* 6(Jan. 1919):6–7; *Railway Age* 66(2 May 1919):1085–86; *Pere Marquette Magazine* 11(June 1919):28–29; U.S. Railroad Administration, Division of Traffic, *Annual Report,* 1919 (Washington, 1920), 20–22.

CHAPTER FOUR

1. Northern Pacific Railway Company, *Successful Central and Western North Dakota* (n.p., n.d.), 36; Luis Jackson, "Railways as Factors in Industrial Development," in *Lectures on Commerce Delivered before the College of Commerce and Administration of the University of Chicago,* ed. Henry R. Hatfield (Chicago, 1907),

82, 84–88; W. W. Finley, "The Railroads' Work in the South," *World's Work* 14(June 1907):8953–54; Finley, "Southern Railroads and Industrial Development," American Academy of Political and Social Science, *Annals* 35(Jan. 1910):99–101; *Railway Age* 45(3 Jan. 1908):14.

2. *Chemical and Metallurgical Engineering* 20(1 June 1919):558; Corliss, *Illinois Central*, 300.

3. *Railroad World* 47(14 Nov. 1903):1299; *Railway Gazette* 39(22 Dec. 1905):574–75; Jackson, "Railways as Factors in Industrial Development," 88, 94–100; Clark, *Then Came the Railroads*, 279; Henry Oyen, "Making Business to Order: How the Santa Fe and Other Railroads Develop the Country They Serve by Means of Their Industrial Departments," *World's Work* 24(July 1912):308–10; Corliss, *Illinois Central*, 300.

4. Erie Railroad Company, *Industrial Map of the Erie Railroad System* (n.p. 1905); Kansas City Southern Railway Company, *Sprays and Spraying* (Kansas City,1927), 29.

5. Edward P. Ripley, "How I Got Customers to See My Side," *System: The Magazine of Business* 29(Apr. 1916):339–45; *Illinois Central Magazine* 18(Jan. 1930):15; American Railway Development Association, *Proceedings*, 1924, 56.

6. Railway Development Association, *Proceedings*, 1917, 34–35; Baltimore and Ohio Railroad Company, *Annual Report*, 1927, 10; John C. Beukema, "The New Science of City Building," *Review of Reviews* 77(Mar. 1928):302.

7. *Manufacturers Record* 86(10 July 1924):71; 92(1 Dec. 1927):73; *Railway Age* 87(26 Oct. 1929):981–82; *Illinois Central Magazine* 18(Feb. 1930):11.

8. *Manufacturers Record* 60(5 Oct. 1911):64; *Commercial West* 3(28 June 1902):32; 5(10 Jan. 1903):39; 6(26 Nov. 1904):43.

9. *Manufacturers Record* 48(5 Oct. 1905):79; *Agricultural and Industrial Bulletin* 1(1 July 1920):8.

10. *Manufacturers Record* 96(11 July 1929):99; 106(Feb. 1937):59.

11. American Railway Development Association, *Proceedings*, 1929, 131–32, 135–36; Railway Development Association, 1917, 43.

12. Corliss, *Illinois Central*, 299; Illinois Central and Yazoo and Mississippi Valley Railroads, *Southern Homeseekers' Guide*, 174; *Southern Farm Magazine* 10(15 Oct. 1905); Illinois Central and Yazoo and Mississippi Valley Railroads, *Locations for Industries* (Chicago, 1905), 3, 16, 196.

13. Hoadley, "How Railroads Aid Industrial Development," 191; Great Northern Railway Company, *Business Openings* (St. Paul, n.d.), 3, 30, 79, 81.

14. *Railway Age* 3(15 Nov. 1941):804; *Chesapeake and Ohio Lines Magazine* 26(Mar. 1941):3–6; *Railway Age* 111(2 Aug. 1941):213; 117(19 Aug. 1944):318–19.

15. *Manufacturers Record*, 48(14 Dec. 1905):574, Norfolk and Western Railway Company, *Industrial and Shippers' Guide*, 67, 69; American Railway Development Association, *Proceedings*, 1920, 7–9.

16. *Manufacturers Record* 51(2 May 1907):467–68; *Illinois Central Magazine* 15(July 1925):64; *Manufacturers Record* 84(29 Nov. 1923):66.

17. American Railway Development Association, *Proceedings*, 1929, 132; *Manufacturers Record* 52(3 Oct. 1907):57; *Missouri Pacific Lines Magazine* 4(Jan. 1927):30, 40.

18. Railway Development Association, *Proceedings*, 1917, 78a; *Missouri Pacific Lines Magazine* 6(Feb. 1929):16; Edward J. Israel, "The Opportunities for Industrial Development on the Railroads," Roadmasters and Maintenance of Way Association of America, *Proceedings*, 1927 (n.p., n.d.), 102; *Maize* 3(Feb. 1914):32–34; *Mutual Magazine* 12(Mar. 1927):6.

19. Shoemaker, "Industrial Department of a Railroad," 134; *Mechanical Engineering* 49(Nov. 1927):1191–94; *Mutual Magazine* 12(Mar. 1927):7–8; Richard H.

Lansburgh, "Recent Migrations of Industries in the United States," *American Academy of Political and Social Science, Annals* 142(Mar. 1929):296-301.

20. American Railway Development Association, *Proceedings,* 1930, 43-45, 46-47; *Railway Age* 87(26 Oct. 1929):981-83.

21. American Railway Development Association, *Proceedings,* 1928, 27; 1930, 45; *Railway Age* 78(25 Apr. 1925):1067; Chicago Great Western Railroad Company, *Annual Report,* 1935, 9.

22. *Railway Age* 92(2 Apr. 1932):576; Union Pacific Railroad Company, *Annual Report,* 1935, 9; 1937, 12; 1939, 21.

23. *Iron Age* 178(26 Apr. 1956):58; American Railway Development Association, *Proceedings,* 1957, 52-56; *Industrial Development* 128(June 1959):42.

24. *Railway Age* 75(15 Sept. 1923):497; Walter R. Armstrong, "Development of Industrial Sites and Trackage Layouts at Kansas City, Kansas, and Los Angeles, California, by the Union Pacific System," American Society of Civil Engineers, *Transactions* 90(1927):994-1102.

25. Waters, *Steel Trails to Santa Fe,* 418-19; Bryant, *Santa Fe,* 246, 248; *Railway Age* 73(23 Sept. 1922):588; American Railway Development Association, *Proceedings,* 1930, 47-48; *Manufacturers Record* 95(30 May 1929):60-61.

26. *Railway Age* 78(2 May 1925):1121; *Manufacturers Record* 109(Sept. 1940):29; Union Pacific Railroad Company, *Annual Report,* 1937, 12; 1938, 11; 1939, 21; 1940, 14; 1941, 14.

27. Illinois Central Railroad Company, *Organization and Traffic,* 222; *In the Matter of Leases and Grants of Property by Carriers,* 73 ICC 671; John Guandolo, *Transportation Law* (Dubuque, 1965), 378-84.

28. Jesse R. Sprague, "Getting Business for the Railroad," *Saturday Evening Post* 198(20 Mar. 1926):50; American Railway Development Association, *Proceedings of the Semi-Annual Meeting,* 1922, 16-17; *Proceedings,* 1923, 58-59; *Railway Age* 88(17 May 1930):1191-92.

29. American Railway Development Association, *Proceedings,* 1927, 84-86; *National Industrial Traffic League v. Aberdeen and Rockfish Railroad Company,* 61 ICC 120.

30. Railway Development Association, *Proceedings of the Semi-Annual Meeting,* 1915, 12-15; *Proceedings,* 1917, 51-52; 1925, 15; *Railway Review* 62(30 Mar. 1918):468; United States Railroad Administration, *General Order* 15, 26 March 1918.

31. American Railway Development Association, *Proceedings,* 1920, 7; 1921, 5-6, 13; 1923, 58-59; 1927, 86-87; 1929, 34-35; *Railway Age* 69(8 Oct. 1920):596-97; 76(19 Apr. 1924):981-84.

32. *Railway Review* 75(6 Sept. 1924):367; American Railway Development Association, *Proceedings,* 1923, 63-64.

33. *Missouri Pacific Lines Magazine* 7(July 1929):77; Israel, "Opportunities for Industrial Development," 104; *Railway Age* 75(15 Dec. 1923):1111; American Railway Development Association, *Proceedings,* 1931, 42-46; 1932, 125-26; *Rail* 20(Dec. 1935), 13.

34. American Railway Development Association, *Proceedings,* 1929, 134; *Illinois Central Magazine* 28(May 1940):11.

35. Israel, "Opportunities for Industrial Development," 101, 106.

CHAPTER FIVE

1. J. W. Haw, "Farm Aid that Builds Business," *Nation's Business* 17(May 1929):149-50; Jones, "Agricultural Development Program of the Chicago, Burlington and Quincy Railroad," 11; American Railway Development Associa-

tion, *Proceedings,* 1921, 9, 46–47; 1922, 52–56; *Commercial West* 51(5 Mar., 4 June 1927):51, 38.

2. Wallace Ashby, "Problems of the New Settler on Reclaimed Cutover Land," *Agricultural Engineering* 5(Feb. 1924):27–29. Before World War I the Duluth and Iron Range maintained a demonstration farm at Meadowlands. *Commercial West* 25(24 Jan. 1914):25.

3. Jones, "Agricultural Development Program of the Chicago, Burlington and Quincy Railroad," 56; *Railway Age,* 76(17 May 1924):1239; Great Northern Railway Company, *Annual Report,* 1923, 9; *Missouri Pacific Lines Magazine* 6(Nov. 1928):17, 144; *Ohio Farmer* 151(17 Mar. 1923):385; *Commercial West* 50(7 Aug. 1926):17.

4. *Manufacturers Record* 88(12 Nov. 1925):89–90; 91(21 Apr. 1927):84; 84(2 Aug. 1923):100; *Santa Fe Magazine* 21(Aug. 1927):19.

5. *Agricultural Development Bulletin* 4(Jan. 1928):11; *Agricultural and Industrial Bulletin* 2(1 Jan. 1921):8; 7(Apr.–May 1926); *Illinois Central Magazine* 15(Oct. 1926):25; Southern Railway Company, *Annual Report,* 1921, 5; Lee A. Dew, "The J. L. C. and E. R. R. and the Opening of the 'Sunk Lands' of Northeast Arkansas," *Arkansas Historical Quarterly* 27(Spring 1968):30–31; *Banker-Farmer* 7(Sept. 1920):4.

6. *Railway Age* 86(20 Apr. 1929):935; *Ohio Farmer* 163(2 Mar. 1929):939; *Great Northern Semaphore* 2(Nov. 1925):3; Frisco Lines, *The Tombigbee Valley of Mississippi and Alabama* (n.p., n.d.).

7. *Agricultural and Industrial Bulletin* 5(Oct. 1924):9; American Railway Development Association, *Proceedings,* 1921, 8–9; 1922, 12; *Railway Age* 77(29 Nov. 1924):999; *Manufacturers Record* 84(2 Aug. 1923):112.

8. *Chicago Evening Post,* 25 Jan. 1921; *Railway Age* 72(11 March 1922):555, 587; *Manufacturers Record* 84(30 Aug. 1923):87–88; 83(8 Feb. 1923):62.

9. American Railway Development Association, *Proceedings,* 1921, 81; *Ohio Farmer* 157(23 Jan., 13 Feb. 1927):125, 228; *Southern Ruralist* 36(15 Oct. 1929):6.

10. Jones, "Agricultural Development Program of the Chicago, Burlington and Quincy Railroad," 219–21; *Railway Age* 80(8 May 1926):1286; *Agricultural Development Bulletin* 3(Mar. 1927):9; Frisco Lines, *Tombigbee Valley of Mississippi and Alabama;* Mobile and Ohio Railroad Company, *Mississippi* (n.p., n.d.).

11. *Illinois Central Magazine* 14(Feb. 1926):26; *Missouri Pacific Lines Magazine* 4(Jan. 1927):17; *Manufacturers Record* 94(2 Aug. 1928):66; Atlantic Coast Line Railroad Company, *Annual Report,* 1928, 11; 1929, 11.

12. American Railway Development Association, *Proceedings,* 1921, 81–82; Atlantic Coast Line Railroad Company, *Annual Report,* 1921, 101; Haw, "Farm Aid that Builds Business," 149–50.

13. Jones, "Agricultural Development Program of the Chicago, Burlington and Quincy Railroad," 225–30; *Commercial West* 44(7 July 1923):36; Dunbar, *Railroads in Michigan,* 172–73; *American Railroads* 1(12 July 1920):4; *Pere Marquette Magazine* 13(Nov. 1920):12.

14. *Manufacturers Record* 83(3 May 1923):109; 81(9 Feb. 1922):56; *Agricultural and Industrial Bulletin* 3(1 Jan. 1922):6; *Agricultural Development Bulletin* 3(Oct. 1927):8.

15. American Railway Development Association, *Proceedings,* 1923, 53–56.

16. *Pacific Dairy Review* 22(11 Apr. 1918):2–3; American Railway Development Association, *Proceedings of the Semi-Annual Meeting,* 1922, 12–16; Maryland Agricultural Extension Service, *Annual Report,* 1921 (College Park, 1922), 42; 1924, 160; 1925, 78.

17. *Railway Age* 78(30 May 1925):1330; American Railway Development Association, *Proceedings,* 1921, 81; Jones, "Agricultural Development Program of the Chicago, Burlington and Quincy Railroad," 132.

18. *Missouri Pacific Lines Magazine* 10(Jan. 1933):10; *Commercial West* 65(4 Mar. 1933):34.

19. *Commercial West* 61(13, 27 June 1931):11, 23; *Railway Age* 89(13 Dec. 1930):1264; Jones, "Agricultural Development Program of the Chicago, Burlington and Quincy Railroad," 247; *Missouri Pacific Lines Magazine* 10(Jan. 1933):10.

20. *Ohio Farmer* 169(9 Jan. 1932):29; *Progressive Farmer* 50(Jan. 1935):38; *Milwaukee Magazine* 18(Oct. 1930):14; Chicago, Milwaukee, St. Paul and Pacific Railroad Company, *Annual Report,* 1939, 10.

21. *Milwaukee Magazine* 22(Sept. 1934):14.

22. Great Northern Railway Company, *Annual Report,* 1937, 8; *Missouri Pacific Lines Magazine* 10(Jan. 1933):59.

23. *Missouri Pacific Lines Magazine* 10(Jan. 1933):59; *Commercial West* 61(27 June 1931):23.

24. Northern Pacific Railway Company, *Annual Report,* 1932, 14; 1936, 15; 1937, 15; Great Northern Railway Company, *Annual Report,* 1931, 7; 1936, 9–10; 1937, 8; *U.S. Federal Extension Service* 6(July 1935):93; *Milwaukee Magazine* 22(July 1934):13; Clark, *Then Came the Railroads,* 256, 296; Agricultural Development—Missouri Pacific Railroad, 12.

25. Chicago, Milwaukee, St. Paul and Pacific Railroad Company, *Annual Report,* 1943, 8; 1945, 19; *Railway Age* 120(18 May 1946):1000, 1004; Jones, "Agricultural Development Program of the Chicago, Burlington and Quincy Railroad," 10–11; *Railway Freight Traffic* 5(Feb. 1957):10.

26. New York Central System, *Finding a Farm in the Land of Shorter Hauls to Bigger Markets,* 3–13; *Santa Fe Magazine,* 50(Apr. 1956):22–23.

CHAPTER SIX

1. Cimco Farm, *Second Annual Bulletin* (Springfield, 1929); Haw, "Farm Aid that Builds Business," 149–50; J. M. Kurn, "The Railroad's Part in Regional Development," *Executive's Magazine* 10(Sept. 1926):7; New York Central Lines, *Industrial Directory and Shippers' Guide,* 1920–21 (New York, 1921), 705; American Railway Development Association, *Proceedings,* 1924, 53–54; 1927, 57.

2. *Missouri Pacific Lines Magazine* 6(Dec. 1928):13; C. Clyde Jones, "The Burlington Railroad and Agricultural Policy in the 1920's," *Agricultural History* 31(Oct. 1957):70; American Railway Development Association, *Proceedings of the Semi-Annual Meeting,* 1928, 22–23; *Manufacturers Record* 93(15 Mar. 1928):63.

3. *Railway Age* 74(10 Mar. 1923):551–52; American Railway Development Association, *Proceedings,* 1922, 27; 1924, 56; 1926, 11.

4. *Manufacturers Record* 90(14 Oct. 1926):102; *Ties* 11(Nov. 1925):4; American Railway Development Association, *Proceedings of the Semi-Annual Meeting,* 1922, 9–11; *Proceedings,* 1927, 62–65.

5. *Long Island Railroad Information Bulletin* 5(Nov.–Dec. 1928):65; Cimco Farm, *Second Annual Bulletin;* American Railway Development Association, *Proceedings,* 1929, 99; *Farm Markets and Maxims* 1(May 1929):3; Jones, "Agricultural Development Program of the Chicago, Burlington and Quincy Railroad," 129.

6. Clark, *Then Came the Railroads,* 291; *Missouri Pacific Lines Magazine* 6(Sept. 1928):7, 112; *Long Island Railroad Information Bulletin* 5(Nov.–Dec. 1928):48–52; *New York Central Lines Magazine* 7(Oct. 1924):54–55.

7. Chicago Great Western Railroad Company, Development Division, *Bulletin* 1(Chicago, n.d.), 2–5; Chicago Great Western Railroad Company, *Annual Report,* 1925, 8; 1927, 10; *Railway Age* 86(11 May 1929):1130.

8. Chicago Great Western Railroad Company, Development Division, *Bul-*

letin 1, 5; Chicago Great Western Railroad Company, *Annual Report,* 1924, 9; *Railway Age* 90(11 Apr. 1931):748.

9. Long Island Railroad Company, *Annual Report,* 1929, 6-7; *Long Island Railroad Information Bulletin* 6(Jan.-Feb. 1930):66; Chicago and Illinois Midland Railway Company, *Cimco Farm* (n.p. 1928); *Newsweek* 36(30 Oct. 1950):72.

10. *Southern Ruralist* 30(15 Feb. 1924):656-57; American Railway Development Association, *Proceedings,* 1924, 55; *United States Investor* 35(21 June 1924):1532.

11. American Railway Development Association, *Proceedings,* 1924, 50; 1929, 117-21; Clark, *Then Came the Railroads,* 290; Jones, "Agricultural Development Program of the Chicago, Burlington and Quincy Railroad," 178.

12. Agricultural Development–Missouri Pacific Railroad, 4-7; *Missouri Pacific Lines Magazine* 4(Jan. 1927):15, 113; *Manufacturers Record* 85(Mar. 1924):113; *Railway Review* 76(11 Apr. 1925):695; *Railway Age* 81(25 Sept., 4 Dec. 1926):569, 1119; *Progressive Farmer* 42(5 Mar. 1927):272.

13. Agricultural Development–Missouri Pacific Railroad, 7-9; Clark, *Then Came the Railroads,* 291; "The Livestock Special Train," Montana State College Extension Service, *Bulletin* 96(Bozeman, 1928), 3-5; "Progress: A Few Steps Forward in Montana's Agricultural Program," Montana Extension Service, *Bulletin* 97 (n.p. 1929), 24-26; *Manufacturers Record* 82(23 Nov. 1922):75; *Railway Age* 84(5 May 1928):1059; Santa Fe System Lines, *Bulletin: Reprint of All Issues* (Chicago, 1928), 106; Illinois Central Railroad Company, *The Illinois Central Railroad in Mississippi* (n.p. 1953), 19; Illinois Central Railroad, *Organization and Traffic,* 246; New York Central Lines, *Industrial Directory,* 706; *New York Central Lines Magazine* 1(Apr. 1920):36-38.

14. *Commercial West* 48(28 Nov. 1925):10; American Railway Development Association, *Proceedings,* 1929, 73-74; *Missouri Pacific Lines Magazine* 2(Mar. 1925):33; *New York Central Lines Magazine* 9(Mar. 1929):63.

15. American Railway Development Association, *Proceedings,* 1922, 17; *National Boys' and Girls' Club News* 5(15 Oct. 1927):2; J. W. Jarvis, "Union Pacific Works with Youth; Agricultural Scholarship," *Electrical West* 86(June 1941):102; *Baltimore and Ohio Magazine* 10(July 1922):27; *Boys' and Girls' Club 4-H Leader* 1(Apr. 1927):9; Baltimore and Ohio Railroad Company, *Annual Report,* 1924, 10; *Rural America* 6(Apr. 1928):7.

16. Scott and Shoalmire, *Cobb,* 105-9; *Railway Freight Traffic* 1(Sept. 1953):32; *Farm Markets and Maxims* 1(15 Nov. 1929):1; *Agricultural and Industrial Bulletin* 6(Feb. 1925):4; *Missouri Pacific Lines Magazine* 6(July 1928):24; Atlantic Coast Line Railroad Company, *Annual Report,* 1929, 12; *U.S. Federal Extension Service* 4(Sept. 1930):77.

17. *New York Central Lines Magazine* 10(Dec. 1929):63-64; *Guernsey Breeders' Journal* 30(1 July 1926):12-13; *Jersey Bulletin* 45(19 May 1926):805; *International Review of Agriculture* 30(Jan.-June 1939):71T; *B and O Magazine* 11(Dec. 1923):36-37; *Ohio Farmer* 158(13 Nov. 1926):493; Illinois Central Railroad Company, *Organization and Traffic,* 246; *L & N Employes' Magazine* 3(June 1927):25-26; 57(15 June 1927):12; Jones, "Burlington Railroad and Agricultural Policy," 71-72; Edward Hungerford, "The Railroad and the Farmer," *Country Gentleman* 90(25 July 1925):13; *Great Northern Semaphore* 1(Oct. 1924):1.

18. American Railway Development Association, *Proceedings,* 1927, 89-90; *United States Investor* 35(21 June 1924):1532, Clark, *Then Came the Railroads,* 294.

19. Malcolm C. Cutting, "How Business Financed the Farmer," *Nation's Business* 17(Feb. 1929):76-81; Haw, "Farm Aid that Builds Business," 149-50; *Commercial West* 61(25 Apr. 1931):11.

20. *Illinois Central Magazine* 10(Aug., Nov. 1921):100, 115-16; Waggener, *Western Agriculture,* 35-36, 40; V. W. Lewis, "Railroads as Co-operators in Live-

stock Development," Association of Southern Agricultural Workers, *Proceedings,* 1931 (n.p., n.d.), 184.

21. *Illinois Central Magazine* 14(Jan. 1926):32; 51(June 1959):6; *Agricultural Development Bulletin* 3(Jan. 1927):9; 3(July 1927):8; *Mississippi Central Round Table* 3(1 Mar. 1929):5-6; *B & O Magazine* 10(Feb. 1923):35-37; *Railway Age* 77(18 Oct. 1924):693.

22. Waggener, *Western Agriculture,* 40-41.

23. Corliss, *Illinois Central,* 419; *Illinois Central Magazine* 15(Oct. 1926):44-45; Agricultural Development–Missouri Pacific Railroad, 9; *Missouri Pacific Lines Magazine* 27(Apr. 1954):46; Jones, "Agricultural Development Program of the Chicago, Burlington and Quincy Railroad," 128.

24. Cimco Farm, *Second Annual Bulletin; New York Central Lines Magazine* 8(June 1927):41-42; *Illinois Central Magazine* 15(Sept. 1926):29; *Mississippi Central Round Table* 1(1 Nov. 1927); *Columbia* (Missouri) *Missourian,* 11 Aug. 1927, 2.

25. Clark, *Then Came the Railroads,* 292-93; Agricultural Development–Missouri Pacific Railroad, 10; *Missouri Pacific Lines Magazine* 11(May 1934):10-11, 24.

26. Kurn, "Regional Development," 7-10; *Manufacturers Record* 87(12 Feb. 1925):93; 91(12 May 1927):87-88; *Missouri Pacific Lines Magazine* 6(Sept. 1928):15; Kansas City Southern Railway Company, *Sprays and Spraying.*

27. American Railway Development Association, *Proceedings,* 1924, 54; 1928, 40; *Manufacturers Record* 86(14 Aug. 1924):86; 92(28 July 1927):84; 90(20 Dec. 1926):63-64; *Rural America* 7(Feb. 1929):6.

28. *Agricultural Development Bulletin* 4(Feb. 1928):13-14; Clark, *Then Came the Railroads,* 290, 293; *Manufacturers Record* 90(30 Dec. 1926):64; 92(29 Dec. 1927):66; 89(4 Mar. 1926):111.

29. *New York Central Lines Magazine* 4(Feb. 1924):53-54; *Ohio Farmer* 162(11 Aug. 1928):107; *Market Growers' Journal* 47(1 Dec. 1930):730; Jones, "Agricultural Development Program of the Chicago, Burlington and Quincy Railroad," 195-96; Waggener, *Western Agriculture,* 33-35.

30. *Commercial West* 50(2 Oct. 1926):29; Jones, "Agricultural Development Program of the Chicago, Burlington and Quincy Railroad," 201-12; Waggener, *Western Agriculture,* 47.

31. *American Railroads* 1(12 July 1920):4; *Manufacturers Record* 81(18 May 1922):69; Atlantic Coast Line Railroad Company, *Annual Report,* 1929, 12-13; *Illinois Central Magazine* 12(Dec. 1923), 54; 14(Nov. 1925):24; *Railway Age* 76(22 Mar. 1924):806; *Southern Cultivator* 81(15 June 1923):5.

32. Jones, "Survey," 241-43; Waggener, *Western Agriculture,* 54; *Manufacturers Record* 90(19 Aug. 1926):92; *Railway Age* 80(8 May 1926):1286.

33. *Manufacturers Record* 84(2 Aug. 1923):89; 86(18 Dec. 1924):83; Lemly, *Gulf, Mobile and Ohio,* 73; Clark, *Then Came the Railroads,* 294-95; *New York Central Lines Magazine* 7(Mar. 1927):3; American Railway Development Association, *Proceedings,* 1921, 75, 77; 1922, 10; 1924, 46-50.

34. American Railway Development Association, *Proceedings,* 1928, 39-41; *American Railroads* 1(12 July 1920):2; *New York Central Lines Magazine* 1(July 1920):60; *Railway Age* 86(6 Apr. 1929):813.

35. Corliss, *Illinois Central,* 293; *Illinois Central Magazine* 9(Aug. 1920):15; *Manufacturers Record* 76(7 Aug. 1919):143.

36. *B & O Magazine* 8(Dec. 1920):21; *Ohio Farmer* 153(3 May 1921):5; American Railway Development Association, *Proceedings,* 1922, 4-6, 13-14; 1926, 10; *New York Central Lines Magazine* 8(Nov. 1927):70-71; *Farm Markets and Maxims* 1(May 1929):1, 3; Cimco Farm, *Third Annual Bulletin.*

37. Chicago and Eastern Illinois Railway Company, *Annual Report,* 1929, 6; Purdue University Department of Agricultural Extension, *Annual Report,* 1929,

19, 26; *B & O Magazine* 11(Oct. 1923):31, 33; *American Fertilizer* 61(26 July 1924):64; *Missouri Pacific Lines Magazine* 4(Nov. 1926):15, 105.

38. *New Reclamation Era* 21(Apr. 1930):69; American Railway Development Association, *Proceedings,* 1924, 61–62; 1927, 66; *Proceedings of the Semi-Annual Meeting,* 1928, 15; *Missouri Pacific Lines Magazine* 2(Sept. 1924):45; John A. Widsoe, *Success on Irrigation Projects* (New York, 1928), 7; *American Railroads* 1(12 July 1920):3; *Commercial West* 48(3 Oct. 1925):38; *Great Northern Semaphore* 2(July 1925):27; 4(Oct. 1927):1; Jones, "Agricultural Development Program of the Chicago, Burlington and Quincy Railroad," 232–34.

39. Jones, "Agricultural Development Programs of the Chicago, Burlington and Quincy Railroad," 263–93; *Milwaukee Magazine* 28(Oct. 1930):12.

40. M. L. Wilson, "Dry Farming in the North Central Montana 'Triangle',"
Montana Agricultural Extension Service, *Bulletin* 66 (Bozeman, 1923); E. A. Starch, "Economic Changes in Montana's Wheat Area," Montana Agricultural Experiment Station, *Bulletin* 295 (Bozeman, 1935); Great Northern Railway Company, *Annual Report,* 1923, 9; 1929, 7; 1930, 7; *Extension Service Review,* 1(Oct. 1930):90.

41. *Manufacturers Record* 92(14 June 1927):68; *Railway Age* 89(9, 23, 30 Aug. 1930):300, 372, 464.

42. American Railway Development Association, *Proceedings,* 1929, 115, 121–23; *Agricultural Development Bulletin* 3(Jan. 1927):11; *New York Central Lines Magazine* 2(21 Oct. 1921):67; *Country Gentleman* 90(25 July 1925):13, 40.

CHAPTER SEVEN

1. Clark, *Then Came the Railroads,* 296; *Railway Age,* 126(18 June 1949):1205; 136(31 May 1954):10–11; 138(31 Jan. 1955):24.

2. Jones, "Agricultural Development Program of the Chicago, Burlington and Quincy Railroad," 247–49; Atlantic Coast Line Railroad Company, *Annual Report,* 1953, 12.

3. American Railway Development Association, *Proceedings,* 1936, 21–27; 1939, 62–63; Jones, "Agricultural Development Program of the Chicago, Burlington and Quincy Railroad," 254–59.

4. Jones, "Agricultural Development Program of the Chicago, Burlington and Quincy Railroad," 250–51; *Railway Age* 96(12 May, 9 June 1934):717, 849; *Commercial West* 62(4 July 1931):9; Great Northern Railway Company, *Annual Report,* 1931, 7; 1938, 8; American Railway Development Association, *Proceedings,* 1936, 52; *L and N Employes' Magazine* 10(Sept. 1934):4–5; *Missouri Pacific Lines Magazine* 9(Dec. 1931):12–13, 68; *Milwaukee Magazine* 24(Sept. 1936):11.

5. Waggener, *Western Agriculture,* 57; *Cimco Fortnightly,* 5(22 May 1937):1; Jones, "Agricultural Development Program of the Chicago, Burlington and Quincy Railroad," 245–46; *Manufacturers Record* 99(19 Feb. 1931):80; *Illinois Central Magazine* 19(Mar. 1931):15.

6. Chicago, Milwaukee, St. Paul and Pacific Railroad Company, *Annual Report,* 1943, 8; *B and O Magazine* 31(Feb. 1943):9; *Railway Age,* 116(4 Mar., 20 May 1944):473, 1004; *Missouri Pacific Lines Magazine* 17(Mar. 1943):8; *Illinois Central Magazine* 31(May 1943):6; Jones, "Agricultural Development Program of the Chicago, Burlington and Quincy Railroad," 298–300; Atlantic Coast Line Railroad Company, *Annual Report,* 1942, 10.

7. *Agricultural Development Bulletin* 6(Nov. 1930):10; *Santa Fe Magazine* 45(July 1951):27; American Railway Development Association, *Proceedings,* 1959, 37; 1963, 33; *Cimco Fortnightly* 21(11 July 1953); *Railway Age* 138(13 June 1955):12.

8. Jones, "Agricultural Development Program of the Chicago, Burlington and Quincy Railroad Company," 244-45; Atlantic Coast Line Railroad Company, *Everglades Pay Dirt: Opportunities for Agriculture, Grazing, Dairying* (Wilmington, n.d.); Great Northern Railway Company, *Annual Report*, 1938, 7; Union Pacific Railroad Company, *Irrigation Guide* (n.p., n.d.); *Railway Freight Traffic*, 2(Dec. 1954):44.

9. American Railway Development Association, *Proceedings*, 1952, 84-86; Illinois Central Railroad Company, Agriculture and Forestry Department, Summary of Activities, 1968, 33-34.

10. American Railway Development Association, *Proceedings*, 1965, 53; *Ties* 22(Oct. 1968):6.

11. *Railway Age* 153(6 Aug. 1962):26; *Ties* 22(Dec. 1968):9-11.

12. *Ohio Farmer* 179(5 June 1937):397; Atlantic Coast Line Railroad Company, *Annual Report* 1937, 14; *U.S. Federal Extension Service* 8(Oct. 1937):147; *Market Growers' Journal* 62(1 Mar. 1938):146-47; Great Northern Railway Company, *Annual Report*, 1939, 9; 1940, 12; *Illinois Central Magazine* 29(Apr. 1941):15-16; 30(Feb. 1942):13-14.

13. *Railway Age* 123(12 July 1947):63, 87; Purdue University Department of Agricultural Extension, *Annual Report*, 1947, 14, 89-90; American Railway Development Association, *Proceedings*, 1949, 101; *Illinois Central Magazine* 35(Feb. 1947):17; *Business Week*, 2 Apr. 1955, 26-27; Union Pacific Railroad Company, *Annual Report*, 1957, 27; American Railway Development Association, *Proceedings*, 1950, 188.

14. Cimco Farm, *Fourth Annual Bulletin*; *Cimco Fortnightly* 2(1 Sept. 1934:) 1; *Railway Age* 91(18 July 1931):108; *Missouri Pacific Lines Magazine* 10(Jan. 1933):9, 53; Lemly, *Gulf, Mobile and Ohio*, 199.

15. *Santa Fe Magazine* 51(June 1958):44; *Rock Island Lines News Digest* 3(Nov. 1944):5; *Boys' and Girls' Club Record* 16 (Oct. 1936):5; Atlantic Coast Line Railroad Company, *Annual Report*, 1941, 16

16. *Electrical West* 86(June 1941):102; Illinois Central Railroad Company, *Annual Report*, 1945, 12; *International Review of Agriculture* 30(Jan.-June 1939):71T; Gulf, Mobile and Ohio Railroad Company, *Annual Report*, 1960, 9; 1968, 5; *GM&O News* 47(15 May 1966):4; Lemly, *Gulf, Mobile and Ohio*, 213; *What's Happening in Community Service*, Apr. 1950; June, 1950; Dec., 1950.

17. American Railway Development Association, *Proceedings*, 1936, 56, 59-60; Atlantic Coast Line Railroad Company, *Annual Report*, 1934, 13-14; 1939, 13; Purdue University Department of Agricultural Extension, *Annual Report*, 1941, 32; *B and O Magazine* 24(July 1938), 10; *Milwaukee Magazine* 24(Sept. 1936):11; *Michigan Extension News* 6(Sept. 1936):5.

18. *Railway Age* 123(5 July 1947):46; 128(22 Apr. 1950):784-85.

19. American Railway Development Association, *Proceedings*, 1954, 26; *Railway Freight Traffic* 4(Nov. 1956):24.

20. American Railway Development Association, *Proceedings*, 1970, 70-72.

21. *Illinois Central Magazine* 29(July 1940):22; *Jersey Bulletin* 64(20 Oct. 1945):1484; Illinois Central Railroad Company, *Annual Report*, 1945, 11; 1951, 23; Illinois Central Railroad Company, Agricultural Development Department, Summary of Activities, 1968, 11; "Fifty Years of Cooperative Extension in Wisconsin, 1912-1962," University of Wisconsin Agricultural Extension Service, *Circular* 602(Madison, 1962),41.

22. *Missouri Pacific Lines Magazine* 9(Nov. 1930):3, 78-79; 10(Nov. 1932):23; American Railway Development Association, *Proceedings*, 1940, 85-90; Purdue University Department of Agricultural Extension, *Annual Report*, 1940, 94.

23. Jones, "Agricultural Development Program of the Chicago, Burlington and Quincy Railroad," 18, 241; Cimco Farm, *Fourth Annual Bulletin*; *Milwaukee*

Magazine 25(Oct. 1937):7, 11; *Railway Age* 123(5 July 1947):48; Great Northern Railway Company, *Annual Report*, 1946, 7; 1947, 11.

24. *B and O Magazine* 24(Mar. 1938):8; Waggener, *Western Agriculture*, 38; *Cimco Fortnightly* 11(31 Oct. 1942); *Milwaukee Magazine* 27(May 1939):10.

25. *Milwaukee Magazine* 30(Dec. 1942):6; *Illinois Central Magazine* 20(Mar. 1932):7; Great Northern Railway Company, *Annual Report*, 1935, 9; 1939, 9; American Railway Development Association, *Proceedings*, 1940, 80–82; 1961, 48; *Railway Age* 123(5 July 1947):45.

26. Illinois Central Railroad Company, *Organization and Traffic*, 248–49; *L and N Employes' Magazine* 8(Jan. 1933):10; 8(Sept. 1932):13; *Missouri Pacific Lines Magazine* 10(Mar. 1933):11, 53; *Market Growers' Journal* 64(Apr. 1939):171–72; Purdue University Department of Agricultural Extension, *Annual Report*, 1938, 97; 1945, 69; 1947, 74.

27. *Market Growers' Journal*, 82(Sept. 1953):10.

28. *Illinois Central Magazine* 30(Aug. 1941):18; 31(Oct. 1942):11; 28(Oct. 1939):16.

29. *Illinois Central Magazine* 24(Jan. 1936):22; Illinois Central Railroad Company, *Organization and Traffic*, 249–50; American Railway Development Association, *Proceedings*, 1946, 24; *Railway Age* 123(5 July 1947):48; *Modern Railroads* 19(July 1964):115.

30. *Engineering News-Record* 114(31 Jan. 1935):167–69; Jones, "Agricultural Development Program of the Chicago, Burlington and Quincy Railroad," 260–61; Oliver Knight, "Correcting Nature's Error: The Colorado-Big Thompson Project," *Agricultural History* 30(Oct. 1956):158.

31. Union Pacific Railroad Company, *Annual Report*, 1958, 25; Jones, "Agricultural Development Program of the Chicago, Burlington and Quincy Railroad," 301–2; A. L. Walker and others, "The Economic Significance of Columbia Basin Development," Washington Agricultural Experiment Station, *Bulletin* 669(Pullman, 1966), 13, 29.

32. *Agricultural Development Bulletin* 6(Jan. 1930):5; Waggener, *Western Agriculture*, 56–57; John J. McCann, "Soil Conservation – All Aboard," *Banking* 40(Jan. 1948):54.

33. American Railway Development Association, *Proceedings*, 1936, 63–66; *Railway Freight Traffic* 1(Sept. 1953):31; Illinois Central Railroad Company, Agricultural and Forestry Department, Summary of Activities, 1965, 3; *Illinois Central Magazine* 57(Mar. 1966):6; Gulf, Mobile and Ohio Railroad Company, *Annual Report*, 1962, 5; 1968, 5; C. W. Burrage to author, 5 Dec. 1969.

34. American Railway Development Association, *Proceedings*, 1949, 85–86, 101.

35. American Railway Development Association, *Proceedings*, 1938, 17–18; 1952, 96–98; 1959, 40–42; 1954, 223; Boston and Maine Railroad Company, *Annual Report*, 1932, 7; *Illinois Central Magazine* 23(Jan. 1935):21.

36. American Railway Development Association, *Proceedings*, 1940, 116; 1946, 28; *Railway Age* 123(5 July 1947):46; 138 (31 Jan. 1955):24.

37. *Ties* 19(Aug. 1965):9; *Modern Railroads* 21(Aug. 1966):160–61; Southern Railway Company, *Annual Report*, 1967, 7.

38. Clark, *Then Came the Railroads*, 297–98; American Railway Development Association, *Proceedings*, 1959, 36; 1960, 48; 1963, 32–36; *Rock Island Lines News Digest*, 3(Oct. 1944):6; *Railway Age* 153(6 Aug. 1962):38.

39. American Railway Development Association, *Proceedings*, 1959, 35–38; 1960, 44–48, 53–55.

40. American Railway Development Association, *Proceedings*, 1948, 60, 68; 1952, 100; 1958, 7, 75–76; 1971, 17–19; *Railway Age* 128(18 Mar. 1950):567;

Railroad Agricultural Colonization and Development, memo supplied by Missouri Pacific Railroad Company, 7–8.

41. American Railway Development Association, *Proceedings,* 1938, 88; 1941, 49.

42. *Traffic World* 93(6 Feb. 1954):82.

CHAPTER EIGHT

1. Sherry H. Olson, *The Depletion Myth: A History of Railroad Use of Timber* (Cambridge, 1971): 36–38; Ridgley, "Railroads and the Development of the Dakotas," 40–45; American Railway Engineering Association, *Proceedings,* 1915 (Chicago, 1915): 989–96.

2. *Manufacturers Record* 43(30 Apr. 1903):293; F. William Rane, "Beautifying the Steel Highway," *Forestry and Irrigation* 12(July 1906):338, 340.

3. Andrews, "Railroads and Farming," 36; *Commercial West,* 6(13 Feb. 1904):43; *Southern Farm Magazine* 10(Oct. 1902):25–26; Rane, "Beautifying the Steel Highway," 338–40; *Forestry and Irrigation* 14(Aug. 1908):426–27.

4. *Manufacturers Record* 41(20 Feb. 1902):75; *Railway Age Gazette* 58(16 Apr. 1915):856; *Railway Purchases and Stores* 49(Mar. 1956):89–90; Olson, *Depletion Myth,* 82–87; *Railway and Engineering Review* 45(8 July 1905):504; 50 (12 Mar. 1910):252–55; *Engineering News* 63(31 Mar. 1910):374.

5. Olson, *Depletion Myth,* 87, 90; *Conservation* 15(June 1909):373; *Railway World* 53(28 May 1909):433; 54(11 Mar. 1910):193; *Commercial West* 11(20 Apr. 1907): 37; *Railway and Engineering Review* 47(2 Feb. 1907):81; *Railway Age* 120(20 Apr. 1946):854.

6. E. A. Sterling, "Forest Management on the Delaware and Hudson Adirondack Forest," *Journal of Forestry* 30(May 1932):569–74; *American Forestry* 17(May 1911):31; *American Railroads* 1(12 July 1920):4; American Railway Development Association, *Proceedings,* 1928, 94.

7. Olson, *Depletion Myth,* 95–104; *Railway Purchases and Stores* 49 (Mar. 1956):89–90.

8. *Railway Age* 79(31 Oct. 1925): 833–34; *Manufacturers Record* 87(7 May 1925):117; R. S. Young, "The Role of Forest Products in Railroad Revenue," *Journal of Forestry* 30(Mar. 1932): 318–22; *Railway Age* 78(28 Mar., 13 June 1925): 849, 1498; Southern Railway Company, *Annual Report,* 1924, 6.

9. *American Forestry* 28(Mar. 1922):191; *Manufacturers Record* 85(5 June 1924):114; 90(7 Oct. 1926):113; *Illinois Central Magazine* 12(Feb. 1924):39; *Missouri Pacific Lines Magazine* 6(Sept. 1928):8, 104.

10. *New York Central Lines Magazine* 7(Apr. 1926):44–45, 100; 10(Aug. 1929):83–84; *Railway Age* 88(3 May 1930):1089.

11. Robert N. Hoskins, "Railroads and Foresters," United States Department of Agriculture, *Yearbook,* 1949(Washington, n.d.), 683; O. K. Quivey, "Railroads Have a Stake in Forestry," *American Forests* 54(Oct. 1948):446; William A. Kluender, "Traffic and Timber," *Journal of Forestry* 44(Dec. 1946):1087–88; Corliss, *Illinois Central,* 419.

12. Illinois Central Railroad Company, *Southern Forestry: A Study of the South's Renewable Resource* (Chicago, 1944), 81; Henry E. Clepper, *Professional Forestry in the United States* (Baltimore, 1971), 232–54; Frank Heyward, *History of Industrial Forestry in the South* (Seattle, 1958), 33–34.

13. *Manufacturers Record* 106(Oct. 1937):50; 108(May 1939):56; James B. Craig, "A Railroad Crusades for Forestry," *American Forests* 56(Feb. 1950):7, 9; Illinois Central Railroad Company, *Annual Report,* 1945, 11–12; American Rail-

way Development Association, *Proceedings*, 1954, 25-26, 40; Hoskins, "Railroads and Foresters," 683-84; *Milwaukee Road Magazine* 38(Feb. 1951):9.

14. William J. Duchaine, "The Railroads' Role in Forest Conservation," *Railway Progress* 3(Feb. 1950):22; Robert N. Hoskins, "Railroads and the Forests," *Journal of Forestry* 45(Apr. 1947):283-84; *Illinois Central Magazine* 57(May 1966):7; *Journal of Forestry* 50(Oct. 1952):803.

15. Seaboard Railway Company, *Forestry Bulletin* 2(Aug. 1944); Craig, "A Railroad Crusades for Forestry," 38; Baltimore and Ohio Railroad Company, *Balancing the Timber Budget in the Bumper Belt* (n.p., n.d.); *Illinois Central Magazine* 51(June 1959):7.

16. *Manufacturers Record* 110(Oct. 1941):34, 68; Hoskins, "Railroads and Forests," 283-84.

17. *Manufacturers Record* 103(Nov. 1934):22; Seaboard Railway Company, *Forestry Bulletin* 1(July 1943); *Railway Age* 128(15 Apr., 18 May 1950):740, 1002.

18. Seaboard Railway Company, *Forestry Bulletin* (June 1947); Duchaine, "Forest Conservation," 18-19; *Railway Age* 128(15 Apr. 1950):740; American Railway Development Association, *Proceedings*, 1951, 112; Chicago, St. Paul, Minneapolis and Omaha Railway Company, *Annual Report*, 1954, 5.

19. American Railway Development Association, *Proceedings*, 1949, 69; 1950, 38-39; 1954, 26; *Illinois Central Magazine*, 51(Aug. 1959):8; *Journal of Forestry* 50(Oct. 1952):803; Illinois Central Industries, *Annual Report*, 1965, 14; *Railway Purchases and Stores* 49(Mar. 1956):90-91.

20. Duchaine, "Forest Conservation," 19-21; *Railway Age* 128(15 Apr. 1950):741; 123(5 July 1947):45; American Railway Development Association, *Proceedings*, 1951, 112; Anderson, *St. Louis Southwestern*, 59, 61.

21. Duchaine, "Forest Conservation," 21; *Railway Age* 131(3 Sept. 1951):44-46; *Milwaukee Road Magazine* 38(Feb. 1951):6-9; 56(May-June 1958):15.

22. Paul F. Sharp, "The Tree Farm Movement: Its Origin and Development," *Agricultural History* 23(Jan. 1949):41; Ralph W. Hidy and others, *Timber and Men: The Weyerhaeuser Story* (New York, 1963), 502-5; *Railway Age* 128(15 Apr. 1950):741; American Railway Development Association, *Proceedings*, 1951, 112.

23. *Railway Age* 137(20 Dec. 1954):34; *Illinois Central Magazine* 51(May 1960):2; 54(Feb. 1963):7; 55 (Sept. 1963):5.

24. *Traffic World* 110 (12 May 1962):47-48; *Southern Pulp and Paper Manufacturer* 35(10 June 1972):18-20, 25-26.

25. Seaboard Air Line Railroad Company, *Annual Report*, 1945, 13; Seaboard Railroad, *Forestry Bulletin* 19(Sept. 1949); (Sept. 1969); *Railway Age* 127 (3 Sept. 1949):443; 123(6 Sept. 1947):390; *Manufacturers Record* 117(May 1948):75; *Traffic World* 110(12 May 1962):48.

26. *Railway Age* 121(28 Dec. 1946):1100; *Illinois Central Magazine* 35(Apr. 1947):28; *Railway Purchases and Stores* 49(Mar. 1956):91; Lemly, *Gulf, Mobile and Ohio*, 213-14; Gulf, Mobile and Ohio Railroad Company, *Annual Report*, 1949, 14; 1960, 9; 1961, 4; *GM&O News*, 43(15 May 1966): 4; C. W. Burrage to author, 5 Dec. 1969.

27. *Railway Age* 138(31 Jan. 1955):24; C. W. Burrage to author, 19 May 1973.

28. Corliss, *Illinois Central*, 409; Illinois Central Railroad Company, *Report upon the Mineral Resources of the Illinois Central Railroad* (New York, 1856); James F. Doster, *Railroads in Alabama Politics, 1875-1914* (University, Ala.,1957), 69; Klein, *Louisville and Nashville*, 263-64, 268; C. H. Vivian, "The N and W-A Progressive Railroad," *Compressed Air Magazine* 41(Oct. 1936):5135; Railway Development Association, *Proceedings of the Semi-Annual Meeting*, 1914, 20.

29. Railway Development Association, *Proceedings*, 1917, 66; 1925, 28; E. T. Dumble, *The Geology of East Texas* (Austin, 1918):2; *Railway Age Gazette* 62(22 June 1917):1383.

30. *Railway Age* 75(15 Dec. 1923):1111; *Missouri Pacific Lines Magazine*

17(Mar. 1943):16; A History of the Industrial Development Department – Missouri Pacific Railroad, memo supplied by the company; *Manufacturers Record* 89(20 May 1926):99; 93(22 Mar. 1928):52; American Railway Development Association, *Proceedings,* 1930, 36; F. H. H. Calhoun, *Geological Resources: Seaboard Air Line Railway Territory* (n.p. 1925), 3.

31. Chicago, Milwaukee, St. Paul and Pacific Railroad Company, *Annual Report,* 1941, 8; American Railway Development Association, *Proceedings,* 1946, 27.

32. *Missouri Pacific Lines Magazine* 7(May 1930):15, 91; *Railway Age* 88(28 June 1930):1599; 153(6 Aug. 1962):26; American Railway Development Association, *Proceedings,* 1946, 76–77; 1930, 37–38; 1971, 75.

33. American Railway Development Association, *Proceedings of the Semi-Annual Meeting,* 1928, 25–26.

34. Baltimore and Ohio Railroad Company, *Annual Report,* 1917, 11; *Milwaukee Magazine* 27(July 1939):10; Chicago, Milwaukee, St. Paul and Pacific Railroad Company, *Annual Report,* 1943, 8; 1946, 9; *Railway Age* 129(11 Nov. 1950):75.

35. Union Pacific Railroad Company, *Annual Report,* 1953, 5; 1961, 21; 1962, 19; 1963, 21; *Railway Age* 136(8 Feb. 1954):16.

36. *Manufacturers Record* 93(22 Mar. 1928):52; *Railway Age* 127(13 Aug. 1949):297; *Railway Freight Traffic* 1(Feb. 1953):61; 5(Sept. 1957):33.

37. *Railway Freight Traffic* 5(Dec. 1957):21, 24; *Ties* 7(Dec. 1953):10–12; *Railway Age* 131(1 October 1951):104, 106; *Railway Freight Traffic,* 1(Feb. 1953):28–30; Clair M. Roddewig, *Address before the Oklahoma State Chamber of Commerce, Tulsa, November 7, 1962* (n.p., n.d.); Great Northern Railway Company, *Annual Report,* 1958, 16.

38. *Manufacturers Record* 82(26 Oct. 1922):63–64; American Railway Development Association, *Proceedings,* 1924, 36, 55–56; 1930, 38; *Manufacturers Record* 87(2 Apr. 1925):93; 97(22 May 1930):45.

39. *Engineering and Mining Journal* 157(Dec. 1956):78–79; E. W. Davis, *Pioneering with Taconite* (St. Paul, 1964); Great Northern Railway Company, *Annual Report,* 1953, 10; 1956, 25; 1957, 23; *Skillings' Mining Review* 53(27 June 1964):27; *U.S. News and World Report* 58(22 Mar. 1965):87; *Modern Railways* 21(Dec. 1966):78; *Goat* 35(Aug. 1965):15.

40. *Book of the Royal Blue* 4(Oct. 1900):19–20; *Railway Age* 155(23 Sept. 1962):20; Turner, *Chessie's Road,* 145–46; Vivian, "The N and W–A Progressive Railroad," 5135–36; *Railway Purchases and Stores* 31(Sept. 1938):300–392; Chesapeake and Ohio Railway Company, *Annual Report,* 1952, 11–12.

41. Union Pacific Railroad Company, *Annual Report,* 1960, 5; 1961, 20; 1962, 18–19; 1963, 20–21; 1965, 20; *Chemical Week* 150(19 May 1962):156.

42. *Mississippi Central Round Table* 1(1 Jan. 1927); *Rock Island Employes' Magazine* 8(Apr. 1915):18.

43. *Railway Age Gazette* 51(24 Nov. 1911):1071; 63(5 Oct. 1917):587; Southern Railway Company, *Annual Report,* 1921, 4; *Railway Age* 83(24 Sept. 1927):594; 128(25 Feb., 4 Mar. 1950):411, 449.

44. Union Pacific Railroad Company, *The Fossil Fields of Wyoming* (Omaha, 1909), 3; *Railway Age Gazette* 51(24 Nov. 1911):1071; *Railway Age* 126 (21 May 1949):1038; Dumble, *Geology of East Texas,* 1–2; Chicago, Burlington and Quincy Railroad Company, *Mines and Mining in the Black Hills* (n.p., n.d.).

45. *Manufacturers Record* 48(17 Aug. 1905):113; Norfolk and Western Railway Company, *Official Guide for the Use of the Company's Patrons and Others Seeking Facts Pertaining to Its Territorial Resources* (n.p. 1905), 1; Central of Georgia Railway Company, *Directory of Commercial Minerals in Georgia and Alabama along the Central of Georgia Railway* (Savannah, n.d.), 3, 51–52; *Railway Age* 75(25 Aug. 1923):358.

46. Calhoun, *Geological Resources; Railway Age* 75(15 Dec. 1923):1111; Ameri-

can Railway Development Association, *Proceedings of the Semi-Annual Meeting,* 1928, 27; *B and O Magazine* 8(Oct. 1920):12–13; *Missouri Pacific Lines Magazine* 6(Sept. 1928):13.

47. Baltimore and Ohio Railroad Company, *High Calcium Limestones in the Area Served by the Baltimore and Ohio Railroad Company* (n.p., n.d.), 1; Baltimore and Ohio Railroad Company, *Salt Report for the B and O Area* (n.p., n.d.), 1; *Railway Age* 131(3 Sept. 1951):61; *Railway Freight Traffic* 6(May 1958):11.

48. St. Louis-San Francisco Railway Company, *Kansas Mineral Wealth in the Frisco Belt* (n.p., n.d.); *Railway Freight Traffic* 1(Feb. 1953):61; Missouri Pacific Railway Company, *The Empire that Missouri Pacific Serves* (St. Louis, n.d.); Southern Pacific Company, *Minerals for Industry* (San Francisco, 1964).

CHAPTER NINE

1. J. L. Townshend to author, 22 May 1973; *Industry Week* 181(15 Apr. 1974):16–17.

2. Anderson, *St. Louis Southwestern,* 92; *Railway Age* 169(31 Aug. 1970):36; *Railway Progress* 4(Apr. 1950):32; *Sales Management* 54(15 Apr. 1945):90; Clark, *Then Came the Railroads,* 307–8; *Missouri Pacific Lines Magazine* 30(Jan. 1957):6; *Traffic World* 92(5 Dec. 1953):70–74.

3. J. L. Townshend to author, 22 May 1973; American Railway Development Association, *Proceedings,* 1952, 39–40; *Traffic World* 93(1 May 1954):82, 84.

4. Penn Central Railway Company, *Annual Report,* 1967, 10; Otto W. Pongrace to author, 24 May 1973; J. C. Bergene to author, 19 June 1973; J. R. Scott to author, 24 May 1973; J. E. Savely to author, 1 June 1973. For a survey of the modern merger movement, see Richard Saunders, *The Railroad Mergers and the Coming of Conrail* (Westport, Conn., 1978).

5. *Magazine of Wall Street* 100(6 July 1957):455; *Railway Age* 171 (30 Aug. 1971):25; *Missouri Pacific Lines Magazine* 30 (Sept. 1956): 10–11.

6. *Railway Freight Traffic* 5(May 1957):31; *Railway Age* 167(25 Aug. 1969):46; *Dun's Review and Modern Industry* 67(May 1956):67.

7. *Railway Age* 171(30 Aug. 1971):25, 27; 138(31 Jan. 1955):24; J. E. Savely to author, 1 June 1973; C. H. Smith to author, 4 June 1973; J. R. Scott to author, 24 May 1973; *Chicago Tribune,* 16 Apr. 1967; *Magazine of Wall Street* 100(6 June 1957):455; *Modern Railroads* 24(May 1969):71.

8. Erie-Lackawanna Railroad Company, *Annual Report,* 1960, 14; Chesapeake and Ohio-Baltimore and Ohio Railroads, *Annual Report,* 1969, 6; *Railway Age* 138(21 Mar. 1955):10.

9. *Railway Age* 155(23 Sept. 1962):20; John R. Hyland to author, 21 May 1973.

10. *Railway Age* 171(30 Aug. 1971):28; 153(6 Aug. 1962):24; J. E. Savely to author, 1 June 1973; *Railway Freight Traffic* 6(Aug. 1958): 26; *Traffic World* 87(3 Mar. 1951):73.

11. Chicago and North Western Railway Company, *Industrial Site Guide* (n.p., n.d.); American Railway Development Association, *Proceedings,* 1963, 53.

12. *Railway Age* 157(31 Aug. 1964):38; 119(4 Aug. 1945):225; Central of Georgia Railway Company, *Annual Report,* 1955, 10; American Railway Development Association, *Proceedings,* 1963, 53.

13. *Traffic World* 90(1 Nov. 1952):80; *Industrial Development* 129(Sept. 1960):50; *Modern Railroads* 19(July 1964):114.

14. Norfolk and Western Railway Company, *Annual Report,* 1948, 6; Norfolk and Western Railway Company, *Successful Plant Site Locations: Where, How, Why*

(n.p., n.d.); Louisville and Nashville Railroad Company, *Full Throttle* (n.p., n.d.); Louisville and Nashville Railroad Company, *Focus on the South* (n.p., n.d.); Santa Fe Railway Company, *North Texas Industrial Empire* (n.p., n.d.); Santa Fe Railway Company, *Six Fine Areas for Industrial Development in Wichita* (n.p., n.d.); Nashville, Chattanooga and St. Louis Railway Company, *Southland Industrial Center: The South's First Planned Industrial District* (n.p., n.d.).

15. *Ties* 9(Mar. 1955):6; *New York Times,* 12 Mar. 1972; John R. Hyland to author, 21 May 1973; *Industrial Development,* 129(Aug. 1960):64; A. F. Hatcher to author, 14 June 1973.

16. Seaboard Air Line Railway Company, *Annual Report,* 1948, 29; 1949, 22; *Railway Age* 131(6 August 1951):70; 146(16 Feb. 1959):60; American Railway Development Association, *Proceedings,* 1963, 53.

17. *Railway Freight Traffic* 2(Nov. 1954):20–21; *Railway Age* 161(29 Aug. 1966):31; *Missouri Pacific Lines Magazine* 36(July–Aug. 1962):10; *Ties* 19(Oct. 1965):14.

18. *Railway Freight Traffic* 2(Dec. 1954):41; *Railway Age* 182(9 Nov. 1981): 30–32; Southern Pacific Transportation Company, *What is the Golden Empire?* (n.p., n.d.); *Traffic World* 130 (15 April 1967):92.

19. Chicago and Eastern Illinois Railroad Company, *Industrial Potentialities of Southern Illinois* (Chicago, 1953); *Railway Age* 143(2 Dec. 1957):23; *Railway Freight Traffic* 1(Oct. 1953):41–42; Norfolk and Western Railway Company, *Annual Report,* 1960, 15; 1961, 16; *Railway Age* 155(23 Sept. 1963):21.

20. *Railway Age,* 157(14 Dec. 1964):8, 23; *Modern Railroads* 26(Oct. 1971):66; Chicago, Milwaukee, St. Paul and Pacific Railroad Company, *Annual Report,* 1968, 9; *Railway Age* 182(9 Nov. 1981):32.

21. *Magazine of Wall Street* 100(6 July 1957):488; American Railway Development Association, *Proceedings,* 1961, 58; *Railway Age* 161(29 Aug. 1966):31; Chicago, Burlington and Quincy Railroad Company, *Annual Report,* 1966, 13; *New York Times,* 12 Mar. 1972.

22. Missouri Pacific Lines, *Industrial Sites Available in Greater St. Louis* (n.p., n.d.); *Milwaukee Road Magazine* 45(July–Aug. 1957):4–5.

23. *Railway Age* 155(23 Sept. 1963):29; 126(21 May 1949):1038; 169(31 Aug. 1970):36; *Railway Freight Traffic* 1(Aug. 1953):25; American Railway Development Association, *Proceedings,* 1962, 56.

24. *Industrial Development* 132(July 1963):35; *Santa Fe Magazine* 49(Feb. 1955):45; *Illinois Central Magazine* 53(Apr. 1962):15; *Dun's Review and Modern Industry* 59(Mar. 1957):51, 122–23; Anderson, *St. Louis Southwestern,* 93; J. C. Bergene to author, 19 June 1973; R. E. Bisha to author, 6 Mar. 1961; Overton, *Burlington Route,* 569; *Railway Age* 169(31 Aug. 1970):36; *Modern Railroads* 23 (July 1968):79; *Traffic World* 87(3 Feb. 1951):69–71; Farrington, *Railroads of the Hour,* 172–73; *Railway Freight Traffic* 3(Mar. 1955):28.

25. American Railway Development Association, *Proceedings,* 1955, 10–11; *Railway Freight Traffic,* 6(June 1958):38; *Railway Age* 150(26 June 1961):68; Memphis *Commercial Appeal,* 28 Mar. 1963, 28 Mar. 1968.

26. James H. Thompson, *Methods of Plant Site Selection Available to Small Manufacturing Firms* (Morgantown, 1961), 102–3; *Railway Age* 157(31 Aug. 1964):47; *Railway Progress* 4(Apr. 1950):29.

27. Gulf, Mobile and Ohio Railroad Company, *Annual Report,* 1950, 10; *Railway Freight Traffic* 2(Nov. 1954):20; John W. Barringer, *Super-Railroads for a Dynamic American Economy* (New York, 1956), 53; *Railway Age* 147(23 Nov. 1959):9; 159(30 Aug. 1965):18; Victor Gruen Associates, *A Proposal for the Development of the East Shore Tidelands of San Francisco Bay Prepared for the Atchison, Topeka and Santa Fe Railway Company* (n.p., 1963).

28. American Railway Development Association, *Proceedings,* 1952, 50–51; Donald R. Gilmore, *Developing the "Little" Economies* (New York, n.d.), 58; *Railway Age* 148(30 May 1960):58.

29. Union Pacific Railroad Company, *Annual Report,* 1953, 26; 1954, 30; 1955, 30; 1956, 29; 1957, 30; 1965, 22; *Railway Age* 159(30 Aug. 1965):21.

30. *Magazine of Wall Street* 100(6 July 1957):488; Chicago, Milwaukee, St. Paul and Pacific Railroad Company, *Annual Report,* 1965, 7; 1966, 8; 1967, 9; Southern Railway Company, *Annual Report,* 1965, 5; American Railway Development Association, *Proceedings,* 1952, 51; *Railway Age* 137(20 Sept. 1954):17; 120(8 May 1946):1004; 161(19 Aug. 1966):54; Northern Pacific Railway Company, *Annual Report,* 1951, 8; 1952, 10; Illinois Central Railroad Company, *Annual Report,* 1958, 13; Chicago, Rock Island and Pacific Railroad Company, *Annual Report,* 1949, 12; 1950, 13; *Railway Age* 157(31 Aug. 1964):41; 169(31 Aug. 1970):41.

31. *Railway Age* 165(26 Aug. 1968):29–30; 159(30 Aug. 1965):20; Southern Railway Company, *Annual Report,* 1973, 10.

32. *Railway Age* 171(30 Aug. 1971):26; 169 (31 Aug. 1970):36; 159(30 Aug. 1965):21; Otto W. Pongrace to author, 24 May, 1973; Burlington Northern, *Annual Report,* 1970, 9; J. L. Townshend to author, 22 May 1973; Atchison, Topeka and Santa Fe Railway Company, *Annual Report,* 1966, 13; *Modern Railroads* 23(July 1968):50; *Southern Pacific Land Company* (n.p., n.d.), 3; *Industrial Development* 139(Jan.–Feb. 1970):9, *Railway Age* 171(3 Aug. 1971):28; J. E. Savely to author, 1 June 1973.

33. American Railway Development Association, *Proceedings,* 1952, 51; 1961, 58; Louisville and Nashville Railroad Company, *Annual Report,* 1957, 19; *Missouri Pacific Lines Magazine* 30(Jan. 1957):6–7.

34. *Iron Age* 178(26 Apr. 1956):58; American Railway Development Association, *Proceedings,* 1952, 51–52; 1957, 52–56; *Industrial Development* 128(June 1959):42; Bryant, *Santa Fe,* 248; Robert R. Johnson, "Role of Railroads in Small Community Industrial Development" (M.A. thesis, Industrial Development Institute, University of Oklahoma, 1967); *Railway Freight Traffic* 3(Aug. 1955):22.

35. *Railway Age* 152(22 Jan. 1962):39; 163(28 Aug. 1967):31; *Modern Railroads* 23(July 1968):50; Clark, *Then Came the Railroads,* 309–10; Santa Fe Railway Company, *A Fine Address for Industry in Houston* (n.p., n.d.).

36. American Railway Development Association, *Proceedings,* 1958, 44–48; *Railway Freight Traffic* 3(Dec. 1955):56–57; Union Pacific Railroad Company, *Annual Report,* 1963, 23; *Railway Age* 150(6 Feb. 1961):36; 160(6 June 1966):46; *Industrial Development* 131(July 1962):55; 135(Feb. 1966):50–51.

37. Clark, *Then Came the Railroads,* 309; *Industrial Development* 118(Jan. 1949):38; *Manufacturers Record* 123(May 1954):40–41; *Railway Age* 157(31 Aug. 1964):45; *Railway Freight Traffic* 3(Dec. 1955):56.

38. *Railway Freight Traffic* 5(May 1957):29–31; *Industrial Development* 131(July 1962):51.

39. St. Louis-San Francisco Railway Company, *Annual Report,* 1965, 11; St. Louis-San Francisco Railway Company, *Frisco Planned Industrial Districts* (n.p., n.d.); *Industrial Development* 133(July 1964):15; Farrington, *Railroads of the Hour,* 168–74; Chicago, Rock Island and Pacific Railroad Company, *Annual Report,* 1949, 12; A. F. Hatcher to author, 14 June 1973.

40. F. B. Stratton, Rail Facilities on Industrial Sites, memo provided by Western Pacific Railroad, 1–6; Daniel T. Daggett, What Should an Industrial Park Developer Expect from a Railroad? MS provided by the author; Chicago, Rock Island and Pacific Railroad Company, *Annual Report,* 1954, 10; American Railway

Development Association, *Proceedings*, 1957, 55; *Railway Freight Traffic*, 3(May 1955):19–20.

41. Union Pacific Railroad Company, *Annual Report*, 1946–1952; Northern Pacific Railway Company, *Annual Report*, 1949, 8; 1950, 8; 1952, 10; *Railway Age* 134(4 May 1953):68–69.

42. *Railway Age* 126(12 May 1949):1034; New York Central System, *The Greater Springfield Ohio Area* (n.p., n.d.); *Railway Age* 180(27 Aug. 1980):34–36.

43. *Railway Freight Traffic* 2(Dec. 1954):43; American Railway Development Association, *Proceedings*, 1949, 60, 63–64; 1952, 59; 1954, 52–53, 64; J. R. Townshend to author, 22 May 1973.

44. *United States v. United Stock Yards and Transit Company*, 226 U.S. 286; American Railway Development Association, *Proceedings*, 1947, 26–27; 1949, 62–64; 1950, 161, 164–73; 1954, 56–58; *Railway Age* 169(31 Aug. 1970):36; *Ties* 10(Feb. 1956):5–6.

45. *Santa Fe Magazine* 49(Dec. 1955):13; *Railway Age* 126(21 May 1949):1037; American Railway Development Association, *Proceedings*, 1954, 64–65; *Railway Freight Traffic* 5(Oct. 1957):34; *Industrial Development* 129(Aug. 1960):56; J. S. Frost to author, 13 Mar. 1961.

46. *Railway Freight Traffic* 3(July 1955):28; American Railway Development Association, *Proceedings*, 1947, 28–29; 1950, 150–53; R. E. Bisha to author, 6 Mar. 1961; J. E. Savely to author, 1 June 1973; Robert M. Edgar, *The Railroad's Place in Industrial Development* (n.p. 1948), 15–19; Daggett, What Should an Industrial Park Developer Expect from a Railroad?; Denver and Rio Grande Western Railroad Company, *Annual Report*, 1965–1969.

47. Daggett, What Should an Industrial Park Developer Expect from a Railroad?; *Railway Age* 173(8 Aug. 1972):52.

48. *Railway Progress* 4(Apr. 1950):30; American Railway Development Association, *Proceedings*, 1952, 52; 1959, 71; *Railway Age* 133(3 Nov. 1952):45; 165(26 Aug. 1968):30.

49. American Railway Development Association, *Proceedings*, 1946, 82–83; 1950, 135–37; 1954, 44–47; *Traffic World* 87(3 Mar. 1951):74; 87(5 May 1951):58.

50. *Railway Age* 174(27 Aug. 1973):33; *Southern Pacific Land Company*, 3; Northern Pacific Railway Company, *Annual Report*, 1956, 12; American Railway Development Association, *Proceedings*, 1954, 68–70; *Industrial Development* 129(Feb. 1960):60; *Southern Pacific Land Company*, 2–5; *Sequoia Pacific: A Southern Pacific Company* (n.p., n.d.).

51. *Modern Railroads* 17(Feb. 1962):61–63; American Railway Development Association, *Proceedings*, 1963, 16; *Illinois Central Magazine* 52(Mar. 1961):7–8; Illinois Central Industries, *Annual Report*, 1966, 2; Pennsylvania Railroad Company, *Annual Report*, 1965, 12; *Railway Age* 174(27 Aug. 1973):31.

52. American Railway Development Association, *Proceedings*, 1959, 43–44; 1963, 113–15; *Railway Freight Traffic* 5(Dec. 1957):19; *Railway Age* 163(28 Aug. 1967):30; Chicago, Burlington and Quincy Railroad Company, *Annual Report*, 1968, 9.

53. *Railway Age* 159(30 Aug. 1965):19.

CHAPTER TEN

1. Leland H. Jenks, "Railways as an Economic Force in American Development," *Journal of Economic History* 4(May 1944):1–20; Leonard J. Arrington, "The

Transcontinental Railroad and the Development of the West," *Utah Historical Quarterly* 37(Winter 1969):14.

2. *Railway and Engineering Review* 46(10 Feb., 4 Aug. 1906):88, 586; *Commercial West* 13(8 Jan. 1908):54; Lester F. Sheffy, *The Life and Times of Timothy Dwight Hobart, 1855–1935* (Canyon, Tex., 1955), 116; *Commercial West* 31(21 Apr. 1917):9.

3. Waters, *Santa Fe*, 251; *Manufacturers Record* 55(25 Mar. 1909):48; *Commercial West* 31(31 Mar. 1917):5, 36–37; 3(22 Feb. 1902):23; 17(4 June 1910):45; Fleming, "Immigration to the Southern States," 289; *Railway Age Gazette* 56(22 May 1914):1164.

4. *Southern Farm Magazine* 9(Apr. 1901):9; 11(Dec. 1903):28; Southern Railway Company, *Annual Report*, 1902, 24; Atlantic Coast Line Railroad Company, *Annual Report*, 1905–1907; Dozier, *Atlantic Coast Line*, 181; *Railway World* 51(4 Jan. 1907):11–12; *Illinois Central Magazine*, 51(June 1959):6; 5(Sept. 1916):43; Gulf and Ship Island Railroad Company, *Annual Report*, 1912–1915.

5. Andrews, "Railroads and Farming," 25–26; John Hamilton to Railroad Presidents and Railroad Industrial Agents, 3 Apr. 1912, Office of Experiment Stations Records; M. C. Wilson and A. L. Clapp, "Extension Results as Influenced by Various Factors: A Study of 532 Farms and Farm Homes in Clay and Sedgwick Counties, Kansas, 1927," United States Department of Agriculture, *Extension Service Circular* 77(Washington, 1928):20; M. C. Wilson, "Extension Methods and Their Relative Effectiveness," United States Department of Agriculture, *Technical Bulletin* 106(Washington, 1929).

6. U.S. *Fourteenth Census: Agriculture,* vol. 4, pt. 1:214–19; pt. 2:575–81; U.S. *Sixteenth Census: Agriculture,* vol. 1, pt. 5:108–9.

7. Corliss, *Illinois Central,* 300; Fairfax Harrison, *The Relation of Southern Railway Company to Southern Progress* (n.p. 1914); Chicago, Rock Island and Pacific Railway Company, *Annual Report,* 1905–1914; Atlantic Coast Line Railroad Company, *Annual Report,* 1905–1914; Central of Georgia Railway Company, *Annual Report,* 1901–1906; Number of New and Expanded Industries Located on Missouri Pacific Railroad, memo supplied by Missouri Pacific Railroad; *Manufacturers Record* 42(23 Oct. 1902):244.

8. Chesapeake and Ohio Railway Company, *Annual Report,* 1921–1927, 1931–1936; *Manufacturers Record* 106(Apr. 1937):41; *Illinois Central Magazine* 21(May 1933):10; 22(Feb. 1934):3; Number of New and Expanded Industries Located on Missouri Pacific Railroad, memo supplied by Missouri Pacific Railroad; *Railway Age* 90(21 Mar. 1931):606.

9. Gulf, Mobile and Ohio Railroad Company, *Annual Report,* 1959–1970; Union Pacific Railroad Company, *Annual Report,* 1954–1969; *Industrial Development* 139(Jan.–Feb. 1970):9; Atlantic Coast Line Railroad Company, *Annual Report,* 1946–1966; Erie-Lackawanna Railroad Company, *Annual Report,* 1960–1963; Dereco, Inc., *Annual Report,* 1968–1971; J. C. Kenady to author, 18 Dec. 1979, 24 Jan. 1980; D. T. Daggett to author, 31 Dec. 1979.

10. Number of New and Expanded Industries Located on Missouri Pacific Railroad, memo supplied by Missouri Pacific Railroad; Farrington, *Railroads of the Hour,* 21; D. T. Daggett to author, 31 Dec. 1979.

11. *Railway Age* 78(31 Jan. 1925):335; 90(31 Jan., 9 May 1931):302, 957; *Manufacturers Record* 105(Mar. 1936):40.

12. New York Central Railroad Company, *Annual Report,* 1965, 11; Otto W. Pongrace to author, 24 May 1973; *Railway Age* 178(29 Aug. 1977):20; Louisville and Nashville Railroad Company, *Annual Report,* 1967, 13; Boston and Maine Corporation, *Annual Report,* 1968, 8; *Railway Age* 159(30 Aug. 1965):17–18; Thomas J. Judge to author, 18 May 1973.

13. Erie Railroad Company, *Annual Report,* 1953, 18; 1954, 17; 1955, 23; Martin M. Pomphrey to author, 26 June 1973; J. C. Kenady to author, 18 Dec. 1979, 24 Jan. 1980.

14. Northern Pacific Railway Company, *Annual Report,* 1956, 10; 1969, 10; Chicago, Rock Island and Pacific Railroad Company, *Annual Report,* 1968, 12, 1973, 8.

15. *Railway Freight Traffic,* 1(Aug. 1953):26; *Railway Age* 157(31 Aug. 1964):30; *Missouri Pacific Lines Magazine* 30(Jan. 1957):6; *Railway Age* 153(6 Aug. 1962):31; 155(23 Sept. 1963):20.

16. *Traffic World* 91(2 May, 1953):74–75; *Railway Freight Traffic* 3(Aug. 1955):21; *Industrial Development* 129(Sept. 1960):52; *Illinois Central Magazine* 58(Apr. 1967):10; *Chemical Week* 90(19 May 1962):153.

17. *Railway Age* 157(31 Aug. 1964):45–48; J. L. Townshend to author, 6 Mar. 1961.

BIBLIOGRAPHY

Primary Sources

MANUSCRIPTS

The Agricultural Department of the Illinois Central Has a Wide Field of Activity. Memo provided by Illinois Central Railroad.

Agricultural Development—Missouri Pacific Railroad. Memo provided by Missouri Pacific Railroad.

Agricultural Extension Service Records. National Archives, Washington.

Bailey, Liberty Hyde. Papers. Cornell University Library, Ithaca.

A Century of Agricultural Progress along the Illinois Central. Memo supplied by Paul K. Farlow.

Daggett, Daniel T. What Should an Industrial Park Developer Expect from a Railroad? MS provided by author.

Hardy, J. C. Papers. Mississippi State University Library, Mississippi State.

History of Industrial Development along the Norfolk and Western. Memo supplied by Norfolk and Western Railway.

A History of the Industrial Development Department, Missouri Pacific Railroad. Memo supplied by Missouri Pacific Railroad.

Illinois Central Railroad: Agricultural Development. Memo supplied by Paul K. Farlow.

Illinois Central Railroad Company. Agriculture and Forestry Department, Summary of Activities, 1965–1968. Copies supplied by Illinois Central Railroad Company.

Industrial Real Estate. Memo supplied by Norfolk and Western Railway.

King, R. C. Letterbooks. Mississippi State University Library, Mississippi State.

Mississippi Extension Service Records. Mississippi State University Library, Mississippi State.

Missouri Agricultural College Papers. University of Missouri Library, Columbia.

Number of New and Expanded Industries Located on Missouri Pacific Railroad. Memo supplied by Missouri Pacific Railroad.

Office of Experiment Stations Records. National Archives, Washington.

Railroad Agicultural Colonization and Development. Memo supplied by Missouri Pacific Railroad.

Secretary of Agriculture Records. National Archives, Washington.

Stratton, F. B. Rail Facilities on Industrial Sites. Memo supplied by Western Pacific Railroad.

LETTERS TO THE AUTHOR

Bergene, J. C.
Bisha, R. E.
Blazowich, Nick
Burrage, C. W.
Daggett, D. T.
Frost, J. S.
Hatcher, A. F.
Hyland, John R.
Judge, Thomas J.
Kenady, J. C.

Martin, T. T.
Nicholas, R. H.
Pomphrey, Martin M.
Pongrace, Otto W.
Sappington, Charles W.
Savely, J. E.
Scott, J. R.
Smith, C. H.
Taylor, J. R.
Townshend, J. L.

GOVERNMENT DOCUMENTS

American Association of Farmers' Institute Workers. "Proceedings, 1902." U.S. Office of Experiment Stations, *Bulletin* 120. Washington, 1902.

Andrews, Frank. "Railroads and Farming." U.S. Bureau of Statistics, *Bulletin* 100. Washington, 1912.

Cullen, George A. "The Relation of the Railroad to the Farmer." Massachusetts State Board of Agriculture, *Circular* 82, 3–15. Boston, 1918.

Edwards, J. L. *Circular Letter* nos. 1, 22, 33, 38-A. United States Railroad Administration.

"Fifty Years of Cooperative Extension in Wisconsin, 1912–1962." University of Wisconsin Agricultural Extension Service, *Circular* 602. Madison, 1962.

Florida Agricultural Extension Service. *Annual Report,* 1921–1952. N.p., n.d.

Hamilton, John. "The Transportation Companies as Factors in Agricultural Extension." U.S. Office of Experiment Stations, *Circular* 112. Washington, 1911.

Hoskins, Robert N. "Railroads and Foresters." U.S. Department of Agriculture, *Yearbook,* 1949, 682–85. Washington, n.d.

"The Livestock Special Train." Montana State College Extension Service, *Bulletin* 96. Bozeman, 1928.

Maryland Agricultural Extension Service. *Annual Report,* 1915–1957. College Park, n.d.

In the Matter of Leases and Grants of Property by Carriers. 73 ICC 671.

Mississippi Agricultural and Mechanical College. *Biennial Report,* 1912–1913. Nashville, 1913.

Montana Farmers' Institutes. *Ninth and Tenth Annual Reports,* 1910–1912. Bozeman, 1912.

National Industrial Traffic League v. Aberdeen and Rockfish Railroad Company. 61 ICC 120.

North Carolina Agricultural Extension Service. *Annual Report,* 1916. Raleigh, 1917.

"Progress: A Few Steps Forward in Montana's Agricultural Program." Montana Extension Service, *Bulletin* 97. N.p. 1929.

Purdue University Department of Agricultural Extension. *Annual Report,* 1927. West LaFayette, n.d.

"Recommended Farm Practices for Northern Montana." Montana Extension Service, *Bulletin* 108. Bozeman, 1930.

Re Transportation of Immigrants from New York. 10 ICC 13.

Richards, M. V. "The Relation of Railroads to Agriculture." U.S. Office of Experiment Stations, *Bulletin* 120, 107–9. Washington, 1902.

Starch, E. A. "Economic Changes in Montana's Wheat Area." Montana Agricultural Experiment Station, *Bulletin* 295. Bozeman, 1935.

U.S. *Fourteenth and Sixteenth Census: Agriculture.*

U.S. Interstate Commerce Commission. *Statistics of Railways in the United States,* 1908–1971. Washington, 1909–1972. Title varies.

———. *Uniform System of Accounts for Railway Companies, January 1, 1968.* Washington, n.d.

United States Railroad Administration. *Colorado.* Washington, n.d.

———. Division of Traffic. *Annual Report,* 1919. Washington, 1920.

———. Division of Traffic. *Circular* no. 3. July 10, 1918.

———. *General Order* no. 15. March 26, 1918.

———. *Louisiana.* Washington, n.d.

———. *Minnesota.* Washington, n.d.

———. *Montana.* Washington, n.d.

United States v. United Stock Yards and Transit Company. 226 U.S. 286.

Walker, A. L., and others. "The Economic Significance of Columbia Basin Development." Washington Agricultural Experiment Station, *Bulletin* 669. Pullman, 1966.

Wilson, M. C. "Extension Methods and Their Relative Effectiveness." U.S. Department of Agriculture, *Technical Bulletin* 106. Washington, 1929.

Wilson, M. C., and A. L. Clapp. "Extension Results as Influenced by Various Factors: A Study of 532 Farms and Farm Homes in Clay and Sedgwick Counties, Kansas, 1927." U.S. Department of Agriculture, *Extension Service Circular* 77. Washington, 1928.

Wilson, M. L. "Dry Farming in the North Central Montana 'Triangle'." Montana Agricultural Extension Service, *Bulletin* 66. Bozeman, 1923.

Wilson, M. L., and H. E. Murdock. "Reducing the Cost of Montana's Dry Land Wheat Harvest." Montana Agricultural Extension Service, *Bulletin* 71. N.p. 1924.

ANNUAL REPORTS (Company Names Vary)

Akron, Canton and Youngstown Railroad Company
Alabama Great Southern Railroad Company
Allegheny Valley Railway Company
Atchison, Topeka and Santa Fe Railway Company
Atlanta and West Point Railroad Company
Atlantic Coast Line Railroad Company
Baltimore and Ohio Railroad Company
Bangor and Aroostook Railroad Company
Bessemer and Lake Erie Railroad Company
Boston and Maine Corporation
Boston and Maine Railroad Company
Burlington Northern, Inc.
Central of Georgia Railway Company
Chesapeake and Ohio–Baltimore and Ohio Railroads
Chesapeake and Ohio Railway Company
Chicago, Burlington and Quincy Railroad Company
Chicago, Indianapolis and Louisville Railway Company
Chicago, Milwaukee, St. Paul and Pacific Railroad Company

Chicago, Rock Island and Pacific Railroad Company
Chicago, St. Paul, Minneapolis and Omaha Railway Company
Chicago and Alton Railway Company
Chicago and Eastern Illinois Railroad Company
Chicago and North Western Railway Company
Chicago Great Western Railway Company
Delaware, Lackawanna and Western Railroad Company
Denver and Rio Grande Western Railroad Company
Dereco, Inc.
Erie-Lackawanna Railroad Company
Erie Railroad Company
Great Northern Railway Company
Gulf, Mobile and Northern Railroad Company
Gulf, Mobile and Ohio Railroad Company
Gulf and Ship Island Railroad Company
Illinois Central Industries, Inc.
Illinois Central Railroad Company
Long Island Railroad Company
Louisville and Nashville Railroad Company
Maine Central Railroad Company
Minneapolis, St. Paul and Sault Ste. Marie Railroad Company
Missouri-Kansas-Texas Railroad Company
Missouri Pacific Railroad Company
Nashville, Chattanooga and St. Louis Railway Company
New York Central Railroad Company
Norfolk and Western Railway Company
Norfolk Southern Railway Company
Northern Pacific Railway Company
Penn Central Company
Pennsylvania Railroad Company
Pere Marquette Railway Company
St. Louis-San Francisco Railway Company
St. Louis Southwestern Railway Company
Soo Line Railroad Company
Southern Pacific Company
Southern Railway Company
Texas and Pacific Railway Company
Union Pacific Railroad Company
Wabash Railroad Company
Western Pacific Railroad Company

RAILROAD COMPANY PERIODICALS

Agents' Bulletin (St. Louis)
Agricultural Development Bulletin (St. Louis)
Agricultural and Industrial Service Bulletin (Kansas City, Mo.). Title varies.
Baltimore and Ohio Employes' Magazine (Baltimore). Title varies.
Book of the Royal Blue (Baltimore)
Chesapeake and Ohio Employes' Magazine (Richmond). Title varies.
Cimco Fortnightly (Havana, Ill.)
Current Events (Kansas City, Mo.)
Erie Railroad Employes' Magazine (New York)

Farm Markets and Maxims (St. Louis)
Frisco-Man (St. Louis)
GM&O News (Mobile)
Goat (St. Paul)
Great Northern Semaphore (St. Paul)
Illinois Central Employes' Magazine (Chicago). Title varies.
L&N Employes' Magazine (Louisville, Ky.)
Long Island Railroad Information Bulletin (New York)
Maize (Chicago)
Milwaukee Railway System Employes' Magazine (Chicago). Title varies.
Mississippi Central Round Table (Hattiesburg, Miss.)
Missouri Pacific Magazine (St. Louis). Title varies.
Mutual Magazine (Philadelphia)
New England Farms (New Haven, Conn.)
New York Central Lines Magazine (New York)
Norfolk and Western Magazine (Roanoke)
Pere Marquette Magazine (Detroit)
Pere Marquette Service (Detroit)
Pilot and Philadelphia and Reading Railway Men (Philadelphia)
Rail (Cleveland)
Rock Island Employes' Magazine (Chicago). Title varies.
Rock Island Lines News Digest (Chicago)
Santa Fe Employes' Magazine (Chicago). Title varies.
Scenic Lines Employes' Magazine (Denver)
Seaboard Railway *Forestry Bulletin* (Richmond)
Southern Field (Washington)
Southwest Trail (Chicago)
Ties (Washington)
Tracks (Richmond)
What's Happening in Community Service (Urbana, Ill.)

OTHER PERIODICALS AND NEWSPAPERS

Agricultural Engineering (St. Joseph, Mich.)
American Fertilizer (Philadelphia)
American Forestry (Washington)
American Railroads (New York)
Annalist (New York)
Banker-Farmer (Champaign, Ill.)
Barron's (New York)
Better Crops (New York)
Boys' and Girls' Club Record (Pullman, Wash.)
Boys' and Girls' 4-H Club Leader (Washington)
Breeder's Gazette (Chicago)
Business Week (New York)
Chemical and Metallurgical Engineering (New York)
Chemical Week (New York)
Chicago Evening Post
Chicago Tribune
College Reflector (Agricultural College, Miss.)
Colman's Rural World (St. Louis)
Columbia (Missouri) *Missourian*

Commercial West (Minneapolis)
Conservation (St. Louis)
Country Gentleman (Philadelphia)
Dun's Review and Modern Industry (New York)
Electrical West (San Francisco)
Engineering News (Chicago)
Engineering Record (New York)
Engineering and Mining Journal (New York)
Extension Service Review (Washington)
Forestry and Irrigation (Washington)
Fruit Grower and Farmer (St. Joseph, Mo.)
Garden Magazine (New York)
Green's American Fruit Grower (Rochester)
Guernsey Breeders' Journal (Peterboro, N.H.)
Hoard's Dairyman (Fort Atkinson, Wisconsin)
Industrial Development (Baltimore)
Industrial Marketing (Chicago)
Industry Week (Cleveland)
International Review of Agriculture (Rome)
Iron Age (Middletown, N. Y.)
Jersey Bulletin (Indianapolis)
Journal of Forestry (Washington)
Literary Digest (New York)
Lumber (New York)
Magazine of Wall Street (New York)
Manufacturers Record (Baltimore)
Market Growers' Journal (Louisville, Ky.)
Mechanical Engineering (New York)
Memphis *Commercial Appeal*
Michigan Extension News (East Lansing)
Missouri Farmer and Breeder (Columbia)
Missouri Ruralist (Kansas City)
Modern Railroads (Chicago)
National Boys' and Girls' Club News (Chicago)
Nation's Agriculture (Fort Wayne, Ind.)
New Breeders' Gazette (Chicago)
New Jersey Agriculture (New Brunswick)
New Mexico Extension News (State College)
New Reclamation Era (Washington)
Newsweek (Dayton, Ohio)
New York *Times*
Ohio Farmer (Cleveland)
Oregon Agriculturist (Portland)
Oregon Horticulturalist and Rural Northwest (Portland)
Pacific Dairy Review (San Francisco)
Power Farming (Detroit)
Prairie Farmer (Chicago)
Progressive Farmer (Raleigh, N.C., and elsewhere)
Progressive Farmer and Southern Farm Gazette (Starkville, Miss.)
Railway Age (Chicago)
Railway Age Gazette (Chicago)
Railway Freight Traffic (Orange, Conn.)
Railway Gazette (London; Manchester)

Railway Progress (Cleveland)
Railway Purchases and Stores (Cleveland)
Railway Review (Chicago)
Railway and Engineering Review (Chicago)
Railway World (Philadelphia)
Reliable Poultry Journal (Quincy, Ill.)
Rural America (New York)
Rural Northwest (Portland)
Sales Management (New York)
Skillings' Mining Review (Duluth)
Southern Cultivator (Atlanta)
Southern Farm Magazine (Baltimore)
Southern Live-Stock Journal (Starkville, Miss.)
Southern Planter (Richmond, Va.)
Southern Pulp and Paper Manufacturer (Atlanta)
Southern Ruralist (Atlanta)
Survey (New York)
Time (New York)
Traffic World (Chicago)
U.S. Federal Extension Service (Washington)
U.S. News and World Report (Washington)
United States Investor (Boston, and elsewhere)
Wallaces' Farmer (Des Moines)
Western Fruit Grower (St. Joseph, Mo.)
West Virginia 4-H Suggestions (Morgantown)
World's Work (New York)

BOOKS, PAMPHLETS AND ARTICLES

American Association of Farmers' Institute Managers. *Proceedings,* 1897. Lincoln, 1898.
American Railroad Development Association. *Proceedings,* 1920–1973. N.p., n.d.
American Railway Engineering Association. *Proceedings,* 1915. Chicago, 1915.
Armstrong, Walter R. "Development of Industrial Sites and Trackage Layouts at Kansas City, Kansas, and Los Angeles, California, by the Union Pacific System." American Society of Civil Engineers, *Transactions* 90 (1927):994–1002.
Ashby, Wallace. "Problems of the New Settler on Reclaimed Cutover Land." *Agricultural Engineering* 5 (Feb. 1924):27–29.
Association of American Railroads. *United States Railroad Administration: A Bibliography.* Washington, 1952.
Atchison, Topeka and Santa Fe Railway Company. *California and Arizona Citrus Fruits.* N.p. 1938.
_____. *Diversified Farming in the Panhandle and South Plains of Texas.* Chicago, 1912.
Atlantic Coast Line Railroad Company. *Everglades Pay Dirt: Opportunities for Agriculture, Grazing, Dairying.* Wilmington, n.d.
Baltimore and Ohio Railroad Company. *Balancing the Timber Budget in the Bumper Belt.* N.p., n.d.
_____. *High-Calcium Limestones in the Area Served by the Baltimore and Ohio Railroad.* N.p., n.d.
_____. *Salt Report for the B and O Area.* N.p., n.d.

Barringer, John W. *Super-Railroads for a Dynamic American Economy.* New York: Simmons-Boardman, 1956.

Beukema, John C. "The New Science of City Building." *Review of Reviews* 77 (Mar. 1928):293–302.

Budd, Ralph. "Agriculture and the Railroads." *Nation's Agriculture* 11 (June 1936):4–5, 15.

Calhoun, F. H. H. *Geological Resources: Seaboard Air Line Railway Territory.* N.p. 1925.

Calkins, Marion C. "The Cutover Country." *Survey* 45 (27 Nov. 1920):301–5.

Central of Georgia Railway Company. *Directory of Commercial Minerals in Georgia and Alabama along the Central of Georgia Railway.* Savannah, n.d.

_____. *Southern Farms for Sale.* Savannah, 1895.

Chicago, Burlington and Quincy Railroad Company. *Mines and Mining in the Black Hills.* N.p., n.d.

_____. *Nebraska: The Great Wheat, Corn, Dairying, Stock and Fruit Country.* N.p. 1904.

_____. *Timber Billions of the Pacific Northwest.* N.p. 1923.

Chicago, Milwaukee and St. Paul Railway Company. *Many Acres Open to Settlers.* N.p. 1907.

_____. *Map of South Dakota and Letters from Settlers.* N.p., n.d.

_____. *Montana.* Chicago, n.d.

_____. *North Pacific Coast Country.* N.p. 1907.

Chicago, Rock Island and Pacific Railway Company. *Colorado: Under the Turquoise Sky.* Chicago, n.d.

_____. *The Golden State: California.* Chicago, 1905.

Chicago, South Shore and South Bend Railroad Company. *Your Plant in One of America's Prime Industrial Sites.* N.p., n.d.

Chicago and Eastern Illinois Railroad Company. *Chicago-Chicago Heights Industrial Economic Blueprint.* Chicago, 1957.

_____. *Industrial Potentialities of Southern Illinois.* Chicago, 1953.

Chicago and Illinois Midland Railway Company. *Cimco Farm.* N.p. 1928.

Chicago and North Western Railway Company. *Alfalfa: The Money Crop of the West and Northwest.* Chicago, 1910.

_____. *Belle Fourche Government Irrigation Project.* N.p., n.d.

_____. *The Black Hills: A Description of a Wonderful and Picturesque Mining Region and Natural Sanitarium.* N.p., 1903.

_____. *Industrial Site Guide.* N.p., n.d.

Chicago Great Western Railroad Company. Development Division, *Bulletin* 1. Chicago, n.d.

Cimco Farm. *Annual Bulletin.* Springfield, Ill., 1929–1931.

Clair, J. C. "The Railroads' Part in the South's Development." In *The Dawn of a New Constructive Era,* Cut-Over Land Conference of the South, 50–54. N.p. 1917.

Clark, Warren T. "Sending College to the Farmer." *Sunset, the Pacific Monthly* 30 (Apr. 1914):383–89.

Council of North American Grain Exchanges, Crop Improvement Committee. *Proceedings of a Meeting in Chicago, February 8, 1911.* N.p., n.d.

Craig, James B. "A Railroad Crusades for Forestry." *American Forests* 56 (Feb. 1950):6–9, 38–39.

Cutting, Malcolm C. "How Business Financed the Farmer." *Nation's Business* 17 (Feb. 1929):76–81.

Davis, E. W. *Pioneering with Taconite.* St. Paul: Minnesota Historical Society, 1964.

Denver and Rio Grande Railroad Company. *The Fertile Lands of Colorado and Northern New Mexico.* N.p. 1912.

Duchaine, William J. "The Railroads' Role in Forest Conservation," *Railway Progress* 3 (Feb. 1950):17–22.

Dumble, E. T. *The Geology of East Texas.* Austin, 1918.

Edgar, Robert M. *The Railroad's Place in Industrial Development.* N.p. 1948.

Elliott, Howard. *Montana: An Address Delivered at the Inter-State Fair, Bozeman, Montana, September 1, 1910.* N.p., n.d.

———. *Relations between the Farmer and the Railroad: An Address at the Tri-State Grain and Stock Growers Association, Fargo, North Dakota, January 17, 1912.* N.p., n.d.

Erie Railroad Company. *Industrial Map of the Erie Railroad System.* N.p. 1905.

Fain, John R. "What Georgia is Doing to Encourage the Utilizing of Cut-Over Lands." In *The Dawn of a New Constructive Era,* Cut-Over Land Conference of the South, 108–11. N.p. 1917.

Finley, W. W. "The Railroads' Work in the South." *World's Work* 14 (June 1907):8953–54.

———. "Southern Railroads and Industrial Development." American Academy of Political and Social Science, *Annals* 35 (Jan. 1910):99–104.

Franklin, Robert. "Teaching Good Roads by Special Train." *Technical World Magazine* 17 (June 1912):448–51.

Frisco Lines. *The Tombigbee Valley of Mississippi and Alabama.* N.p., n.d.

Great Northern Railway Company. *Business Openings.* St. Paul, n.d.

Gulf, Mobile and Northern Railroad Company. *Time Tables,* 20 Dec. 1938.

Haines, Henry S. *Railway Corporations as Public Servants.* New York: Macmillan, 1907.

Harder, Worth C. "For Better Roads: How the Good-Roads Special Is Teaching the Science of Improved Peripateticism." *Harper's Weekly* 56 (14 Sept. 1912):15.

Harrison, Fairfax. *The Relation of Southern Railway Company to Southern Progress: An Address before the Manufacturers and Merchants of Atlanta, Georgia, June 10, 1914.* N.p., n.d.

———. *The South and the Southern Railway: An Address before the Virginia Bankers' Association, Old Point Comfort, Virginia, June 23, 1916.* N.p., n.d.

Haw, J. W. "Farm Aid that Builds Business." *Nation's Business* 17 (May 1929):149–50, 152.

Henry, Robert S. "The Contribution of Railroad Agricultural Workers." In *Proceedings,* 1935, Association of Southern Agricultural Workers, 417–20. N.p., n.d.

Hill, James J. "Our Wealth in Swamp and Desert." *World's Work* 19 (Feb. 1910):12595–617.

Hines, Walker D. *War History of American Railroads.* New Haven: Yale Univ. Press, 1928.

Hoadley, Francis W. "How Railroads Aid Industrial Development." *Cassier's Magazine* 41 (Feb. 1912):189–92.

Hoskins, Robert N. "Railroads and the Forests." *Journal of Forestry* 45 (Apr. 1947):283–84.

———. "The Seaboard's Program for Promoting Forestry." *Journal of Forestry* 45 (May 1947):340–41.

Hungerford, Edward. "The Railroad and the Farmer." *Country Gentleman* 90 (25 July 1925):13, 40.

———. "When Railroad and Farm Work Together." *Business America* 12(Sept. 1912): 5–11.

Illinois Central Railroad Company. *About the South.* Chicago, 1904.

Illinois Central Railroad Company. *Farming with Dynamite*. Chicago, 1911.
_____. *The Illinois Central Railroad in Mississippi*. N.p. 1953.
_____. *Opportunities Unlimited: The Story of Our Southern Forests*. Chicago, 1950.
_____. *Organization and Traffic of the Illinois Central System*. Chicago, 1938.
_____. *Report upon the Mineral Resources of the Illinois Central Railroad*. New York: J. W. Foster, 1856.
_____. *Southern Forestry: A Study of the South's Renewable Natural Resource*. Chicago, 1944.
Illinois Central and Yazoo and Mississippi Valley Railroads. *Locations for Industries*. Chicago, 1905.
_____. *Official Directory of Classified Industries for Buyers and Shippers*. Chicago, 1925.
_____. *Southern Homeseekers' Guide*. Louisville, 1898.
Israel, Edward J. "The Opportunities for Industrial Development on the Railroads." In *Proceedings, 1927*, Roadmasters and Maintenance of Way Association of America, 100–106. N.p., n.d.
Jackson, Luis. "Railways as Factors in Industrial Development." In *Lectures on Commerce Delivered before the College of Commerce and Administration of the University of Chicago*, ed. Henry R. Hatfield, 82, 84–88. Chicago: Univ. Chicago Press, 1907.
Jarvis, J. W. "Union Pacific Works with Youth; Agricultural Scholarship." *Electrical West* 86 (June 1941):102.
Johnson, Emory R., and Grover G. Huebner. *Railroad Traffic and Rates*. 2 vols. New York: D. Appleton, 1911.
Kansas City Southern Railway Company. *Eastern Oklahoma*. Kansas City, Mo., 1913.
_____. *The Ozark Region of Western Missouri and Arkansas*. Kansas City, Mo., n.d.
_____. *Sprays and Spraying*. Kansas City, Mo., 1927.
_____. *Tomato Plant Culture*. Kansas City, Mo., 1927.
Kelley, George B. "How Environmentalists Cost Us New and/or Expanded Plants". In *Proceedings, 1970*, Texas Industrial Development Conference, 20, 25. College Station, 1970.
Kendrick, J. W. *A Report upon the Missouri, Kansas and Texas Railway System*. Chicago, 1917.
Kluender, William A. "Traffic and Timber." *Journal of Forestry* 44 (Dec. 1946):1087–88.
Kurn, J. M. "The Developing Ozarks." *Executive's Magazine* 10 (May 1927):9–10.
_____. "The Railroad's Part in Regional Development." *Executive's Magazine* 10 (Sept. 1926):7–8.
Leedy, E. C. "The West Okanogan Irrigation Project." *Western Magazine* 7 (Nov. 1915):9–15.
Lewis, V. W. "Railroads as Co-operators in Livestock Development." In *Proceedings, 1931*, Association of Southern Agricultural Workers, 181–85. N.p., n.d.
Livingston, Carl D. "Stumps and Their Removal." In *The Dawn of a New Constructive Era*, Cut-Over Land Conference of the South, 188–95. N.p. 1917.
Louisville and Nashville Railroad Company. *Directory of Industries*. N.p., n.d.
_____. *Focus on the South*. N.p., n.d.
_____. *Full Throttle*. N.p., n.d.
_____. *Pass Christian, Mississippi*. Louisville, n.d.
McCann, John J. "Soil Conservation–All Aboard." *Banking* 40 (Jan. 1948):54.
McPherson, Logan G. *The Working of the Railroads*. New York: H. Holt, 1907.
Manss, William H. "The Industrial Commissioner." In *Railway Organization and*

Working, ed. Ernest R. Dewsnup, 44–62. Chicago: Univ. Chicago Press, 1906.

Mayo, Earl. "The Good Roads Train." *World's Work* 2 (July 1901):956–60.

Merry, J. F. "Methods of Developing Traffic, Industry and Immigration." *Science* 23 (20 Apr. 1906):610–11.

Missouri-Kansas-Texas Lines. *Southwest: The New Industrial Giant.* N.p., n.d.

Missouri Pacific–Iron Mountain Route. *Louisiana.* St. Louis, n.d.

Missouri Pacific–Iron Mountain System. *Home Builder in Arkansas.* St. Louis, 1911.

Missouri Pacific Lines. *Industrial Sites Available in Greater St. Louis.* N.p., n.d.

Missouri Pacific Railroad Company. *The Empire that Missouri Pacific Serves.* St. Louis, n.d.

Missouri Pacific Railway Company. *Facts about Kansas: A Book for Home-Seekers and Home-Builders.* St. Louis, 1903.

––––––. *Louisiana.* N.p., n.d.

––––––. *Statistics and Information Concerning the State of Missouri.* N.p. 1905.

Mobile and Ohio Railroad Company. *Mississippi.* N.p., n.d.

Nashville, Chattanooga and St. Louis Railway Company. *Southland Industrial Center: The South's First Planned Industrial District.* N.p., n.d.

New York Central Lines. *Improving Crop Yields by the Use of Dynamite.* Baltimore, 1911.

––––––. *Industrial Directory and Shippers' Guide,* 1920–21. New York, 1921.

New York Central System. *Finding a Farm in the Land of Shorter Hauls to Bigger Markets.* N.p. 1946.

––––––. *The Greater Springfield Ohio Area.* N.p., n.d.

Norfolk and Western Railway Company. *Industrial and Shippers' Guide.* Roanoke, 1916.

––––––. *Official Guide for the Use of the Company's Patrons and Others Seeking Facts Pertaining to Its Territorial Resources.* N.p. 1905.

––––––. *Successful Plant Site Locations: Where, How, Why.* N.p., n.d.

Northern Pacific Railway Company. *All about Fruit and Hop Raising, Dairying and General Farming, Lumbering, Fishing and Mining in Western Washington.* N.p., n.d.

––––––. *Montana: The Treasure State.* N.p. 1913.

––––––. *Report of Agricultural Extension Department,* 1913. St. Paul, 1914.

––––––. *Report of Agricultural Extension Department and of Operations on Demonstration Farms,* 1914. St. Paul, 1915.

––––––. *Report of Agricultural Department,* 1916. St. Paul, 1917.

––––––. *Report of Operations on Demonstration Farms in Western North Dakota and Report on Marquis Wheat,* 1915. St. Paul, 1916.

––––––. *Successful Central and Western North Dakota.* N.p., n.d.

––––––. *What Settlers Say over Their Own Signatures.* N.p., n.d.

Oyen, Henry. "Making Business to Order: How the Santa Fe and Other Railroads Develop the Country They Serve by Means of Their Industrial Departments." *World's Work* 24 (July 1912):308–12.

Pennsylvania Railroad Company. *How This Railroad Helps the Farmer.* Philadelphia, 1914.

––––––. *The Pennsylvania Railroad Farmers' Instruction Train.* Philadelphia, 1913.

Pittsburgh and Lake Erie Railroad Company. *Region of Opportunity: Industrial Potential along the Pittsburgh-Youngstown Axis.* N.p. 1961.

Powell, T. C. "The Work of Railroads for Agricultural Development." In *Proceedings,* 1914, Conference for Education in the South, 110–12. Washington, n.d.

Powell, T. F. "Opportunities Afforded the Railroads of the United States for Profitable Agricultural Development Work." *Proceedings of the Second Pan American Scientific Congress,* 3:451–56. 11 vols. Washington, 1917.

Quivey, O. K. "Railroads Have a Stake in Forestry." *American Forests* 54 (Oct. 1948):446–47, 468.

"Railroads as Aids to Farmers: How the Need for More Traffic Had Led Them to Help in the Revival of Agriculture." *Craftsman* 19 (Nov. 1910):186–91.

"Railroads Co-operating with Farmers: Colleges on Wheels." *Harper's Weekly* 54 (5 Feb. 1910):31.

Railway Development Association. *Proceedings,* 1913–1919. N.p., n.d.

Railway Industrial Association. *Proceedings,* 1911–1912. N.p. 1911–1912.

Railway Systems and Management Association. *Creative Railroad Real Estate Development.* Chicago: Railway Systems and Management Association, 1965.

Rane, F. William. "Beautifying the Steel Highway." *Forestry and Irrigation* 12 (July 1906):336–40.

Renehey, Robert H. "On Long Island's Worst Ten Acres She Runs a Model Farm." *American Magazine* 107 (Apr. 1929):73–74.

Ripley, Edward P. "How I Got Customers to See My Side." *System: The Magazine of Business* 29 (Apr. 1916):339–45.

Roddewig, Clair M. *Address before the Oklahoma State Chamber of Commerce, Tulsa, November 7, 1962.* N.p., n.d.

St. Louis and San Francisco Railway Company. *The Houston Mid-Coast Country of Texas.* N.p., n.d.

_____. *Irrigation in the Gulf Coast Country of Texas.* N.p., n.d.

_____. *North and Central Texas along the Frisco Lines.* N.p., n.d.

St. Louis-San Francisco Railway Company. *Frisco Planned Industrial Districts.* N.p., n.d.

_____. *Frisco and Industrial Development in Mississippi.* N.p. 1953.

_____. *Kansas Mineral Wealth in the Frisco Belt.* N.p., n.d.

St. Louis Southwestern Railway Company. *The St. Francis Country: Southeast Missouri and Northeast Arkansas.* St. Louis, 1906.

Santa Fe Railway Company. *A Fine Address for Industry in Houston.* N.p., n.d.

_____. *North Texas Industrial Empire.* N.p., n.d.

_____. *Six Fine Areas for Industrial Development in Wichita.* N.p., n.d.

Santa Fe System Lines. *Bulletin: Reprint of All Issues.* Chicago, 1928.

Schoffelmayer, Victor H. *Southwest Trails to New Horizons.* San Antonio: Naylor, 1960.

Sequoia Pacific: A Southern Pacific Company. N.p., n.d.

Shedd, H. G. "Securing Settlers for Private Irrigation Projects." In *Proceedings of the Second Pan American Scientific Congress* 3:518–24. 11 vols. Washington, 1917.

Shoemaker, Ira H. "The Industrial Department of a Railroad." *Independent* 67 (15 July 1909):134–35.

Southern Pacific Company. *Minerals for Industry.* San Francisco, 1964.

Southern Pacific Land Company. N.p., n.d.

Southern Pacific Railroad Company. *The Gulf Coast of Louisiana.* New Orleans, 1912.

_____. *Southern Pacific Guide to Sites for Industry in Northern California.* N.p., n.d.

Southern Pacific Transportation Company. *What is the Golden Empire?* N.p., n.d.

Sprague, Jesse R. "Getting Business for the Railroad." *Saturday Evening Post* 198 (20 Mar. 1926): 48, 50, 52.

Sterling, E. A. "Forest Management on the Delaware and Hudson Adirondack Forest." *Journal of Forestry* 30 (May 1932):569–74.

Stevens, F. R. "What Farmers Can Do to Facilitate the Transportation and

Marketing of Produce." *American Academy of Political and Social Science,*
  Annals 50 (Nov. 1913):37–43.
Union Pacific Railroad Company. *Colorado: Resources, Population, Industries, Op-*
  portunities, and Climate. Omaha, 1909.
———. *The Fossil Fields of Wyoming.* Omaha, 1909.
———. *Handling Potatoes.* N.p., n.d.
———. *Irrigation Guide.* N.p., n.d.
———. *Oregon Wheat Lands.* N.p., n.d.
———. *Wyoming: Its Resources and Attractions.* Omaha, 1903.
Victor Gruen Associates. *A Proposal for the Development of the East Shore Tide-*
  lands of San Francisco Bay Prepared for the Atchison, Topeka and Santa Fe
  Railway Company. N.p: Sante Fe Railway Co., 1963.
Vivian, C. H. "The N and W–A Progressive Railroad," *Compressed Air Magazine*
  41 (Oct. 1936):5132–38.
Waggener, O. O. *Western Agriculture and the Burlington.* Chicago: Chicago,
  Burlington and Quincy Railroad, 1938.
Wallace, Henry. *Uncle Henry's Own Story of His Life.* 3 vols. Des Moines: Wallace,
  1917–1919.
Welty, D. C. "The Railroads' Interest in Cut-Over Land Development." In *The*
  Dawn of a New Constructive Era, Cut-Over Land Conference of the South,
  151–55. N.p. 1917.
"What the Railroads are Doing for Farming in the East." *Craftsman* 18 (Aug.
  1910): 603–4.
Widsoe, John A. *Success on Irrigation Projects.* New York: John Wiley, 1928.
Young, R. S. "The Role of Forest Products in Railroad Revenue." *Journal of*
  Forestry 30 (Mar. 1932):318–22.

Secondary Materials

BOOKS AND ARTICLES

Anderson, Jacob E. *80 Years of Transportation Progress: A History of the St. Louis*
  Southwestern Railway. Tyler: Story-Wright, 1957.
Armitage, Merle. *Operations Santa Fe.* New York: Duell, Sloan and Pearce, 1948.
Arrington, Leonard J. "The Transcontinental Railroad and the Development of
  the West." *Utah Historical Quarterly* 37 (Winter 1969):3–15.
Athearn, Robert G. *Rebel of the Rockies.* New Haven: Yale Univ. Press, 1962.
———. *Union Pacific Country.* New York: Rand McNally, 1971.
Bailes, Kendal. "The Mennonites Come to Kansas." *American Heritage* 10 (Aug.
  1959):30–33, 102–5.
Berthoff, Rowland T. "Southern Attitudes toward Immigration, 1865–1914."
  Journal of Southern History 17 (Aug. 1951):328–60.
Billingsly, William C. "The FW&DC Railroad: Giving Birth to a Line of Communi-
  ties in West Texas." *Texas Humanist* 5 (May–June 1983):16–18.
Boening, Rose M. "History of Irrigation in the State of Washington." *Washington*
  Historical Quarterly 10 (Jan. 1919): 21–45.
Bradley, Glenn D. *The Story of the Santa Fe.* Boston: R. G. Badger, 1920.
Brandfon, Robert L. *Cotton Kingdom in the New South: A History of the Yazoo*
  Mississippi Delta from Reconstruction to the Twentieth Century. Cambridge:
  Harvard Univ. Press, 1967.

Brandfon, Robert L. "The End of Immigration to the Cotton Fields." *Mississippi Valley Historical Review* 50 (Mar. 1964):591–611.

Brunet, Patrick J. " 'Can't Hurt, and May Do You Some Good': A Study of the Pamphlets the Southern Pacific Railroad Used to Induce Immigration to Texas." *East Texas Historical Journal* 16 (1978):35–45.

Brunson, B. R. *The Texas Land and Development Company: A Panhandle Promotion, 1912–1956.* Austin: Univ. Texas Press, 1970.

Bryant, Keith L., Jr. *History of the Atchison, Topeka and Santa Fe Railway.* New York: Macmillan, 1974.

Burgess, George H., and Miles C. Kennedy. *Centennial History of the Pennsylvania Railroad Company.* Philadelphia: Pennsylvania Railroad Company, 1949.

Casey, Robert J., and W. A. S. Douglas. *The Lackawanna Story.* New York: McGraw-Hill, 1951.

――――. *Pioneer Railroad: The Story of the Chicago and North Western System.* New York: Whittlesey House, 1948.

Chu Chang Liang. *A Study of the Industrial and Agricultural Development Departments of American Railroads.* Peiping, 1933.

Clark, Ira G. *Then Came the Railroads: The Century from Steam to Diesel in the Southwest.* Norman: Univ. Oklahoma Press, 1958.

Clark, James I. *Cutover Problems: Colonization, Depression, Reforestation.* Madison: State Historical Society of Wisconsin, 1956.

――――. *Farming the Cutover: The Settlement of Northern Wisconsin.* Madison: State Historical Society of Wisconsin, 1956.

Clepper, Henry E. *Professional Forestry in the United States.* Baltimore: Johns Hopkins Univ. Press, 1971.

Cochran, John S. "Economic Importance of Early Transcontinental Railroads: The Pacific Northwest." *Oregon Historical Quarterly* 71 (Mar. 1970): 27–98.

Cochran, Thomas C. *Railroad Leaders, 1845–1890: The Business Mind in Action.* Cambridge: Harvard Univ. Press, 1953.

Combs, Barry B. "The Union Pacific Railroad and the Early Settlement of Nebraska, 1868–1880." *Nebraska History* 50 (Spring 1969):1–26.

Corliss, Carlton J. *Main Line of Mid-America: The Story of the Illinois Central.* New York: Creative Age, 1950.

Cotroneo, Ross R. "Western Land Marketing by the Northern Pacific Railway." *Pacific Historical Review* 37 (Aug. 1968):299–320.

Coulter, Calvin B. "The Victory of National Irrigation in the Yakima Valley, 1902–1906." *Pacific Northwest Quarterly* 42 (Apr. 1951):99–122.

Delaware and Hudson Company. *A Century of Progress: History of the Delaware and Hudson Company, 1823–1923.* Albany: J. B. Lyon, 1925.

Derleth, August. *The Milwaukee Road: Its First Hundred Years.* New York: Creative Age, 1948.

Dew, Lee A. *The JLC&E: The History of an Arkansas Railroad.* State University: Arkansas State Univ., 1968.

――――. "The J. L. C. and E. R. R. and the Opening of the 'Sunk Lands' of Northeast Arkansas." *Arkansas Historical Quarterly* 27 (Spring 1968):22–39.

Donovan, Frank P., Jr. *Mileposts on the Prairie: The Story of the Minneapolis and St. Louis Railway.* New York: Simmons-Boardman, 1950.

Doster, James F. *Railroads in Alabama Politics, 1875–1914.* University: Univ. Alabama Studies, 1957.

Dozier, Howard D. *A History of the Atlantic Coast Line Railroad.* New York: A. M. Kelley, 1971.

Drache, Hiram M. *The Day of the Bonanza: A History of Bonanza Farming in the Red River Valley of the North.* Fargo: North Dakota Institute for Regional Studies, 1964.

Drache, Hiram M. "The Economic Aspects of the Northern Pacific Railroad in North Dakota." *North Dakota History* 34 (Fall 1967):321–72.

Dunbar, Willis F. *All Aboard! A History of Railroads in Michigan.* Grand Rapids: W. B. Erdmans, 1969.

Emmons, David M. *Garden in the Grasslands: Boomer Literature of the Central Great Plains.* Lincoln: Univ. Nebraska Press, 1971.

Fahey, John. *Inland Empire: D. C. Corbin and Spokane.* Seattle: Univ. Washington Press, 1965.

Farrington, S. Kip, Jr. *Railroads of the Hour.* New York: Coward-McCann, 1958.

Fleming, Walter L. "Immigration to the Southern States." *Political Science Quarterly* 20 (June 1905):276–97.

Ganoe, John T. "The Origin of a National Reclamation Policy." *Mississippi Valley Historical Review* 18 (June 1931):34–52.

Gates, Paul W. *The Farmer's Age: Agriculture, 1815–1860.* New York: Holt, Rinehart and Winston, 1960.

————. *History of Public Land Law Development.* Washington, 1968.

————. *The Illinois Central Railroad and Its Colonization Work.* Cambridge: Harvard Univ. Press, 1934.

————. "The Promotion of Agriculture by the Illinois Central Railroad, 1855–1870." *Agricultural History* 5 (Apr. 1931):57–76.

————. "The Railroad Land-Grant Legend." *Journal of Economic History* 14 (Spring 1954):143–46.

Gilmore, Donald R. *Developing the "Little" Economies.* New York: Committee for Economic Development, n.d.

Gjevre, John A. *Saga of the Soo: West from Shoreham.* N.p. 1973.

Godfrey, Aaron A. *Government Operation of the Railroads: Its Necessity, Success, and Consequences, 1918–1920.* Austin: Jenkins, 1974.

Gracy, David B. *Littlefield Lands: Colonization on the Texas Plains, 1912–1920.* Austin: Univ. Texas Press, 1968.

Greever, William S. *Arid Domain: The Santa Fe Railway and Its Western Land Grant.* Stanford: Stanford Univ. Press, 1954.

————. "A Comparison of Railroad Land-Grant Policies." *Agricultural History* 25 (Apr. 1951): 83–90.

Guandolo, John. *Transportation Law.* Dubuque: W. C. Brown, 1965.

Hampton, Taylor. *The Nickel Plate Road: The History of a Great Railroad.* Cleveland: World, 1947.

Harlow, Alvin F. *The Road of the Century: The Story of the New York Central.* New York: Creative Age, 1947.

Hargreaves, Mary W. M. *Dry Farming in the Northern Great Plains, 1900–1925.* Cambridge, Harvard Univ. Press, 1957.

————. "Hardy Webster Campbell (1850–1937)." *Agricultural History* 32 (Jan. 1958):62–65.

Hays, Samuel P. *Conservation and the Gospel of Efficiency: The Progressive Conservation Movement, 1890–1920.* New York: Atheneum, 1969.

Heathcote, Lesley M. "The Montana Arid Land Commission, 1895–1903." *Agricultural History* 38 (Apr. 1964):108–17.

Hedges, James B. "The Colonization Work of the Northern Pacific Railroad." *Mississippi Valley Historical Review* 13 (Dec. 1926):311–42.

————. "Promotion of Immigration to the Pacific Northwest by the Railroads." *Mississippi Valley Historical Review* 15 (Sept. 1928):183–203.

Helgeson, Arlan C. *Farms in the Cutover: Agricultural Settlement in Northern Wisconsin.* Madison: State Historical Society of Wisconsin, 1962.

Henry, Robert S. "The Railroad Land Grant Legend in American History Texts." *Mississippi Valley Historical Review* 32 (Sept. 1945):171–94.

Heyward, Frank. *History of Industrial Forestry in the South.* Seattle: Univ. Washington, College of Forestry, 1958.

Hidy, Ralph W., Frank Ernest Hill, and Allan Nevins. *Timber and Men: The Weyerhaeuser Story.* New York: Macmillan, 1963.

Howard, Dick, ed. *Guide to Industrial Development.* Englewood Cliffs, N. J.: Prentice-Hall, 1972.

Howard, Joseph K. *Montana, High, Wide, and Handsome.* New Haven: Yale Univ. Press, 1943.

Hungerford, Edward. *The Modern Railroad.* Chicago: A. C. McClure, 1918.

_____. *The Story of the Baltimore and Ohio Railroad, 1827-1927.* 2 vols. New York: G. P. Putnam's Sons, 1928.

Hunter, William C. *Beacon Across the Prairie: North Dakota's Land-Grant College.* Fargo: North Dakota Institute for Regional Studies, 1961.

Jenks, Leland H. "Railroads as an Economic Force in American Development." *Journal of Economic History* 4 (May 1944):1-20.

Jones, C. Clyde. "The Burlington Railroad and Agricultural Policy in the 1920's." *Agricultural History* 31 (Oct. 1957):67-74.

_____. "A Survey of the Agricultural Development Program of the Chicago, Burlington and Quincy Railroad." *Nebraska History* 30 (Sept. 1949):226-56.

_____. "Val Kuska, Agricultural Development Agent." *Nebraska History* 38 (Dec. 1957):285-93.

Kinnard, William N. *Industrial Real Estate.* Washington: Society of Industrial Realtors, 1967.

Klein, Maury. *History of the Louisville and Nashville Railroad.* New York: Macmillan, 1972.

_____. "Southern Railroad Leaders, 1865-1893: Identities and Ideologies." *Business History Review* 42 (Autumn 1968): 288-310.

Knight, Oliver. "Correcting Nature's Error: The Colorado Big Thompson Project." *Agricultural History* 30 (Oct. 1956):157-69.

Lansburgh, Richard H. "Recent Migrations of Industries in the United States." American Academy of Political and Social Science, *Annals* 142 (Mar. 1929): 296-301.

Lee, Ivy L. "The Place of the Interstate Railroad in Reducing Food Distribution Costs." American Academy of Political and Social Science, *Annals* 50 (Nov. 1913):10-19.

Lemly, James H. *The Gulf, Mobile and Ohio: A Railroad that Had to Expand or Expire.* Homewood, Ill.: Richard D. Irwin, 1953.

Loewenberg, Bert J. "Efforts of the South to Encourage Immigration, 1865-1900." *South Atlantic Quarterly* 33 (Oct. 1934):363-85.

Luebke, Frederick C. *Immigrants and Politics: The Germans of Nebraska, 1880-1900.* Lincoln: Univ. Nebraska Press, 1969.

Lux, Mabel. "Honyockers of Harlem, Scissorbills of Zurich." *Montana, the Magazine of Western History* 13 (Autumn 1963):2-14.

McConnell, Grant. *The Decline of Agrarian Democracy.* Berkeley and Los Angeles: Univ. California Press, 1953.

McCorkle, James L., Jr. "Nineteenth Century Beginnings of the Commercial Vegetable Industry in Mississippi." *Journal of Mississippi History* 30 (Nov. 1968):260-74.

MacPherson, Ian. "Better Britons for the Burlington: A Study of the Selective Approach of the Chicago, Burlington and Quincy in Great Britain, 1871-1875." *Nebraska History* 50 (Winter 1969):373-407.

Marshall, James. *Santa Fe: The Railroad that Built an Empire.* New York: Random House, 1945.

Martin, Albro. *Enterprise Denied: Origins of the Decline of American Railroads,*

1897-1917. New York: Columbia Univ. Press, 1971.

———. *James J. Hill and the Opening of the Northwest.* New York: Oxford Univ. Press, 1976.

Martin, Robert L. *The City Moves West: Economic and Industrial Growth in Central West Texas.* Austin: Univ. Texas Press, 1969.

Meinig, Donald W. *The Great Columbia Plain: A Historical Geography, 1805-1910.* Seattle: Univ. Washington Press, 1968.

Mercer, Lloyd J. "Land Grants to American Railroads: Social Cost or Social Benefit?" *Business History Review* 43 (Summer 1969):134-51.

Miller, Thomas L. *The Public Lands of Texas, 1819-1970.* Norman: Univ. Oklahoma Press, 1971.

Miner, H. Craig. *The St. Louis-San Francisco Transcontinental Railroad: The Thirty-Fifth Parallel Project, 1853-1890.* Lawrence: Univ. Kansas Press, 1972.

Murray, Stanley N. "Railroads and the Agricultural Development of the Red River Valley of the North." *Agricultural History* 31 (Oct. 1957): 57-66.

———. *The Valley Comes of Age: A History of Agriculture in the Valley of the Red River of the North, 1812-1920.* Fargo: North Dakota Institute for Regional Studies, 1967.

Olson, Sherry H. *The Depletion Myth: A History of Railroad Use of Timber.* Cambridge: Harvard Univ. Press, 1971.

Overton, Richard C. *Burlington Route: A History of the Burlington Lines.* New York: Knopf, 1965.

———. *Burlington West: A Colonization History of the Burlington Railroad.* Cambridge: Harvard Univ. Press, 1941.

———. *Gulf to Rockies: The Heritage of the Fort Worth and Denver-Colorado and Southern Railways, 1861-1898.* Austin: Univ. Texas Press, 1953.

Parker, Edna M. "The Southern Pacific Railroad and the Settlement of Southern California." *Pacific Historical Review* 6 (June 1937):103-19.

Peterson, Harold F. "Some Colonization Projects of the Northern Pacific Railroad." *Minnesota History* 10 (June 1929):127-44.

Rae, John B. "The Great Northern's Land Grant." *Journal of Economic History* 12 (Spring 1952): 140-45.

Ridgley, Ronald. H. "The Railroads and Rural Development in the Dakotas." *North Dakota History* 36 (Spring 1969):163-87.

Rogers, William W. "Reuben F. Kolb: Agricultural Leader of the New South." *Agricultural History* 32 (Apr. 1958): 109-19.

Saunders, Richard. *The Railroad Mergers and the Coming of Conrail.* Westport, Conn.: Greenwood, 1978.

Schell, Herbert S. *History of South Dakota.* Lincoln: Univ. Nebraska Press, 1961.

Scobie, James R. *Argentina: A City and a Nation.* New York: Oxford Univ. Press, 1964.

Scott, Roy V. "American Railroads and Agricultural Extension, 1900-1914: A Study in Railway Developmental Techniques." *Business History Review* 39 (Spring 1965):74-98.

———. "Railroads and Farmers: Educational Trains in Missouri, 1902-1914." *Agricultural History* 36 (Jan. 1962):3-15.

———. *The Reluctant Farmer: The Rise of Agricultural Extension to 1914.* Urbana: Univ. Illinois Press, 1970.

Scott, Roy V., and J. G. Shoalmire. *The Public Career of Cully A. Cobb: A Study in Agricultural Leadership.* Jackson: Univ. and College Press Mississippi, 1973.

Sharp, Paul F. "The Tree Farm Movement: Its Origin and Development." *Agricultural History* 23 (Jan. 1949):41-45.

Sheffy, Lester F. *The Life and Times of Timothy Dwight Hobart, 1855-1935.*

Canyon, Tex.: Panhandle-Plains Historical Society, 1955.

Soule, George. *Prosperity Decade from War to Depression: 1917–1929.* New York: Rinehart, 1947.

Stover, John F. *History of the Illinois Central Railroad.* New York: Macmillan, 1975.

———. *The Life and Decline of the American Railroad.* New York: Oxford Univ. Press, 1970.

Taylor, George Rogers. *The Transportation Revolution, 1815–1860.* New York: Rinehart, 1951.

Thompson, James H. *Methods of Plant Site Selection Available to Small Manufacturing Firms.* Morgantown: West Virginia Univ. Press, 1961.

Throne, Mildred. "Suggested Research on Railroad Aid to the Farmer, with Particular Reference to Iowa and Kansas." *Agricultural History* 31 (Oct. 1957):50–56.

Toole, K. Ross. *Montana: An Uncommon Land.* Norman: Univ. Oklahoma Press, 1959.

Traxler, Ralph N., Jr. "The Texas and Pacific Railroad Land Grants: A Comparison of Land Grant Policies of the United States and Texas." *Southwestern Historical Quarterly* 6 (Jan. 1958):359–70.

Turner, Charles W. *Chessie's Road.* Richmond: Garrett and Massie, 1956.

Unruh, John D., Jr. "The Burlington and Missouri River Railroad Brings the Mennonites to Nebraska, 1873–1878." *Nebraska History* 35 (Mar., June 1964):3–30, 177–206.

Waters, L. L. *Steel Trails to Santa Fe.* Lawrence: Univ. Kansas Press, 1950.

Wilson, Neill C., and Frank J. Taylor. *Southern Pacific: The Roaring Story of a Fighting Railroad.* New York: McGraw-Hill, 1952.

Winther, Oscar O. *The Transportation Frontier: Trans-Mississippi West, 1865–1890.* New York: Holt, Rinehart and Winston, 1964.

Wolfe, Jonathan J. "Background of German Immigration to Arkansas." *Arkansas Historical Quarterly* 25 (1966):151–82, 248–78, 354–85.

THESES AND MISCELLANEOUS PAPERS

Baiamonte, John V., Jr. "Immigrants in Rural America: A Study of the Italians of Tangipahoa Parish, Louisiana." Ph.D. diss., Mississippi State University, 1972.

Bennett, Howard F. "The Hannibal and St. Joseph Railroad and the Development of Northern Missouri, 1847–1870: A Study of Land and Colonization Policies." Ph.D. diss., Harvard University, 1951.

Burt, Jesse C. "History of the Nashville, Chattanooga and St. Louis Railway, 1873–1916." Ph.D. diss., Vanderbilt University, 1950.

Cotroneo, Ross R. "The History of the Northern Pacific Land Grant, 1900–1952." Ph.D. diss., University of Idaho, 1967.

Cranford, Sammy O. "The Fernwood, Columbia and Gulf: A Railroad in the Piney Woods of South Mississippi." Ph.D. diss., Mississippi State University, 1983.

Daniels, David D. "Railroad Industrial Development: The Influence of Selected Railroads upon Manufacturing Location." Ph.D. diss., University of North Carolina, 1974.

Hammer, Kenneth M. "Dakota Railroads." Ph.D. diss., South Dakota State University, 1966.

Johnson, Robert R. "Role of Railroads in Small Community Industrial Development." M.A. thesis, Industrial Development Institute, University of Oklahoma, 1967.

Jones, C. Clyde. "The Agricultural Development Program of the Chicago, Burlington and Quincy Railroad." Ph.D. diss., Northwestern University, 1954.

Lowe, Ida M. W. "The Role of the Railroads in the Settlement of the Texas Panhandle." M.A. thesis, West Texas State College, Canyon, 1962.

Oden, Jack P. "Development of the Southern Pulp and Paper Industry, 1900–1970." Ph.D. diss., Mississippi State University, 1973.

Patterson, William H. "Through the Heart of the South: A History of the Seaboard Air Line Railroad Company, 1832–1950." Ph.D. diss., University of South Carolina, 1952.

Petrowski, William R. "The Kansas Pacific: A Study in Railroad Promotion." Ph.D. diss., University of Wisconsin, 1966.

Ridgley, Ronald H. "Railroads and the Development of the Dakotas: 1872–1914." Ph.D. diss., Indiana University, 1967.

Shoalmire, J. G. "The Good Roads Trains, 1901–1902." Graduate seminar paper in possession of the author.

Spencer, Morris N. "The Union Pacific's Utilization of Its Land Grant with Emphasis on Its Colonization Program." Ph.D. diss., University of Nebraska, 1950.

Young, J. Frank. "Land Development for Industry by Railroads and Communities." M.A. thesis, Industrial Development Institute, University of Oklahoma, n.d.

INDEX

ROY V. SCOTT, Distinguished Professor of History, Mississippi State University, received his B.S. from Iowa State University and his M.S. and Ph.D. degrees from the University of Illinois. He served as president of the Agricultural History Society, 1978–1979. Professor Scott's contributions to agricultural history include: *The Agrarian Movement in Illinois, 1880–1896* (1962); *The Reluctant Farmers: The Rise of Agricultural Extension to 1914* (1970); (with J. G. Shoalmire) *The Public Career of Cully A. Cobb: A Study of Agricultural Leadership* (1973); and (with George L. Robson, Jr., editor) *Southern Agriculture Since the Civil War: A Symposium* (1979).